THE
PRESS IN TIMES
OF CRISIS

Recent Titles in
Contributions to the Study of Mass Media and Communications

THE
PRESS IN TIMES
OF CRISIS

Edited by
LLOYD CHIASSON JR.

Contributions to the Study of Mass Media and Communications,
Number 48

GREENWOOD PRESS
Westport, Connecticut • London

Library of Congress Cataloging-in-Publication Data

The Press in times of crisis / edited by Lloyd
Chiasson Jr.
     p. cm.—(Contributions to the study of mass media and
communications, ISSN 0732–4456 ; no. 48)
   Includes bibliographical references and index.
   ISBN 0–313–29364–3 (alk. paper)
   1. Press and politics—United States. 2. United States—History.
I. Chiasson, Lloyd E. II. Series.
PN4888.P6P67 1995
071′.3—dc20   95–2903

British Library Cataloguing in Publication Data is available.

A paperback edition of *The Press in Times of Crisis* is available from
Praeger Publishers, an imprint of Greenwood Publishing Group, Inc.
(ISBN 0–275–95340–8).

Library of Congress Catalog Card Number: 95–2903
ISBN: 0–313–29364–3
ISSN: 0732–4456

First published in 1995

Greenwood Press, 88 Post Road West, Westport, CT 06881
An imprint of Greenwood Publishing Group, Inc.

Printed in the United States of America

The paper used in this book complies with the
Permanent Paper Standard issued by the National
Information Standards Organization (Z39.48–1984).

10 9 8 7 6 5 4 3 2 1

As promised, this book is dedicated to my sister Susanne.
I hope you like it, Sis.

Lloyd

CONTENTS

PREFACE

History shows that what we think about, we talk about and take action on—and change usually ensues. The change may not occur in ways we expect or be in our best interests. But change is often the residue of public awareness, and the press has always been incredibly adept at making us aware, if only for brief snatches of time. The history of the press in times of crisis is in many ways the story of public attitudes. And if nothing else is true, the history of a democracy can be traced through the attitudes and beliefs of the populace. The story—the countless stories—of the American press in conflict is the story of America.

This book is about the press coverage of 13 events that span a time frame that includes the birth of the United States; its political, economic, and social struggles as a young country; and its civil war. It tells how a young agrarian society grew into an industrial giant in the course of one century and how it changed from isolationist to world power in the next. It relates how this country coped with the growth of socialism, two world wars, and civil unrest. It concludes with perhaps the most important story that has never been told, at least in full, in the United States or anywhere else.

Throughout American history, the press has performed various functions. At the end of the colonial period, it served as a vehicle of discussion, then debate, and finally agitation. In the process, it may also have defined itself and laid a groundwork for its role(s) in future crises. Sometimes it has led public opinion, sometimes it has mirrored attitudes, and sometimes it has set its agenda after public opinion has crystallized. The press has agitated, advocated, persuaded. It has been duped, it has been unfair, and it has misled. There have been times when the press has served as the people's watchdog of the government and times when it has acted as the government's passive lapdog.

All along the way the press has recorded events that, for the most part, are what we know as American history. In the 18th century, American newspapers told the colonists of British injustice. Depending on the geographic region, newspapers in the 19th century either criticized or defended slavery. In the 20th century, newspapers alternately lambasted those they thought were Communists and those who attempted to restrict the freedoms of those who might have been. Newspapers reported the horrors and frustrations of Vietnam, the civil rights movement, and environmental problems that are enveloping us as we enter the 21st century.

Probably no country in history has a greater legacy of news reporting than the United States. And no country has had a greater affinity for news and newspapers. From the colonial period to the space age, Americans have relied upon the news media to keep them abreast of events, to provide insight into their meaning, to record history on a daily basis. In a democracy, this is essentially the job of the press, and except for limitations in time and space, in economics and politics, in ability and understanding, the press has attempted to fulfill its role. But whether it's across a backyard fence, in a coffee room, or in a newspaper, the story that gets told is never the whole story—and it is sometimes the wrong story.

Like old man Adam, the press is fatally flawed. No matter how hard it tries, it simply cannot achieve its goals. The reason is simple: The press is us. It is people with different ideas and beliefs who are trying to present, and preserve, the truth, whatever that may be. And like the rest of us, the press sometimes fails on the job.

This book looks at both the failures and the successes of the press. It also tries to show how the press functions in an agenda-setting capacity, not on a day-to-day basis but in periods of crisis. In times of normalcy, the press seems most adept at accomplishing its tasks of informing, educating, and persuading. But what happens when the environment in which the press functions becomes volatile? What happens when the public or the government or the press views a moment in time as being critical? It is in this environment that the authors attempt to document what the press reported, how it was reported, and why it was reported. They also attempt to look at something else: how the press reacted when its right to perform its job was challenged.

Along the long river of American history, the press has played a significant role in shaping events. One wonders, however, what course the river would have run if the words would have been different—or had not been written.

Lloyd Chiasson Jr.

ACKNOWLEDGMENTS

A special thanks to the contributors who gave both of their time and of their expertise to make this a very special book. A particularly big thanks goes out to my friend Al Delahaye, for reminding me that good historiography is good storytelling. Thanks to good friend Joe McKerns, who worked through the rain and finished in the sunlight. And thanks to my wife Shannon for her belief in a good idea, the vision to see the end product, and the willingness to put a fire under me to get it done.

Lloyd Chiasson Jr.

THE
PRESS IN TIMES
OF CRISIS

1 ⟫

SELLING THE
AMERICAN REVOLUTION

Carol Sue Humphrey

About four thirty in the morning of April 19, 1775, British troops under the command of Major John Pitcairn approached the little town of Lexington, Massachusetts. Instead of a sleepy hamlet of empty streets, an armed group of local militia waited in the center of town for the British. Under the command of Captain John Parker, the militiamen had originally assembled at midnight after being alerted by Paul Revere that "the British are coming."

As the redcoats approached, the untrained military men of Lexington took what seemed to be an insane action. Just over 70 of them lined up on the village green to protest the march of the six companies of British troops. When told to disperse by the British commander, the Americans hesitated, then began to leave the green. The militiamen, however, refused to leave their guns as ordered by Pitcairn. Angry words were spoken, and suddenly someone fired a shot. The immediate response was two volleys from the British troops, with some weak fire from the Americans. When it was over, 8 Americans were dead and 10 were wounded. In the few moments it took to fight this first battle, the colonists had embarked on a journey that would end with the formation of a new, bold form of government.

Following the skirmish at Lexington, the British forces continued toward Concord, their planned destination. They reached Concord about seven in the morning and searched the town for the munitions supposedly stored there. In the course of the search, the blacksmith shop and the courthouse were set on fire. Whether done deliberately or by accident, these events served to anger the colonial militia, which prior to these fires had stayed out of the way of the British to avoid a conflict. At North Bridge, however, the two opposing forces exchanged fire. Neither group proved well-disciplined, and they both retreated in disarray. By noon, the British were retreating back to Boston.

The return to Boston went smoothly at first, but fighting began again one mile outside of Concord. From there to Cambridge, the British faced a gauntlet as the militiamen fired from whatever cover they could find. The colonials inflicted heavy casualties but proved too disorganized to capitalize on this success. The British struck back when possible but could not respond in a traditional military fashion because of the limited space available on the road to Boston. Frustration at their inability to deal adequately with the enemy led to attacks on civilians as well as looting and pillaging. British officers did little to stop such activity because they, too, were frustrated at the day's results.

The British finally reached the safety of Boston shortly after sundown. The total casualty number for the British that day was 273. For the Americans, the number was 95. But more important than the numbers was the fact that British troops, representing the mother country, had fired on the colonial militia. The rift between the two had become nearly impossible to heal—the shedding of colonial blood almost guaranteed an eventual decision for independence. With those few shots that early morning at Lexington, the American Revolution had begun.[1]

News of events quickly spread throughout the colonies via newspapers. Beginning even before the actual fighting, and continuing throughout the war, the weekly gazettes of the 13 colonies would serve to keep the people informed concerning the events related to the fighting and the American attempt to break away from British control. Most American newspapers came to support independence, and increasingly, their pages urged their readers to do the same. By and large, the American press set a positive agenda concerning the war by emphasizing the certainty of American success. Even the early reports of Lexington and Concord discussed the British retreat and the casualties inflicted by the militia rather than the two skirmishes in which the colonials did not fare as well. This pattern would continue throughout the war, as exemplified by the newspapers of one small, but not insignificant town in Virginia: Williamsburg.

News of Lexington and Concord finally reached Williamsburg a week after the battles took place.[2] Stories of the fighting appeared in the pages of the Williamsburg newspapers, all titled the Virginia *Gazette*, but many Virginians already knew that war was coming. Armed conflict had come to Virginia on April 21, 1775, when the governor, Lord Dunmore, had seized the colony's supply of gunpowder and carried it to a ship anchored offshore.

As soon as the news of this manoeuvre took wind the whole city was alarmed and much exasperated; and numbers got themselves in readiness to repair to the Palace; to demand from the Governour a restoration of what they so justly supposed was deposited in this magazine for the country's defense.[3]

With the report of this incident in a supplement of Alexander Purdie's Virginia *Gazette*, the citizens of Williamsburg became aware that the growing conflict between the colonies and Great Britain had taken a more militaristic turn, at least in their colony. The news of Lexington and Concord only served to solidify the growing realization that war had arrived. All of these events were covered in the pages of the Virginia *Gazettes*, publications that became the major source of information about the war for the people of Virginia.

The following year, the editor of a Loyalist paper in New York, Ambrose Serle, wrote to Lord Dartmouth concerning the potential impact of the colonial newspapers: "One is astonished to see with what avidity they are sought after, and how implicitly they are believed, by the great Bulk of the People. . . . Government may find it expedient, in the sum of things, to employ this popular Engine."[4]

From the beginning of the war, everyone involved perceived the important influence of the colonial press. Prior to the outbreak of hostilities, the newspapers had played a crucial role in making the problems of each individual colony general issues in all of the colonies, but the total impact would be difficult to measure.[5] Proprietors of taverns and other public gathering places commonly bought one or more newspapers for the benefit of their customers,[6] and "the readers always greatly outnumbered the purchasers."[7] Because of the availability of newspapers in places where the public congregated, numerous conversations about the issues of the day took place on a regular basis; so the media helped the war effort by providing news to large numbers of people. The conflict was not always easy for newspaper printers, but the press of this period survived as an institution throughout the vicissitudes of war, and its contribution to the unity of the colonies cannot be underestimated.[8]

Behind the influential newspapers stood their printers, craftsmen skilled at their trade. While doing little of the actual writing, these men and women, described by Daniel Boorstin as "servants of the general public," played an important role in gathering intelligence and disseminating it to the people of their colony.[9] Obviously, "newspapers influence readers by the method of presenting the contents and by the contents themselves."[10] All available materials could not be published. The revolutionary printer controlled the content of the paper, deciding what would and would not be published.

Whether done consciously or not, decisions influenced public opinion and helped to shape future events.[11] By publishing some stories and not others, the printer told readers what was and was not important. Printers helped set the public agenda by emphasizing some items and downplaying others. Stories concerning battles always emphasized the success of the Americans and the failures of the British, whether that was actually the truth or not. American leaders and troops were pictured as heroes to be emulated, while the British were portrayed as the scum of the earth, deserving only of contempt.

The wartime newspapers of Williamsburg provide a good case study of the impact of the press during the American Revolution. They show how printers, through their news reporting, helped set the public agenda and produce public support for the war effort. They show how newspapers coalesced public opinion throughout the colonies.

At the time of the Battle of Lexington, there were 37 newspapers published in the colonies. Twenty of these failed during the war, with 18 new ones beginning, then failing before the war ended. Other new publications, however, survived through the war, and when General Charles Cornwallis surrendered at Yorktown, 35 news sheets were being printed. In all, the colonies issued 70 different papers during the war, 15 of which supported the Tory cause during at least part of their existence. Of the 37 papers at the beginning of the war, 3 were published in Williamsburg.[12]

The three Williamsburg papers in 1775 were printed by John Pinkney, Alexander Purdie, and John Dixon and William Hunter. Pinkney's Virginia *Gazette*, the most radical of the three, continued the paper begun by William Rind in 1766. Pinkney had taken control in September 1774 and continued publishing until shortly before his death in the spring of 1776.[13]

Alexander Purdie began issuing his paper on February 3, 1775, following the dissolution of his partnership with John Dixon. Purdie, appointed the official printer of the colony by the House of Burgesses in 1775, published numerous debates and proclamations of the assembly during the war. Purdie printed his Virginia *Gazette* until his death in 1779, when the paper continued under new printers, Purdie's nephew, John Clarkson, and his partner, Augustine Davis. They published the paper until December 1780, when they moved their operations to Richmond.[14]

The third paper, John Dixon and William Hunter's, began publication early in 1775 following the dissolution of the Purdie and Dixon partnership. This paper actually continued one begun in 1751 by Hunter's father, but it came to a sudden end in December 1778 when Hunter deserted to the British. Dixon, however, soon established another paper in partnership with Thomas Nicolson. This one appeared until late 1780, when Dixon and Nicolson also moved their press to Richmond.[15]

All of Williamsburg's wartime papers preached the patriot cause. They apparently did this willingly, but it might have been dangerous for them to have done otherwise. Freedom of the press had not become a fixed legal principle. Very little legal censorship occurred during the Revolution, and the press openly discussed government officials on occasion; however, criticism of the American cause usually brought public action, and the mob censored those whom the government failed to quiet. An exchange between several of the Williamsburg printers indicated the pressure that could be applied by the public to influence the contents of the newspapers. On September 9, 1775, Dixon and Hunter published a letter from John Pinkney's paper. Included with the letter was the following comment from Pinkney:

I am exceedingly sorry that I am compelled by the officers of the volunteer companies to transmit to you a copy of the paragraph, inserted in my paper this week, relative to Mr. Hardcastle. I leave it to yourselves whether you will comply with this requisition or not.[16]

Failure to comply by either of these printers could have easily resulted in more direct encouragement. During the American Revolution, freedom of speech, and press as well, "belonged solely to those who spoke the speech of liberty."[17] For whatever reason, the Virginia *Gazettes* supported the patriots, or the "right" side, providing one of Virginia's most important news sources throughout the war.

The material in colonial papers, including Virginia's, usually consisted of news and advertisements. Little original material appeared in the news columns, but each printer added to the total news supply by producing some local stories. These locally produced stories enabled the exchange system to function so that other newspapers provided most of the news items, both foreign and domestic. In addition to clippings from other papers, gossip acquired from returning sailors and other travelers and letters from other colonies and countries to local residents provided a source of information.

The use of such haphazard and inconsistent sources, coupled with slow, unreliable transportation and communication systems, produced an often considerable time lag between event and publication. The mails, because of the use of regularly scheduled post riders, ran fairly consistently during the colonial era, but once the local British governments ceased to function, mail delivery increasingly had to wait on someone going to an area on business. Since newspapers went with the post, printers depended on the mails for most of their newspaper content. In 1775, Dixon and Hunter commented that such delays had become common: "The latest Philadelphia papers are not come to hand this week, as usual."[18] An example of this type of delay occurred following the Battle of Lexington, when six weeks passed before all newspapers in the colonies had printed an account.[19]

In the colonial Virginia *Gazettes*, foreign news predominated. Following the Battle of Lexington, however, the emphasis shifted. A small amount of local news remained the norm, but now the emphasis rested on provincial news, particularly from New England, the site of most of the fighting. This trend continued until mid-1788, when another news shift occurred. As the entrance of France into the war became a distinct possibility and then a reality, foreign news once more predominated and continued to do so until publication of the Williamsburg papers ceased.

Even though news sources varied from time to time, the most important type of intelligence throughout the war continued to be battle accounts. From the first shots at Lexington, the Williamsburg printers inundated their readers with rumors and/or reports of battles and skirmishes throughout the colonies. And most of these accounts, even when describing defeat, aimed at gaining support for the patriot cause.[20]

The first accounts of Lexington and Concord to appear in Williamsburg fit the above description. One early report not only reported the skirmish but sought to rally the people to the cause:

To all friends of American liberty, be it known, that this morning, before break of day, a brigade consisting of about 1000 or 1200 men landed at Phipp's Farm, at Cambridge, and marched to Lexington, where they found a company of our colony militia in arms, upon whom they fired without any provocation, and killed six men, and wounded four others. By an express from Boston we find another brigade are now upon their march from Boston, supposed to be about 1000. The bearer, Trail Brissel, is charged to alarm the country quite to Connecticut; and all persons are desired to furnish him with fresh horses, as they may be needed.[21]

Pinkney published a patriot version of the battles in a supplement dated April 28, 1775, and the other printers soon followed suit,[22] all three continuing to publish various reports of the battles until June. Only Dixon and Hunter printed a nonpatriot account—General William Gage's report of the battle.[23] The other Williamsburg printers felt no obligation to do likewise, and all the other stories seemed to agree that the "late transaction was a most unprovoked attack upon the lives and property" of the colonials, and the New England militia had "given a good drubbing to 2000 regulars."[24] All three papers contained discussions of the battle by members of the British army in which some officers said that they "never were in a hotter engagement," and one regular declared that "the militia had fought like bears, and that he would as soon attempt to storm Hell as to fight against them a second time."[25]

A major controversy surrounding the battles of Lexington and Concord, both then and now, concerned the question of who fired first. All three Williamsburg papers supported the patriot view that the British had fired initially on both occasions. Purdie, as well as Dixon and Hunter, published depositions from regulars wounded and captured at Lexington and Concord, stating that the British had opened fire at both places.[26] In printing some intercepted letters from soldiers in Boston that blamed the militia, Pinkney emphasized "the pains taken by their superiors to have it thought that the provincials began the fire, and behaved with savage bar-

barity during the action."[27] Obviously, he disagreed with the British assessment of what had happened.

The publications of Dixon and Hunter and Purdie agreed with
Pinkney on this subject. They both ended their discussion of who fired
first with a story designed not only to increase colonial dislike for the British but also to increase colonial hatred for the provincials who supported
the Crown:

Some officers in the King's army, it is said, have sworn that the Americans fired
first. Their method of cheating the Devil, we are told, has been by some means
brought out. They procured three or four traitors to their God and country, born
among us, and took with them, and they first fired upon their countrymen, which
was immediately followed by the regulars. It is also said these wretches were
dressed in soldiers' clothing.[28]

Accounts in the Virginia *Gazettes* of later actions in the war resembled
those of Lexington and Concord. American successes and British losses
sparkled and shone, while American losses and British successes were
played down and almost ignored. Many reports read as if the British could
do nothing right and the Americans nothing wrong.

Following Lexington and Concord, several skirmishes took place near
Boston. Dixon and Hunter claimed victory for the colonials in all of them.
They, along with Purdie, published several favorable accounts of the Battle
of Bunker Hill, describing the valiant efforts of the colonial militia to retain possession of the hill. Neither printer criticized the militia for the loss
of the position. Rather, they blamed unforeseeable accidents. At first, the
guilt fell to a withdrawal order mistaken for a command to retreat, producing a loss with victory nearly won. Later, reproach rested on a lack of
enough ammunition to fight off the third British charge. In both cases, the
honor and bravery of the militia remained intact.[29] In response to this loss,
a Virginia delegate to the Continental Congress wrote home that the British "had little to boast of, for being able to force our troops from Bunker's
hill. It is no wonder they did so, with superior numbers, ships of war,
floating batteries, and field artillery."[30]

Later, an unforeseen calamity was a reason for the failure of the American army to hold the field at Germantown. Dixon and Hunter printed a
letter blaming the loss on the Americans' mistaking their own forces for a
British reinforcement and precipitately retreating.[31] That victory at
Germantown was within the Americans' grasp was supported by a report
in which British officers described the Germantown actions as their worst
"drubbing since Bunkers' Hill."[32] Thus, in these stories, the patriot printers attributed American defeats to accidental causes rather than to the inability of the Continental army or cowardice in battle. The press portrayed
the American fighting force as without defects, or more likely, editors at-

tempted to bolster morale by blaming anyone but the army for American losses.

This type of reasoning seemed even more evident in accounts of American retreats. Both Dixon and Hunter and Purdie published reports praising George Washington for "having effected a safe retreat for our army out of Long Island, in spite of the great numbers in that commanded by Howe."[33] Following the withdrawal, New York was described as untenable because it resulted in a division of the army.[34] As Washington retreated further across New Jersey, the media praised him for preserving the Continental army and its provisions.[35] Furthermore, a Williamsburg correspondent of Dixon and Hunter applauded the withdrawal because, as a result, the British had "marched so far into the country as to put it in our power to cut off their retreat, and by a dicisive [sic] blow perhaps finish the war."[36]

Accompanying the thought that the Americans could do no wrong was the idea that each battle produced heavy British losses and minimal American casualties. Numerous examples of this abound throughout all the Virginia *Gazettes* and are somewhat reminiscent of the "scorecard" reporting of the Vietnam War in which statistics of casualties almost always favored the U.S. forces. An early account of the British retreat from Concord stated that at least one half of the regulars had been killed. A later report listed 302 casualties for the British (killed, wounded, and taken prisoner) as opposed to 37 for the provincials. Other battles produced similar accounts. These included Bunker Hill—150 British dead, 810 British prisoners, and only 20 American dead.[37] Following Bunker Hill, Dixon and Hunter and Purdie printed a story that General Howe had compared the battle to Minden and Fontenoy because of the tremendous losses among his troops.[38] The Williamsburg printers published casualty counts frequently, using figures to support the contention that the Americans, though losing specific engagements, were always winning the war.

All of the battle accounts published by patriot newspapers, including the Virginia *Gazettes*, aimed to increase local support for the war effort.[39] The Williamsburg printers usually published reports more favorable to the patriots than the British. In 1780, the following critical description of the American press was reprinted by Dixon and Nicolson:

When any untoward accident has happened to the Americans, or their great and good ally, the King of slaves, they are totally silent as to matters of news; but, if the least favourable turn happens to their affairs, they . . . will boast of victories never gained, battles never fought, and successes they had no right to expect.[40]

Although an exaggeration, this description held true in Williamsburg because the local printers filled the battle accounts in the Virginia *Gazettes* full of praise when the Americans won but remained relatively quiet when they lost. Disasters were always minimized as much as possible, and each story always ended on a note of hope.[41]

Numerous recitals of other British actions, all aimed at gaining support for the war, accompanied the battle account in the Virginia *Gazettes*. Most numerous of these were reports of British destruction of American property. British raids occurred in all the colonies, and tales of pillage and plunder appeared in the Williamsburg papers throughout the war. The press condemned all the raids, but several expeditions received more censure from the Williamsburg printers than did others. In 1775, Governor John Dunmore conducted raids along the Virginia coast, including the seizure of the printing press used by John Holt of Norfolk to publish his newspaper. Dixon and Hunter declared that the city of Norfolk was in a "distressed situation" because of "the wanton, unjust, and cruel behaviour of the tools of tyranny and oppression on board the ships of war in that harbour."[42]

The Williamsburg newspapers also severely criticized the British for wreaking havoc and destruction as they marched across New Jersey in 1777. According to one story from Morristown, "the British army burnt, stripped, and destroyed, all as they went along. Women and children were left without food to eat, or raiment to put on. . . . The enemy even destroyed all the bibles and books of divinity they came across."[43] Not surprisingly, alongside accounts of the destruction of private property appeared tales of atrocities on the part of the British. A story in Dixon and Hunter's paper accused the British of torturing recent Scottish emigrants to America in order to secure their aid against the colonials.[44] Most numerous among these tales were reports of rape and cruelty toward women. In reporting a threatened bombardment of Newport, Purdie's paper declared that the terrified pregnant women of the town "absolutely miscarried by the fright."[45]

In describing British actions in New Jersey, Dixon and Hunter printed a British threat "to destroy the poor helpless women, by burning them in their houses."[46] Rumors of other intended atrocities also appeared in the Virginia *Gazettes*. In 1775, Pinkney published a London story that stated "the three Boston generals have issued orders to give no quarters to the provincials."[47] The press first accused General Howe of trying to spread smallpox around Boston and then of leaving arsenic mixed in with medicines left in Boston following the British withdrawal.[48] These rumors and tales of British attacks on the unarmed citizenry of the colonies appeared in the Williamsburg papers throughout the war.

Letters and articles describing British treatment of American prisoners were also intended to increase colonial hatred of the British. A letter from Philadelphia to Williamsburg published in Purdie's paper declared that American soldiers captured during the New Jersey fighting "were put to death after they had surrendered."[49] Stories such as this one, however, appeared infrequently. Most tales about American prisoners described their situation after confinement in British prisons, reporting that they fared terribly at the hands of their British keepers, with many dying.

Few specific descriptions of the treatment of American prisoners of war appeared in the press, but several publications written by General George Washington indicate that he felt the care was inadequate. In a letter to British General William Howe, Washington stated that:

[A]iry buildings were chosen to confine our men in, is a fact I shall not dispute. But whether this was an advantage or not in the winter season, I leave you to decide. I am inclined to think it was not, especially as there was a general complaint, that they were destitute of fire the greater part of the time, and were only prevented from feeling the inclemency of the weather, in its extremest rigour, by their crowded situation. This I must believe was not very conducive to their health, and if we may judge by comparison, we must conclude, they endured similar inconveniences on board the transports. As to the supplies of provisions, I know not what they were. My ideas of the matter were drawn from their united testimony, confirmed by their appearance, which represented the allowance as insufficient in quantity, bad in quality, and irregularly served.[50]

A report from Boston declared that many died "merely for the want of the common support of life, and that several brave Americans, only to save themselves from perishing, have enlisted into the British tyrant's army."[51] Other accounts related how the British forced Americans into the army against their will. One Boston extract published by Purdie even alleged that the British government had offered American prisoners to the East India Company for transport to India as workers.[52]

All newspaper narratives concerning the "barbarity and insults" of the British in America sought to convince colonials of the cruelty and degeneracy of the British and instill in Americans a hatred for the British.[53] Aimed at destroying any reputation the British may have once held, the Virginia *Gazettes* described the colonials' former countrymen as "royal thieves,"[54] "savage brutes,"[55] "uncivilized banditti,"[56] and "pirates and bloodsuckers."[57] In 1775, Pinkney declared that "the repeated insults which this distressed country has suffered call aloud for everything tending to its preservation and protection."[58] All wartime efforts on the part of the Williamsburg printers to picture the British as cruel, depraved, and undeserving of American support aimed at ensuring that Virginians answered Pinkney's call.

In addition to picturing the British government and its people as being unworthy of American loyalty, the Virginia *Gazettes* also portrayed the British army as being unhappy with the war. In the months after Lexington, the Williamsburg printers carried several reports of the uneasiness and low morale present in the army in Boston. One described the British regulars as "universally disheartened,"[59] while another attributed the suicide of a lieutenant in Thomas Gage's army "to the chagrin and terror of mind arising from his being employed in so bad a cause."[60] In December 1775, Dixon and Hunter published an extract from a London paper that stated that part of the army at Boston had been recalled to Britain "on account of their dislike for the service."[61]

Associated with the tales of low British morale were numerous reports of British desertions. Accounts of British desertions began to appear immediately after the Battle of Lexington and continued until the end of the war.[62] Many of those fleeing claimed that many others still hoped to do the same when an opportunity presented itself.[63] In 1778, an article from the Philadelphia Evening Post reprinted by Dixon and Hunter declared that "there never was an instance of so much desertion in a British army as what now prevails in the Jerseys."[64] The reasons for the desertions ranged from dislike of the duty to sickness to ill-forebodings over a proposed attack,[65\] but whatever the reasons, the Williamsburg press carried them as proof of discontent in the British army, which greatly increased the chances of an overall American victory.

Although numerous attacks against the army abounded, they were not the only censures against the British in the Virginia *Gazettes*; they also strongly assailed Britain's allies whenever possible. Britain's primary foreign allies (if one can call them that) came from Germany as mercenaries hired to replace British regulars. Several reports in the colonies described the raising of German troops for use not only in America but throughout the empire.[66] It is generally accepted that the colonial press primarily attacked the Hessians for their cruelty and barbarity,[67] but the Williamsburg press did not fit this description. One such account printed by both Dixon and Hunter and Purdie declared that the Hessians at Halifax had taken "an oath to spare neither man, woman, nor child."[68]

The primary type of discussion concerning the Hessians found in the Virginia *Gazettes*, however, concerned their unhappiness with American service.[69] Several articles stated that the Germans had been forced into the army and had to be carefully watched in order to "prevent mutiny and desertion."[70] According to reports from the northern colonies, the Germans deserted whenever possible.[71] All of the Williamsburg papers agreed that the Hessians were really not enemies of the colonies and waited only for a favourable opportunity of laying down their arms.[72]

While discussions of the Hessians in the Virginia *Gazettes* seemed fairly tame, references to Britain's American allies, the Tories, were hate filled and polemical. Adjectives such as "vile"[73] and "perfidious"[74] appeared to describe the Loyalists along the labels such as "deluded miscreants,"[75] "Judases,"[76] and "traitors to their country."[77] The patriots attacked the Tories for hoarding goods in order to raise prices and depreciate the currency.[78] Dixon and Hunter accused the Loyalists of murder,[79] while Purdie reviled them for planning "to spare neither men, women, nor children"[80] in suppressing the rebellion.

In attempts to further undermine the Tories, the Williamsburg papers published several accounts of Tory military failures, ranging from the Battle of Moore's Creek Bridge to the loss of a Tory ship at sea.[81] Numerous reports of the suffering of the Loyalists at the hands of the British also appeared.[82] Included in these were tales of British impressment of Tories for service overseas,[83] and one rumor of particular interest stated that Loyalists would be sent to Germany to replace Hessians killed or captured in America.[84] In their attacks on the Tories as both traitors and failures, the printers of Williamsburg hoped not only to encourage further patriot support for the war but also to convince many to return to the "right side" of the conflict.

While maligning the allies of Britain, the Williamsburg press created a promising image of support forthcoming from Europe. As early as June 1775, Pinkney printed a rumor that a shipload of Prussians had arrived in New England to help in the fight against British tyranny.[85] Frequent reports of European sympathy and forthcoming aid from such countries as Spain, Holland, and Prussia appeared throughout the war.[86] Dixon and Hunter and Purdie even printed a rumor in 1777 that all the courts of Europe except Portugal had recognized American independence and had requested that Congress send ambassadors immediately.[87] Such a hopeful outlook, however, did not maintain itself as the war progressed without the expected overflow of help. In 1779 and 1780, accounts concerning the Dutch usually stressed their neutrality rather than their support of the Americans.[88] Discussions of other European nations concentrated on their failure to aid Britain in her time of need. This proved particularly true in accounts of Russia.[89]

Not surprisingly, most newspaper accounts dealing with hoped-for European support concerned the one country that actually did greatly help the colonies: France. Rumors, reports, and descriptions of French aid began to appear early in 1776 and continued to be printed long after France openly joined the Americans. Many early discussions stated that the French considered a declaration of American independence an essential precondition for aid because the "war with England can only be looked on as a domestic broil" without such a stand on the part of the colonies.[90]

After the adoption of the Declaration of Independence, printed rumors of forthcoming French assistance increased steadily until the announcement in mid-1778 of the signing of a treaty between the French government and American emissaries in Paris.[91] Following approval of the treaty by Congress, rumors and reports of French aid continued to appear in the Virginia *Gazettes*, but most of these only praised the efforts of the French on behalf of American independence.[92] In the printed accounts of forthcoming European help, the Williamsburg printers hoped to convince Virginians that the entire world sided with America rather than

Britain in the struggle. The open support of France supposedly confirmed this beyond a shadow of a doubt, and thus the stress on European aid became less pronounced in the newspapers of Williamsburg.

Also common were rumors concerning the Indians. The position of the Indians in the conflict posed one big unanswered question at the beginning of the war. The extensive coverage of the problem in the Virginia *Gazettes* mirrored the colonials' great fear that the Indians would be used by the British. Several accounts of British attempts to incite the Indians appeared during the early months of the struggle. Articles in the Williamsburg press evinced the special fear of Virginians because they could be attacked from two directions: by the Cherokees to the south and the Ohio Valley Indians to the north. In the summer of 1775, both Dixon and Hunter and Purdie carried extracts of letters from British agents among the Cherokees that said the Cherokees would be used against the colonials.[93] Purdie confirmed the report in September with a letter stating that "the Cherokees, after several iniquitous expedients, have been prevailed on to take up arms against this colony."[94]

Several articles appeared in all three Virginia *Gazettes* of attempts by Governor Guy Carleton and Guy Johnston to arouse the Indians in Canada and, of more importance to Virginians, in the Ohio Valley to attack frontier settlements.[95] One rumor originating in Baltimore stated that the British had told the Ohio Valley Indians the Virginians "were a people not to be depended on" and "their attacking them would not be resented by the other colonies."[96] According to Purdie (and the other printers would have agreed), these accounts provided "a full proof that the ministerial servants have attempted to engage the savages against us."[97]

The printers of the Virginia *Gazettes* continually attacked the British for trying to incite the Indians, but early reports were accompanied by categorical denials that the British were having any success. In 1775, all three papers contained a letter stating that the Canadian Indians had declared that "they have received no offence from the people, so will not make war with them."[98] Several accounts declared that many Indians desired to remain neutral in the conflict between the British and the Americans[99] and that they "should not take up the hatchet on either side."[100] Other news stories described the Indians as "very staunch friends to the colonies"[101] and said "that if they did fight at all they would fight against the regulars, for they did not like them."[102] Several reports of active Indian aid for the Americans, including the offer of warriors for use in battle, accompanied these accounts.[103]

Even though the Williamsburg printers tried to show the lack of any Indian aid for the English, tales soon circulated detailing their appearance in battle alongside British regulars.[104] Replies to these rumors in the Virginia *Gazettes* included scathing attacks on the use of Indians in battle by the British (although it had apparently been appropriate for the Americans to use them in a similar manner). In 1775, Pinkney printed this description of the Indians in the Canadian campaign: "The savages appear barbarous to the last degree. Not content with scalping, they dug up our dead, and mangled them in the most shocking manner."[105]

Action in New York in 1776 produced accusations that "many of our people were sacrificed to their fury, butchered with tomahawks and other instruments of murder"[106] and that the British had readily acquiesced in these actions.[107] The newspapers particularly reviled General John Burgoyne for his use of Indians because he supposedly offered rewards for scalps brought in by his warriors.[108]

One incident in particular during his invasion of New York produced a great deal of criticism in the press. During the summer of 1777,

a Miss McCrea, who was to have been married to one Jones, a Tory who had joined the enemy and who she daily expected to bring her off, was dragged by the savages out of her house, shot twice through her body, her clothes torn off her back, and left scalped in the bushes. This brutal scene was transacted by four Indians, under cover of three hundred British regulars.[109]

The murder of Jane McCrea horrified many people throughout the colonies, destroyed almost any real support Burgoyne might have had in New York, and greatly increased colonial hatred and disgust for the British.[110]

While attacking the Indians for their barbarity, the Virginia *Gazette* printers also painted a glorious picture of the Indians' defeat at the hands of the colonials.[111] Following the uprising of 1776, Purdie urged Americans to "make a severe, lasting, and salutary example, of the treacherous Cherokees."[112] Later descriptions of battles with the Indians showed that the colonials agreed with Purdie's advice and intended to make examples of all cases.[113] In 1779, Dixon and Nicolson declared that the Indians were "taught by severe experience, the power of the American empire, which must secure our frontiers from future molestation."[114] Accounts of these defeats preceded reports that the Indians were unhappy with the British, and on one occasion, several tribes accused the British of being "the cause of all their misfortunes, by prevailing on them to strike the Americans."[115]

Many colonials, including the Williamsburg printers, probably considered this the just fate of the British and the Indians. With their stories concerning the Indians, the printers hoped to gain further adherents to the idea of the savagery of both the Indians and the British in hopes that this would keep people agitated in favor of the war.

The Indians undoubtedly produced a great deal of concern among Virginians, but other fears predominated. The people of the southern colonies shuddered over the possibility of a slave insurrection instigated by the British—and Virginians more than the others because of the activities of their royal governor, Lord Dunmore.[116] Dunmore, having fled the capital in early June 1775, was ensconced on a small fleet of ships in Norfolk harbor. From there, he directed numerous raids in the surrounding countryside in search of necessary provisions and in attempts to break up patriot forces and recover control of his government.[117]

At this time, Dunmore basically controlled Norfolk and its surrounding environs, but following the defeat of his forces at the Battle of Great Bridge in December 1775,[118] he had to abandon Norfolk and retire his entire force to the ships.[119] Following his withdrawal, Dunmore ordered a bombardment, producing fires that destroyed most of the city.[120] Dunmore then left his untenable position in Norfolk harbor and looked elsewhere for refuge. He remained at sea for a time, then occupied Gwynn's Island in Chesapeake Bay.[121] After the Virginia forces compelled him to withdraw from Gwynn's Island, his fleet went to the mouth of the Potomac River.[122] Finally, in August 1776, Dunmore and his fleet left the coast of Virginia, never to return.[123] Dunmore went to New York and served with Howe until the end of the year, at which time the former governor of Virginia sailed for England.[124]

The printers of Williamsburg strongly attacked Dunmore for his actions and tried in any way possible to ruin his credibility. They censured him for cruelty to a group of recent emigrants who refused to aid him in his fight, and they tried to show his unpopularity with his men by reporting desertions from the fleet.[125] But, more than for any other reason, the Williamsburg newspapermen violently assaulted Governor Dunmore in print for inciting slave insurrections. This is a particularly interesting point for the South in general, and Virginia in particular, because it marks the beginning of a pattern of fear that the region did not resolve until after the Civil War. Fear of a slave uprising, as the reader will subsequently see, was due in part to a mixture of press, propaganda, and events: the abolitionist press; the proliferation of antislavery literature and the anti-slavery societies; the Denmark Vesey and Nate Turner slave uprisings and subsequent news coverage; and the famous, and infamous, raid at Harper's Ferry, Virginia, by John Brown in 1859.

Fears of a possible British-inspired slave insurrection appeared early in the Revolution. Purdie printed one such rumor in August 1775, laying blame for the plan at the feet of Sir William Draper.[126] Pinkney, however, quickly accused Dunmore of harboring such a plan,[127] and Purdie soon attacked him for using the threat as a sword over the heads of the people of Virginia.[128] When Dunmore finally issued his proclamation offering freedom to slaves in exchange for fighting for the British, all three Virginia *Gazettes* assailed it as an unthinkable and dangerous proposition.[129] Purdie carried accounts of two incidents showing the effect of the proclamation among the blacks: A black openly insulted a white woman in the streets of Philadelphia, declaring, "Stay . . . till Lord Dunmore and his black regiment come, and then we will see who is to take the wall;"[130] and a Negro mother from New York proudly named her new son after the governor.[131] Reports soon appeared of Dunmore's successful recruiting efforts as a result of the proclamation.[132]

All three printers in Williamsburg hurriedly tried to undermine Dunmore's proclamation by whatever available method. They tried to ruin Dunmore's reputation in the colony in hopes of reversing his successes. Pinkney called Dunmore the "king of the blacks,"[133] while Purdie said his actions "would even have disgraced the noted pirate Blackbeard,"[134] and Dixon and Hunter accused him of using blacks to spread smallpox among the inhabitants of Virginia.[135]

Most of the efforts of the Williamsburg press, however, were aimed at convincing people that slaves would not or should not listen to Dunmore's entreaties. Several stories appeared about blacks who failed to believe the governor.[136] Pinkney printed a statement exemplary of these shortly after the publication of the proclamation: "An honest negro (Caesar, the famous barber of York) being asked what he thought of Lord Dunmore's setting negroes free, said, that he did not know any one foolish enough to believe him, for if he intended to do so, he ought first to set his own free."[137]

Further reports, supposedly meant to be passed on to the slaves by their masters, were designed to frighten them so they would not even try to join Dunmore. Dixon and Hunter reported great sickness and death among the blacks with Dunmore, and they expressed a hope that "Dunmore's neglect of those poor creatures, suffering numbers of them to perish for want of common necessaries and the least assistance, one would think enough to discourage others from joining him."[138] The printers of all three papers published reports declaring that Dunmore sold many of the slaves joining him in the West Indies in order to raise money to cover his expenses.[139]

Finally, accounts appeared of the quick recapture of the runaway slaves.[140] Quickly following these stories was the sentence of several to death by Virginia authorities "as an example to others."[141]

Press coverage of Dunmore's actions and the printers' efforts to stir up people as a safeguard against an insurrection occurring exemplified the hysteria present among the people concerning their former governor. The departure of Dunmore from the colony removed the immediate threat of an insurrection, but the fear of a slave uprising remained throughout the war and grew in the antebellum period.

The Williamsburg printers attempted to cover the war as thoroughly as possible in their reports and published numerous material concerning various aspects of the Revolution. However, the news reporting in the Virginia *Gazettes* could be seen as propaganda of a sort. The papers contained numerous essays and poems obviously meant to influence public opinion.

More interesting, however, were the news reports that, while not always obviously propaganda, were designed in such a way as to serve both the news function of reporting the war and the propaganda function of increasing morale and support for the war effort. Reports of the cruelty of the British, the low morale among the British and the Hessians, the attempted use of Indians and slaves against the colonies—all of these, while only news reports on the surface, also aimed to inflame the people and to increase the active support of Virginians for the war.

All of the colonial papers, including those in Williamsburg, helped to set the public agenda concerning the Revolution and to develop "a feeling of solidarity against the mother country."[142] The war was a long one, and the efforts of the media had to be maintained throughout. In 1782, Benjamin Franklin, writing about the usefulness of newspapers, declared that "by the press we can speak to nations. . . . And we now find, that it is not only right to strike while the iron is hot, but that it may be very practicable to heat it by continually striking."[143]

The printers of the Virginia *Gazettes* in Williamsburg made an important contribution in this area through a persistent discussion of the war and its ramifications for their readers. In doing so, they exemplified the work of many others throughout the colonies and kept the iron hot enough, long enough, to achieve military victory and freedom from Great Britain.

NOTES

1. Description of the battles of Lexington and Concord from Robert Middlekauf, *The Glorious Cause: The American Revolution, 1763–1789* (New York: Oxford University Press, 1982), 267–273.

2. Virginia *Gazette* (Dixon and Hunter), 29 April 1775.

3. Virginia *Gazette* (Pinkney), 21 April 1775.

4. John Tebbel, *The Compact History of the American Newspaper* (New York: Hawthorn Books, 1963), 53.

5. Philip Davidson, *Propaganda and the American Revolution, 1763–1783* (Chapel Hill: University of North Carolina Press, 1941), 225, 235; Martin Mayes, *An Historical–Sociological Inquiry Into Certain Phases of the Development of the Press in the United States* (Richmond: Missourian Press, 1935), 41; Sidney Kobre, *Development of American Journalism* (Dubuque, IA: William C. Brown, 1969), 71–72.

6. Don Higginbotham, *The War of American Independence: Military Attitudes, Policies, and Practice, 1763–1789* (New York: Macmillan Company, 1971), 258; Richard L. Merritt, "Public Opinion in Colonial America: Content–Analying the Colonial Press," *Public Opinion Quarterly* 27 (1963):363–364.

7. Arthur M. Schlesinger, *Prelude to Independence: The Newspaper War on Britain, 1764–1776* (New York: Alfred A. Knopf, 1958), 303.

8. Tebbel, *Compact History*, 54; Merritt, "Public Opinion," 367.

9. Daniel J. Boorstin, *The Americans: The Colonial Experience* (New York: Random House, 1958), 335–336, 340; Frank Luther Mott, *American Journalism: A History of Newspapers in the United States Through 250 Years, 1690 to 1940* (New York: Macmillan Company, 1941), 103; Willard Grosvenor Bleyer, *Main Currents in the History of American Journalism* (Boston: Houghton Mifflin Company, 1927), 93.

10. Davidson, *Propaganda*, 233.

11. Merritt, "Public Opinion," 369; Davidson, *Propaganda*, 226–227; Schlesinger, *Prelude to Independence*, 61.

12. Mayes, *Development of the Press*, 38; S.N.D. North, *History and Present Condition of the Newspapers and Periodical Press of the United States with a Catalogue of the Publications of the Census Year* (Washington, DC: Government Printing Office, 1909), 27; Mott, *American Journalism*, 95.

13. Schlesinger, *Prelude to Independence*, 259–260; Clarence S. Brigham, *History and Bibliography of American Newspapers, 1690–1820* (Worcester, MA: American Antiquarian Society, 1947), 2:1161; Isaiah Thomas, *The History of Printing in America with a Biography of Printers & an Account of Newspapers*, 2nd ed. (Albany, NY: American Antiquarian Society, 1874; reprint ed., Barre, MA: Imprint Society, 1970), 557.

14. Brigham, *American Newspapers*, 2:1162; Thomas, *History of Printing*, 557; Schlesinger, *Prelude to Independence*, 239.

15. Brigham, *American Newspapers*, 2:1159–1160, 1163; Schlesinger, *Prelude to Independence*, 290–291.

16. Virginia *Gazette* (Dixon and Hunter), 9 September 1775.

17. Kobre, *Development of American Journalism*, 63; Tebbel, *Compact History*, 38; Mott, *American Journalism*, 103–104; Boorstin, *The Americans*, p. 331; Schlesinger, *Prelude to Independence*, 189; Higginbotham, *War of American Independence*, 259–260; John Tebbel, *The Media in America* (New York: Mentor Books, 1974), 43, 52; Leonard W. Levy, *Emergence of a Free Press* (New York: Oxford University Press, 1985), 173.

18. Virginia *Gazette* (Dixon and Hunter), 8 July 1775.

19. Lawrence C. Wroth, *The Colonial Printer* (Portland, ME: Southworth–Athoensen Press, 1938), 234; Mayes, *Development of the Press*, 36; Mott, *American Journalism*, 99–100; Lester J. Cappon and Stella F. Duff, *Virginia Gazette Index, 1736–1780* (Williamsburg, VA: Institute of Early American History and Culture, 1950), 2:vi; Merritt, "Public Opinion," 361; Frank Luther Mott, "The Newspaper Coverage of Lexington and Concord," *New England Quarterly* 17 (1944): 497.

20. Jim Allee Hart, *The Developing Views on the News: Editorial Syndrome, 1500–1800* (Carbondale: Southern Illinois University Press, 1970), 160–161.

21. Virginia *Gazette* (Dixon and Hunter), 29 April 1775.

22. Virginia *Gazette* (Pinkney), 28 April 1775; (Dixon and Hunter), 29 April 1775; (Purdie), 5 May 1775.

23. Davidson, *Propaganda*, 232; Virginia *Gazette* (Dixon and Hunter), 20 May 1775.

24. Virginia *Gazette* (Purdie), 5 May 1775; (Dixon and Hunter), 10 June 1775. Both newspapers used the same quotation.

25. Virginia *Gazette* (Purdie), 5 May 1775; (Dixon and Hunter), 6 May 1775; (Pinkney), 11 May 1775. Each of the newspapers used the same quotation.

26. Virginia *Gazette* (Dixon and Hunter), 3 June 1775; (Purdie), 2 June 1775.

27. Virginia *Gazette* (Pinkney), 22 June 1775.

28. Virginia *Gazette* (Dixon and Hunter), 3 June 1775; (Purdie), 2 June 1775. Both of the newspapers used the same quotation.

29. Virginia *Gazette* (Dixon and Hunter), 24 June 1775, 8 July 1775, 15 July 1775; (Purdie), 7 July 1775, 14 July 1775.

30. Virginia *Gazette* (Purdie), 21 July 1775.

31. Virginia *Gazette* (Dixon and Hunter), 17 October 1777.

32. Virginia *Gazette* (Purdie), 24 October 1777; (Dixon and Hunter), 24 October 1777.

33. Virginia *Gazette* (Purdie), 13 September 1776; (Dixon and Hunter), 14 September 1776. Both newspapers used the same quotation.

34. Virginia *Gazette* (Purdie), 4 October 1776.

35. Virginia *Gazette* (Dixon and Hunter), 29 November 1776.

36. Virginia *Gazette* (Dixon and Hunter), 13 December 1776.

37. Virginia *Gazette* (Dixon and Hunter), 6 May 1774, 13 May, 8 July 1775; (Clarkson and Davis), 21 October 1780. The actual casualty count was much worse for both sides. The British lost 226 dead and 828 wounded, while the Americans lost 140 killed and 271 wounded. Middlekauf, *The Glorious Cause*, 292.

38. Virginia *Gazette* (Dixon and Hunter), 15 July 1775; (Purdie), 14 July 1775.

39. For a similar conclusion concerning Maryland, see David C. Skaggs, "Editorial Policies of the *Maryland Gazette*, 1765–1783," *Maryland Historical Magaine* 59 (1964): 341–349.

40. Virginia *Gazette* (Dixon and Nicolson), 22 January 1780.

41. Davidson, *Propaganda*, 400–401.

42. Virginia *Gazette* (Dixon and Hunter), 23 September 1775, 7 October 1775, 21 October 1775, 28 October 1775; (Purdie), 22 September 1775, 6 October 1775; (Pinkney), 5 October 1775.

43. Virginia *Gazette* (Dixon and Hunter), 29 June 1776, 27 December 1776, 29 August 1777; (Purdie), 27 December 1776, 29 August 1777; (Dixon and Nicolson), 7 August 1779; Davidson, *Propaganda*, 368, 369.

44. Virginia *Gazette* (Dixon and Hunter), 20 January 1776.

45. Virginia *Gazette* (Purdie), 18 August 1775.

46. Virginia *Gazette* (Dixon and Hunter), 18 July 1777.

47. Virginia *Gazette* (Pinkney), 19 October 1775.

48. Virginia *Gazette* (Pinkney), 10 January 1776; (Dixon and Hunter), 11 May 1776.

49. Virginia *Gazette* (Purdie), 16 October 1778 (unable to confirm this story from other sources).

50. Virginia *Gazette* (Dixon and Hunter), 4 July 1777.

51. Virginia *Gazette* (Dixon and Hunter), 21 February 1777.

52. Virginia *Gazette* (Purdie), 30 May 1777, 22 August 1777; (Dixon and Hunter), 15 August 1777.

53. Davidson, *Propaganda*, 365, 403.

54. Virginia *Gazette* (Dixon and Nicolson), 12 June 1779.

55. Virginia *Gazette* (Purdie), 12 April 1776.

56. Virginia *Gazette* (Dixon and Hunter), 24 January 1777.

57. Virginia *Gazette* (Dixon and Hunter), 20 April 1776.

58. Virginia *Gazette* (Pinkney), 22 June 1775.

59. Virginia *Gazette* (Pinkney), 24 August 1775.

60. Virginia *Gazette* (Dixon and Hunter), 14 October 1775.

61. Virginia *Gazette* (Dixon and Hunter), 2 December 1775.

62. Virginia *Gazette* (Pinkney), 4 May, 13 December 1775; (Dixon and Hunter), 3 June 1775, 16 September 1775, 7 September 1775, 22 November 1776,10 July 1778, 17 July 1778; (Purdie), 12 July 1776, 6 September 1776; (Dixon and Nicolson), 12 June 1779, 3 July 1779; (Clarkson and Davis), 3 July 1779.

63. Virginia *Gazette* (Dixon and Hunter), 30 September 1775; (Purdie), 15 December 1775, 8 March 1776, 26 July 1776, 18 October 1776.

64. Virginia *Gazette* (Dixon and Hunter), 10 July 1778.

65. Virginia *Gazette* (Purdie), 26 July 1776, 18 October 1776; (Dixon and Nicolson), 3 July 1779; (Clarkson and Davis), 3 July 1779.

66. Virginia *Gazette* (Purdie), 5 January 1776; (Dixon and Hunter), 3 February 1776; (Pinkney), 3 February 1776.

67. Davidson, *Propaganda*, 371.

68. Virginia *Gazette* (Dixon and Hunter), 28 February 1777; (Purdie), 28 February 1777.

69. Virginia *Gazette* (Dixon and Hunter), 29 June 1776, 7 September 1776, 4 July 1777, 1 August 1777; (Purdie), 6 September 1776.

70. Virginia *Gazette* (Purdie), 29 November 1776, 12 September 1777; (Dixon and Hunter), 18 April 1777, 15 August 1777.

71. Virginia *Gazette* (Purdie), 30 August 1776, 11 July 1777; (Dixon and Hunter), 4 July 1777, 11 July 1777, 1 August 1777.

72. Virginia *Gazette* (Purdie), 6 September 1776; (Dixon and Hunter), 7 September 1776.

73. Virginia *Gazette* (Purdie), 10 May 1776.

74. Virginia *Gazette* (Dixon and Hunter), 21 February 1777; (Purdie), 21 February 1777.

75. Virginia *Gazette* (Dixon and Hunter), 13 June 1777.

76. Virginia *Gazette* (Pinkney), 26 October 1775.

77. Virginia *Gazette* (Purdie), 19 January 1776.

78. Davidson, *Propaganda*, 373; Virginia *Gazette* (Purdie), 6 June 1777.

79. Virginia *Gazette* (Dixon and Nicolson), 5 June 1779.

80. Virginia *Gazette* (Dixon and Hunter), 13 June 1777.

81. Virginia *Gazette* (Dixon and Hunter), 20 June 1777; (Purdie), 15 March 1776, 13 June 1777, 27 June 1777; (Dixon and Nicolson), 26 March 1779, 8 May 1779, 5 June 1779, 3 July 1779; (Clarkson and Davis), 3 July 1779.

82. Virginia *Gazette* (Dixon and Hunter), 11 May 1776, 7 March 1777, 15 August 1777, 5 December 1777; (Dixon and Nicolson), 22 January 1780.

83. Virginia *Gazette* (Dixon and Hunter), 18 July 1777; (Purdie), 18 July 1777, 20 March 1778.

84. Virginia *Gazette* (Purdie), 28 February 1777.

85. Virginia *Gazette* (Pinkney), 22 June 1775.

86. Virginia *Gazette* (Pinkney), 3 February 1776; (Dixon and Hunter), 27 January 1776, 5 December 1777; (Purdie), 22 August 1777, 5 December 1777; (Dixon and Nicolson), 26 February 1779, 9 April 1779, 22 May 1799, 14 August 1779, 28 August 1779.

87. Virginia *Gazette* (Dixon and Hunter), 6 June 1777; (Purdie), 6 June 1777.

88. Virginia *Gazette* (Dixon and Nicolson), 9 April 1779, 30 October 1779, 27 No-

vember 1779, 25 December 1779,11 March 1780; (Clarkson and Davis), 25 December 1779.

89. Virginia *Gazette* (Dixon and Nicolson), 19 March 1779, 9 April 1779, 24 April 1779, 19 February 1780.

90. Virginia *Gazette* (Dixon and Hunter), 4 April 1776, 10 August 1776; (Purdie), 7 June 1776, 11 October 1776. Each newspaper printed the same quotation.

91. Virginia *Gazette* (Purdie), 25 October 1776, 15 August 1777, 27 March 1778; (Dixon and Hunter), 27 December 1776, 14 February 1777, 18 April 1777, 12 December 1777, 8, 15 May 1778.

92. Virginia *Gazette* (Dixon and Hunter), 9 October 1778; (Dixon and Nicolson), 24 April 1779, 22 May 1779, 11 December 1779; (Clarkson and Davis), 11 December 1779.

93. Virginia *Gazette* (Dixon and Hunter), 22 July 1775; (Purdie), 22 July 1775.

94. Virginia *Gazette* (Purdie), 22 September 1775.

95. Virginia *Gazette* (Dixon and Hunter), 8 July, 5 August 1775, 11 October 1776; (Pinkney), 3 August 1775; (Purdie), 4 August, 8 September 1775.

96. Virginia *Gazette* (Dixon and Hunter), 16 September 1775.

97. Virginia *Gazette* (Purdie), 5 January 1776.

98. Virginia *Gazette* (Dixon and Hunter), 15 July 1775; (Pinkney), 13 July 1775; (Purdie), 14 July 1775.

99. Virginia *Gazette* (Pinkney), 7 September 1775; (Purdie), 21 September 1775, 30 August 1776; (Dixon and Hunter), 18 November 1775, 13 July 1776.

100. Virginia *Gazette* (Dixon and Hunter), 9 September 1775.

101. Virginia *Gazette* (Dixon and Hunter), 16 September 1775.

102. Virginia *Gazette* (Pinkney), 13 July 1775.

103. Virginia *Gazette* (Dixon and Hunter), 9 March 1776, 22 June 1776; (Purdie), 2 June 1775, 15 September 1775, 22 December 1775, 26 February 1776, 5 December 1777, 29 May 1778, 23 October 1778.

104. Virginia *Gazette* (Purdie), 9 February 1776, 7 June 1776, 2 August 1776, 23 October 1778, 26 February 1779; (Dixon and Hunter), 4 October 1776, 25 July 1777, 12 February 1779, 22 May 1779.

105. Virginia *Gazette* (Pinkney), 12 October 1775.

106. Virginia *Gazette* (Dixon and Hunter), 6 July 1776.

107. Virginia *Gazette* (Dixon and Hunter), 7 September 1776.

108. Virginia *Gazette* (Dixon and Hunter), 12 September 1777; (Purdie), 25 September 1777.

109. Virginia *Gazette* (Dixon and Hunter), 29 August 1777.

110. Davidson, *Propaganda*, 371–372; James Austin Holden, "Influence of Death of Jane McCrea on Burgoyne Campaign," *Proceedings of the New York Historical Association* 12 (1913): 286; Virginia *Gazette* (Dixon and Hunter), 3 October 1777; (Purdie), 15 August 1777.

111. Virginia *Gazette* (Dixon and Hunter), 6 July 1776, 10 August 1776, 17 August 1776, 27 September 1776; (Purdie), 22 November 1776, 29 November 1776; (Dixon and Nicolson), 1 May 1779, 22 May 1779, 25 September 1779, 13 November 1779, 29 January 1780.

112. Virginia *Gazette* (Purdie), 26 July 1776.

113. Virginia *Gazette* (Dixon and Nicolson), 29 May 1779, 31 July 1779, 9 October 1779.

114. Virginia *Gazette* (Dixon and Nicolson), 30 October 1779.

115. Virginia *Gazette* (Clarkson and Davis), 19 February 1780; (Dixon and Nicolson), 8 April 1780. Both newspapers printed the same quotation.

116. Benjamin Quarles, "Lord Dunmore as Liberator," *William and Mary Quarterly*, 3rd Series, 15(1958): 494–507.

117. Virginia *Gazette* (Dixon and Hunter), 12 August 1775, 23 September 1775, 21 October 1775, 13 April 1776; (Purdie),15 September 1775, 20 October 1775, 5 January 1776, 2 August 1776.

118. Virginia *Gazette* (Pinkney), 6 December 1775; (Dixon and Hunter), 9 December 1775, 16 December 1775; (Purdie), 15 December 1775.

119. Virginia *Gazette* (Dixon and Hunter), 23 December 1775; (Pinkney), 23 December 1775.

120. Virginia *Gazette* (Purdie), 5 January 1776; (Dixon and Hunter), 6 January 1776; (Pinkney), 6 January 1776.

121. Virginia *Gazette* (Purdie), 31 May 1776.

122. Virginia *Gazette* (Purdie), 19 July 1776.

123. Virginia *Gazette* (Purdie), 9 August 1776.

124. Virginia *Gazette* (Dixon and Hunter), 31 August 1776, 14 September 1776; (Purdie), 30 August 1776, 13 September 1776, 3 January 1777.

125. Virginia *Gazette* (Pinkney), 6 July 1775, 30 December 1775; (Dixon and Hunter), 8 July 1775, 27 January 1776.

126. Virginia *Gazette* (Purdie), 11 August 1775.

127. Virginia *Gazette* (Pinkney), 1 June 1775, 6 July 1775.

128. Virginia *Gazette* (Purdie), 22 March 1776.

129. Virginia *Gazette* (Pinkney), 23 November 1775; (Purdie), 24 November 1775; (Dixon and Hunter), 25 November 1775.

130. Virginia *Gazette* (Purdie), 29 December 1775.

131. Virginia *Gazette* (Purdie), 24 May 1776.

132. Virginia *Gazette* (Pinkney), 30 November 1775; (Dixon and Hunter), 2 December 1775, 11 May 1776; (Purdie), 22 March 1776.

133. Virginia *Gazette* (Pinkney), 16 November 1775.

134. Virginia *Gazette* (Purdie), 9 August 1776.

135. Virginia *Gazette* (Dixon and Hunter), 5 June 1776, 29 July 1776.

136. Virginia *Gazette* (Dixon and Hunter), 6 January 1776; (Purdie), 12 January 1776.

137. Virginia *Gazette* (Pinkney), 9 December 1775.

138. Virginia *Gazette* (Dixon and Hunter), 20 July 1776.

139. Virginia *Gazette* (Pinkney), 30 November 1775; (Dixon and Hunter), 31 August 1776; (Purdie), 2 May 1777.

140. Virginia *Gazette* (Purdie), 29 March 1776, 26 April 1776.

141. Virginia *Gazette* (Dixon and Hunter), 13 April 1776.

142. Bleyer, *Main Currents*, 76.

143. Benjamin Franklin to Richard Price, 13 June 1782, *Writings*, ed. J.A. Leo Lemay (New York: Library of America, 1987), 1049–1050.

2

BATTLE WITHOUT
A RULE BOOK

Donald Avery

It's not a new story. The President's private life becomes the subject of vicious rumor; there are strategic leaks to the press, threatening not only to undermine the presidency but to reduce it to impotence. Claims are made about a staffer's illicit liaisons with the President; others, that the President is a philanderer; that the President has children outside of wedlock, that the President and the First Lady are not actually married; that the President is about to deliver the nation to the enemy or, worse, to Satan; that a vote for the President is a vote against God—and indeed, God is telling His flocks that the President is the Anti-Christ.[1]

It reads like a work of modern fiction or at least as if it came from the pages of America's tabloid newspapers and television programs. The subject has to be a modern president, Bill Clinton, perhaps. But it isn't. All of America's early presidents, George Washington, John Adams, Thomas Jefferson, James Madison, James Monroe, Andrew Jackson, along with other political leaders, were subject to scathing attack in the form of rumors in newspapers.[2] Newspapers, however, were merely reflective of the times, and similar invectives were commonplace in correspondence, song, pamphlets, and the like.

Some of the claims made against political leaders in the early years of the Republic were devastating. Jackson, along with presidential hopeful Alexander Hamilton, were both accused of adultery.[3] Jefferson was charged in the opposition press with "frolicking with his 'Congo Harem' and adding to the labor force at Monticello by an annual increment of mulattoes."[4] Not unlike the abuse heaped upon Hillary Rodham Clinton today by opponents of her husband, Rachel Jackson suffered some of the most scurrilous attacks against a First Lady in American history. The following is a good example of the kind of attack that found its way to news-papers:

I make a solumn [sic] appeal to the reflecting part of the community, and beg of them to think and ponder well before they place their tickets in the box, how they can justify it to themselves and posterity to place such a woman as Mrs. Jackson! at the head of the female society of the U. States.[5]

At one time or another, all of America's early presidents were accused of consorting with the enemy, both worldly and temporal. Accusations were thrown back and forth between Federalists and Republicans[6] over which faction represented the greatest threat to the Republic's well-be-ing.[7] In a time of deeply held religious convictions, an implication of athe-ism could be devastating to a public figure. Most of the leadership of the political faction associated with Thomas Jefferson, as well as Jefferson him-self, was accused of atheism by its opponents. A striking example ap-peared in the New England *Palladium* in 1800:

Should the Infidel Jefferson be elected to the Presidency, the seal of death is that moment set on our holy religion, our churches will be prostrated, and some infa-mous prostitute, under the title of the Goddess of Reason, will preside in the Sanc-tuaries now devoted to the Most High.[8]

However, while it was Washington and Jefferson who were most of-ten identified as ungodly, Jefferson's Republicans as a group were gener-ally attacked by Federalists and the clergy.[9]

Although modern tabloid journalism looks somewhat like the jour-nalism of the early years of the Republic, there is a fundamental differ-ence. While the journalistic rumor mill in the early national period was generated by political expediency, it was also a response to pressing politi-cal, economic, and cultural differences among Americans and the myriad crises facing the new nation. However—and this is no small *however*—while the modern journalistic rumor mill still has to deal with the conflict it finds itself in as it responds to the crises facing America, it is driven by competitive pressures rather than political motivations that often look the same in practice. Ultimately, the press has throughout its history faced crises along with the society of which it is a part.

Almost from its meager beginning in 1704,[10] the American newspaper has exerted influence.[11] Occasionally brilliant, often mediocre, it has rarely been insignificant. Donald Stewart's assessment seems near the mark: "Despite the unevenness of its influence, the press has almost from its in-ception in America come consistently to reflect the life and interests of the nation's citizenry."[12] Indeed, he argues that at times the press has "both molded public opinion and mirrored it."[13] One of those times was what has come to be called the party press period. The concerns of the nation's newspapers during this 50-year period (1783–1833) were those of society at large.

How Americans thought of themselves and viewed the rest of the world were colored by a number of political factors. It was differences over these factors that led to the creation of political parties. The issues that were of concern to the nation in the early years of the Republic were themselves the raw material of the newspapers. In a sense, historians have only continued discussions that began during the period. Maritime issues, including infringement upon American trade and the rights of neutral nations, along with the controversy surrounding the impressment of seamen, expansionism into Canada and east Florida, along with land hunger and Indian hostilities, the failures of diplomacy, threats to national honor, and the abiding faith in republicanism—all were division points that promoted political factions. These were all matters for debate and discussion in newspapers, the period's only widely disseminated medium. The ebb and flow of news pushed the newspapers first one way and then another. Just as is true today, they may not have been the only subject on the individual's agenda, but these issues were the overriding concerns of the day. In a period when communication could hardly be termed *mass*, letter writing was a major means of communication and tied closely to newspapers. Letters were often the raw material of journals, and the ideas and opinions of the citizenry spread more widely through the instrument of the newspaper than any other means of communication.[14]

While the newspaper reports were often less than accurate, they usually represented the only source of information the common American had of events in far-off places, which in most cases was the next town. The United States was not as developed as Europe, had fewer roads, more difficult means of travel, and was not as physically isolated. In such an environment, communication of any nature was vital and represented a means to satiate curiosity about the outside world. Throughout the 18th century, newspapers showed remarkable popularity as the American public developed an infatuation with the medium beyond that of the Europeans. For this reason alone, American newspapers' social and political importance throughout this period, no matter their content, should not be underestimated.

When viewed from the perspective of the 20th century, the party press period in American history appears to be a "period of black journalism"[15] or the "Dark Ages of Journalism"[16] with few of the positive attributes of journalism as the modern age believes it should be practiced. It was a time of back-stabbing, name-calling, lies and liars, and partisanship. Generally, the newspapers were devoted to one political persuasion or another with little concern for the middle ground, running the gamut from the vitriolic *Wasp* of Harry Cromwell, so scurrilous that it was often disavowed by the very Federalists whom it supported,[17] to the Washington (D.C.) *National Intelligencer*, a newspaper that began life as a mouthpiece for the Jefferson administration but that grew more independent over the years.[18]

James Lee argues the traditional view: "Those who look over the papers of this era will find that all of the customary courtesies of life were put aside; that the papers of both parties employed the vilest, grossest epithets found in the English language."[19] Even family members were not immune.[20]

The name-calling was brutal, and there was little to differentiate the party factions when it came to mudslinging.[21] Among the epithets found in newspapers were many that would be considered fighting words, such as *dog, skunk, coward, hypocrite, criminal, blasphemous, corrupt, worthless, immoral, atheist, adulterer, insane, drunk, assassin, vile, carouser*, among a litany of others.[22] Among those much more politically oriented aimed at Federalists by Republicans were terms such as *Tory, aristocrat, royalist, monarchist*, and *enemy of liberty*. Those terms aimed at Republicans by Federalists included *democrat, atheist*, the pro-French word *Jacobins*, and *anarchist*.[23] While many of the attacks were personal, the differentiating factor was still partisan politics.

There is little question that the two countries that caused the most profound political rifts in the young United States were England and France. In addition to promoting political divisions in America, the French Revolution created a demand in Europe and particularly in France for the food staples that the United States produced in abundance. Where England had controlled the trade of such goods in the past, after the Revolution, Americans were in a position to establish their own trade. It was a brisk trade that strongly competed with English commercial supremacy.[24] Such competition with English trade was certain to cause conflict. The United States was scorning English laws, cutting into English trade, and creating a merchant marine that competed with English sea power; English seamen were deserting and signing on American ships; and contraband was being carried on American vessels to England's enemy, France. Clearly, such activity ran counter to England's traditional role as a sea power.[25] The English reaction was to limit American trade just as it had in the colonial period. It was this English interference with American trade that constituted "the maritime issues."[26]

Almost every American reaction to the maritime issues was to limit American trade in some way. This was almost certain to generate hostility between New England's commercial interests and farmers, usually supported by Federalists, and the federal government. One of the many American reactions to the maritime issues in the early Republic years was the Embargo Act of 1807.[27] Open defiance by New England and the late-arriving but nearly as vehement opposition of farmers suggested just how unpopular the measure was and, like most matters involving England or France, provided political attack opportunities.

The Federalists attempted to take advantage of the discontent, much of which they fomented themselves. There seemed to be little middle ground on the matter from the beginning. The New Haven Connecticut *Journal*'s commentary on the embargo was typical of the Federalist, pro-British position: "I will stake my life on it, the hand of Napoleon is in this thing. It will have no effect on Europe and will only harm Americans."[28] The tact of the administration's newspaper, the Washington (D.C.) *National Intelligencer,* was to support the Republican line and President Jefferson's handling of foreign policy. It was also inclined to attack those opposed to the embargo: "The embargo will produce a happy effect, inasmuch as it will determine in the estimation of European nations the importance of American commerce and the value of her friendship."[29]

Since the end of the Revolution, American Federalist leaders had recognized that cordial relations with England were in America's best interests because England controlled the Atlantic and the shipping routes that American trade required. Republicans were openly hostile toward England, the former master, and considered an association with France more acceptable—even if proved less advantageous to American commercial interests. It would be years before Republicans understood that American commerce was such that an alliance with the prevailing sea power was in the nation's best interest.[30] In a letter to James Monroe, Jefferson, toward the end of his life, wrote: "Great Britain is the nation which can do us the most harm of any one . . . on earth; and with her on our side we need not fear the whole world."[31]

Perhaps the most baffling issue was the impressment of Americans to crew English ships. While it was not new—it had occurred to a limited extent in the colonial period[32]—it began in earnest following the Revolution when, due to continuing warfare with France, the English had an increasing need for naval personnel. The legal basis for impressment was contained in the King's Proclamation of October 16, 1807:

It commands all British seamen serving in foreign vessels, merchantmen or ships of war, to return to their native country, . . . and authorizing all officers commanding his majesty's ships of war to reclaim all such seamen.[33]

The major event in the impressment controversy concerned the American frigate *Chesapeake*. It embodied all aspects of the disagreement. The ship was an American naval vessel, both English and American seamen were impressed, and the American ship sustained considerable damage during a brief and decidedly one-sided cannon battle. Even the British government agreed the attack was illegal but refused to do more than negotiate. The attack provided considerable fodder for the partisan press.

Congress was in session when the attack occurred, and the Embargo of 1807 was passed in the heat of that incident. Despite the matter passing Congress, the embargo itself was attacked or defended by the press strictly along party lines.

When the vote was taken in the House on whether the United States should go to war with the British in 1812, the frontier states and Deep South were unanimous in their support for war. Because the frontier states were somewhat removed from the coast and many of the maritime issues, some historians have suggested that "land hunger"[34] and "Indian troubles"[35] were major underlying reasons for the vote. Few would seriously argue the land hunger thesis, but Indian problems were recognized at the time and provided a fine controversy for the newspapers. Fears of a massacre of Americans by Indians by the Republican Washington (D.C.) *National Intelligencer*[36] were in sharp contrast to a report in the Federalist New Haven Connecticut *Journal*[37] that the Indians in the Northwest wanted peace.

The Indian issue gave newspapers an excellent means of expressing their politics on a subject with which most Americans could agree. The Portland (Maine) *Eastern Argus*, always outspoken whether the subject concerned the British, Federalists, or Indians, reported boldly on the specifics. Under the headline "Most Horrid!" appeared a report that the British were paying $6 for the scalps of white settlers, "men, women, and children." The final line of the report was strong, to say the least: "Gracious God, in thy omnipotent justice—STRIKE!"[38] Federalist newspapers attempted to allay fears by reporting that Indians wanted peace and that treaties were being signed.[39]

Along with the issues concerning Indians was the matter of American expansionist tendencies in east Florida and Canada. Threats against East Florida and Canada appear to have been merely tools of diplomacy, a matter of achieving a better bargaining position with the English.[40] However, when combined with the Indian issues, expansionism made for a particularly powerful newspaper tool to use against the opposition. As with all issues of the day, the newspapers adopted predictable positions.

The failure of American diplomacy in the early years of the 19th century and even the *Chesapeake* attack itself can be seen in terms of British attempts to prevent American economic growth; they certainly reduced American prestige around the world. Madison, and the Republicans, saw the British demands leading up to the War of 1812 as "not sought in a belligerent right or even in a policy merely belligerent, but in one which had no origin or plan but those of commercial jealousy and monopoly."[41] In short, Madison knew that Great Britain was worried about, and envious of, the rising American empire, an empire growing both in pride and in power.[42]

Perhaps one of the overriding concerns of the early years of the Republic were fears that republicanism and the experiment with the republican form of governance might fail or the government might be overthrown. American leaders felt they had to show the world that the republican form of government led to greater human well-being than any other form of government. While Federalists and Republicans could agree on the importance of maintaining the republican form of government, they simply could never agree on how to do it as a practical matter.

These were the central issues of the early years of the Republic. They not only helped to define American foreign and domestic policy, they were the means by which political factions defined themselves. A key element in the defining process was the newspaper, a means of stating the national leadership's evolving politics but also a way of getting political stances to the local supporters in a way that made it more difficult for internal party differences to spread into the public arena.

Whether the newspapers' concern for partisan politics was as overwhelming as journalism historians have suggested is debatable, but that editors were much taken with political issues is clear.[43] That they performed a major role in the developmental political history of both the nation, generally, and political parties, specifically, is less arguable. Newspapers were viewed by contemporaries of the period as an essential part of the evolving American political system.[44] They were the instrument by which the political faithful were kept informed and given their marching orders. In short, the press may never have been more critical to the political debate, to the formation of political concepts, to the political life of the nation as it was during the party press period.[45]

The party press is usually discussed as if it represented a single event, process, or period of time.[46] However, historians today consider the evolutionary period collectively called the party press period as actually consisting of two time frames separated by what has been called the "Era of Good Feelings,"[47] which ran approximately from 1816 to 1824. A number of these writers have pointed out that the Era of Good Feelings really wasn't. The period was marked mostly by "political turmoil" as the Republican Party devolved into warring camps.[48] After the disaster of the Adams administration, Federalists spent the next few years trying to find a new political identity.

Not surprisingly, the politics of the party press period were perhaps more volatile than at any other time in American history. This is particularly true of the first period, from 1783 to 1816, which seemed to consist of a multitude of politicians/editors painting the opposition in the vilest terms. Historians know all the names: Benjamin Russell, John Fenno, William Cobbett, Benjamin Bache, William Duane, Philip Freneau, and William Harrison Smith, just to mention the more prominent. The second party press period, roughly from 1824 to 1833, told the story of many politicians and their newspaper supporters but was marked by the dominance of one man, Andrew Jackson; most others paled next to "Old Hickory."[49] Historians know those names as well: Francis Blair, Duff Green, Thurlow Weed, Amos Kendall, Thomas Ritchie, Edwin Croswell, and Joseph Gates. There were many other, lessor knowns, found in virtually every town with a newspaper.

One of the mainstays of modern journalism is the concept of objectivity, what many during the party press period called *impartiality*. However, it was not enough to be independent during this period—an editor needed to be partisan, unashamedly so.[50] Federalist William Cobbett and his *Porcupine's Gazette and Daily Advertiser* were good examples of a newspaper and an editor who actively promoted the concept of partisanship: "Professions of impartiality I shall make none," Cobbett wrote in attacking editors who were not partisan.[51] There simply was no attempt to be impartial. To do so was to invite invective from one's own party. Most editors did not pretend to be impartial. Indeed, advocacy of a cause was imperative.[52]

In modern America, only conservatives and the Religious Right appear to come close to the venom level found in the newspapers of the two periods. Accusations against President Clinton from the Religious Right when they know the charges are untrue read and sound in the media very much like what readers found in the newspapers of the party press period. It was simply the contemporary means of taking on the opposition. Cobbett thought the best way to deal with Republicans was tit for tat: "to set foot to foot; dispute every inch and every hair's breadth; fight them at their own weapons, and return them two blows for one."[53]

One writer contrasted the new freedom editors enjoyed with how they used the freedom: "In America where newspapers were enjoying a greater freedom of comment than ever had been known anywhere in the world ... journalists soon became known for the vituperativeness of their writing."[54] For example, the Philadelphia *Aurora*, a Jeffersonian paper, referred to prominent Federalist Noah Webster as an "impious, disorganized wretch!"[55] and printed an advertisement to the Federalist editor of the *Gazette of the United States*: "To Mr. Fenno: This is to announce you to the world as a scoundrel and a liar; and though you may be generally known as such, I will prove what I say."[56]

Several writers have looked at the absence of a sense of responsibility to describe the media of this period.[57] However, the media of the party press period must be understood in terms of the practices of the period and not in terms of attributes developed and assigned later.[58] Still, that mitigating circumstances existed does not change the fact that among the most frequently used techniques to support political causes was the personal attack.[59] At the roots of the conflict was politics, and despite research on the agenda-setting function,[60] newspapers responded to environmental pressures then just as they do today.[61]

Viewed from a modern perspective, newspapers of the early Republic were usually gray, used small type,[62] were monotonous, and lacked continuity.[63] Considering the primitive state of the craft, nothing more should be expected.[64] They rarely printed headlines in the modern sense. For each one-column headline that read "War with Algiers,"[65] there were dozens that might have only a simple label such as "Europe."[66] Unlike modern publications, no attempt was made to give readers sufficient background so that they could understand the nature of the story. Clearly, editors believed they were producing for a select and informed audience.[67] Because newspapers were costly,[68] concerned with commerce, politics, and high matters of state, and often given to classical allusions,[69] the conclusion that readers were often the educated elite of society is inescapable.[70]

While there were partisan newspapers in every state and territory, those that carried the greatest influence were to be found in the major cities, at least during the first party press period. Of course, those journals with the greatest influence often created the greatest agitation.

Agitated-dissenters-turned-mob were nothing new to Benjamin Franklin Bache, founder of the independent[71] Philadelphia *General Advertiser* (also called the *Aurora*) and grandson of Benjamin Franklin. When the mob, fortified with alcohol and Federalist fervor, came for him the first time, Bache was trapped in his home with wife and children. The crowd's catcalls and ineffectual but noisy attempts to beat on the Bache house attracted the notice of neighbors who were able to disperse the mob. The second attack was met by Bache and his friends, armed and ready for a fight. The only damage was a few broken windows.

The kind of hate generated by Bache among Federalists is probably unique in American history. Perhaps the only modern comparison is with the late William Loeb of the Manchester (New Hampshire) *Union Leader*, which has been a thorn to nonconservatives for decades. Bache was the grandson of Benjamin Franklin, but that cut no ice with Federalists. Unlike his famous grandfather, Bache was passionate, impetuous, narrow, and intolerant.[72] One writer points out that as a journalist Bache displayed "a degree of virulence, vindictiveness and scurrility that distinguished him even among the journalists of his generation."[73] Republicans loved him and thought him a patriot, while Federalists thought he was the devil. Whether loved or hated, Bache remained undeterred in bashing Federalists, especially Washington:

If ever a nation was debauched by a man, the American nation has been debauched by Washington. If ever a nation has suffered from the improper influence of a man, The American Nation has suffered from the influence of Washington. If ever a nation was deceived by a man, the American nation has been deceived by Washington. Let his conduct then be an example to future ages. Let it serve to be a warning that no man may be an idol.[74]

Merciless to the end, Bache commented at the first president's death that "if ever there was a period for rejoicing, this is the moment."[75]

When mobs failed, Federalists in government tried other informal and more formal means of silencing the "vicious"[76] Bache, including congressional action, and even led advertising and distribution boycotts against his newspaper. The Adams administration's major attempt against Bache came on the heels of the passage of the Alien and Sedition Acts of 1798. However, before he could be tried, his death in a Philadelphia yellow fever outbreak did what the most fervent Federalist could not do. The Alien and Sedition Acts went far beyond any Federalist feud with Bache, however. As can be seen in the following chapter, they embodied the antagonistic spirit of the times and represented the most serious threat the press faced as the young Republic grappled with what it was and what it wanted to be.

With Bache's death it fell to his assistant, William Duane, to carry on the Republican crusade. Immediately, the Adams administration redirected its attention to Duane, who was charged under the Alien and Sedition Acts. And Duane had the company of other Republicans. Illustrative of the animosity between Federalists and Republican editors (also known as democrats) are the following comments by one Federalist editor:

Why did the Democrats call the Federal sedition-law the "gag law"? It only punished them for lying, while it left them free liberty to publish truth. "Aye, there's the rub!" Nothing can so completely gag a Democrat as to restrain him from lying. If you forbid his lying, you forbid his speaking.[77]

Following the demise of the Alien and Sedition Acts, Duane continued to support Republicans and was instrumental in the election of Thomas Jefferson in 1800. Despite the partisan nature of the *Aurora*, Duane's antics in political brokerage were so divisive that Jefferson shifted his support after 1801 to the Washington (D.C.) *National Intelligencer*. The *Aurora* remained a powerful voice in Republican politics long after it had been supplanted by other favored Republican newspapers.

Along with the Washington (D.C.) *National Intelligencer*, the *National Gazette* was one of two newspapers of national stature that James Madison and Jefferson helped establish to carry the Republican message. Edited by Philip Freneau, a classmate of Madison, the *National Gazette* was the early voice of republicanism, a powerful counterpoint to the Federalists. Founded in 1791, the *National Gazette* was created to have a national scope through being identified as the voice of Republican leadership at the national level.[78] It provided guidance for Republicans at all political levels[79] and no small amount of humor, given Freneau's knack with sarcastic verse, often aimed at his Federalist counterpart, Fenno.

One national paper, you think is enough
To flatter and lie, to pallaver and puff;
To preach up in favor of monarchs and titles,
And garters and ribbons, to prey on our vitals:
Who knows but our Congress will give it in fee,
And make Mr. Fenno the grand patentee![80]

When Jefferson resigned as secretary of state in 1793, Freneau lost the department's printing business, the newspaper's only means of support, and folded.

The Washington (D.C.) *National Intelligencer* was by far the most long-lived, successful, and ultimately, independent of those newspapers that began as voices for national political leadership. It became the model for a maturing newspaper industry that outgrew its rabid political partisanship. When the seat of government was moved from Philadelphia to the wilderness of Virginia, Jefferson convinced Samuel Harrison Smith to leave the old Capitol and begin a newspaper to support Jefferson's administration. While a voice for Republicans, Smith's newspaper often tended to be positive about the administration and generally was not as rabid in its attacks on the opposition as many other newspapers. This, coupled with the fact that it also printed the activities of Congress, often verbatim, made it a resource for other newspapers and made it possible for the newspaper to outlive the party it was founded to serve.

There were also a number of prominent regional or local newspapers that supported the Republican cause, often taking their cue from the national newspapers. Among the more conspicuous were the Richmond (Virginia) *Enquirer*, Portland (Maine) *Eastern Argus*, Worcester (Massachusetts) *National Aegis*, Raleigh (North Carolina) *Register*, the Missouri *Gazette* (today's St. Louis *Globe Democrat*), and the Nashville (Tennessee) *Gazette*.[81]

Three newspapers comprised the most important Federalist voices: John Fenno's *Gazette of the United States*, William Cobbett's *Porcupine's Gazette and Daily Advertiser*, and William Coleman's New York *Evening Post*. The first national and arguably most powerful Federalist newspaper was the *Gazette of the United States*, edited by Freneau's great editorial adversary, John Fenno. Thanks to government patronage and the support of Alexander Hamilton and other Federalist leaders, Fenno's publication helped define many of the political issues of the day.[82] Fenno gave as good as he got. His newspaper was every bit as strident and uncompromising as any Republican voice. He referred to Republicans as "the monster of Jacobinism," which was merely another way of calling them traitors.[83] So zealous was he that when yellow fever swept Philadelphia in 1793, he refused to leave the city. He survived to carry on the newspaper for another five years. However, in 1798, his failure to leave the city was fatal. Ironically, two major opponents in the party press period (Fenno and Bache) died in the same yellow fever outbreak.

The best writer of the party press period probably was William Cobbett.[84] For a man who lived in America only from 1794-1800, he spent those years well. A constant pain to Republicans and particularly Benjamin Franklin Bache, Cobbett and his *Porcupine's Gazette* replaced Fenno's *Gazette of the United States* as the most powerful voice for the Federalist cause.[85] That voice was strident, vitriolic, and rarely concerned with truth. He called Bache "an ill-looking devil" and said his "eyes never get above your knees."[86] Toward the end of his tenure in the United States, Cobbett disagreed with Adams over the president's handling of diplomacy with France. Cobbett's attacks on Adams were as strong as any that he had directed at Republicans. Adams considered using the Alien Act to get Cobbett deported, but when the editor lost a libel suit and fled to England in 1800, Cobbett was no longer a problem for either party.[87]

William Coleman's New York *Evening Post* was the inheritor of the Fenno and Cobbett legacy. Founded and supported by a group of prominent New York Federalists, including Alexander Hamilton, the newspaper almost immediately challenged the *Gazette of the United States* for leadership among Federalists. Called by one Federalist editor the "Field-Marshall of the Federalist editors,"[88] Coleman was perhaps a bit more even-tempered in his writings than many other partisan editors. However, as the leading Federalist voice, the newspaper became a severe critic of the Jefferson administration. Coleman remained editor until 1829, long past the demise of the Federalists.

There were other important, but not national, Federalist newspapers. Among the most important were Noah Webster's *American Minerva*, published in the early years of the Federalist cause, Warren Dutton's New England *Palladium*, poorly supported by the Federalists it served, and Benjamin Russell's *Columbian* (Massachusetts) *Centinel*, a Federalist newspaper that followed the party line but was also a successful publication because it provided the news of the day.[89]

The second party press period saw a major realignment of political parties. Federalists had managed to fatally shoot themselves in the foot over their mean-spirited and uneven handling of the Alien and Sedition Acts from 1797 through 1800. The effect of the legislation designed to destroy opposition was to kill the Federalist Party and get Jefferson and his Republicans elected in 1800. However, by the Era of Good Feelings, the Republican Party was beginning to disintegrate. During that rancorous time, party unity broke down and the party broke into a number of factions. In the election of 1824, there were actually three political entities, Republicans, supporting John Quincy Adams, Whigs, supporting Henry Clay, and Democrats, supporting Andrew Jackson.

By the 1828 election, only two parties remained, the Whigs and the

Democrats. The Federalist cause was espoused by the Whig Party, which consisted of the remnants of Federalist groupings and more conservative Republicans. The new entry was the party of Andrew Jackson. The Jackson Democrats represented the main body of Republicans. Many of the same newspapers that had existed under the old groupings, particularly those supportive of the Republican Party, continued in the 1820s and early 1830s.

Owing to its editor's connections, the *Argus of Western Kentucky* was probably the most important non national newspaper in the entire party press period. Amos Kendall, who would later become a crucial part of Jackson's "kitchen cabinet" (which carried more power than any official agency of government), was a superb promoter and effective editor. Kendall's newspaper became the instrument through which Jackson's policies were disseminated during the 1828 presidential campaign, and Kendall created much of the image used by Jackson to get elected.

The most important Democrat (the inheritor of the Republican label) newspaper was Duff Green's United States *Telegraph*, also instrumental in Jackson's presidential bid in 1828. Called "a political adventurer" by some,[90] Green was a hard headed, partisan editor who was accurately called "rough" by his opposition. His assertive style became the model for most Jacksonian newspapers. Green edited the newspaper until 1836. However, over time it became clear that Green's support for Jackson was waning and that Green's preferred choice was the vice president, John Calhoun. In 1830 Jackson decided to underwrite another newspaper as the official voice of the administration.[91]

The new official voice was Francis Blair's Washington (D.C.) *Globe*. Blair was a member of Jackson's "kitchen cabinet," hand picked by Kendall but a relative unknown to Washington politics.[92] Blair was closer to Jackson than any newspaper editor has been to a president.[93] As part of the "kitchen cabinet," Blair was instrumental in setting government policy as well as promoting the cause of the Democrats. Political office holders came to understand that a subscription to Blair's newspaper was a necessary prerequisite to appointment.[94]

Generally, the second party press period is seen as less rancorous than the first. However, as is so true of the modern presidency, the president was a lightning rod for opposition attack, and it was, and still is, often personal. James's comment in discussing the 1828 campaign seems to apply down through the years too often: "The sulphurous clouds of personal abuse all but obscured the only issues of policy before the country."[95]

Although politicians do not own media vehicles today, the effect is often the same. The distortion of events still provides considerable opportunity for the dark side of the human spirit to show through. Take the juxtaposition in 1994 of a mother's murder of her two small children in South Carolina and the political fervor of a congressman from Georgia. In the best tradition of the worst of times during the party press period, Congressman Newt Gingrich asserts that the Democratic Party is responsible for the murders because Democrats are not normal people, and after all, God is not on their side, a position slowly repudiated by some in the leadership of the Republican Party. It all sounds so much like Harry Cromwell's vicious attacks in his *Wasp*.

Despite the admitted rancor of the party press era, the media response to politics was often to help define political factions, issues, and personalities, a role that has not changed all that much. Still, the party press is a time-bound artifact of the early years of the Republic and, as such, should not be judged based on later, alien precepts.

NOTES

1. While all the events described apply to President Bill Clinton, they apply equally to previous presidents who served during the party press period, 1789 to 1833.

2. For the best treatment of newspaper political attack in the early party press period see William David Sloan, "Scurrility and the Party Press, 1789-1816," *American Journalism* 5, no. 2 (1988): 97-112.

3. Marguis James, *The Life of Andrew Jackson* (Indianapolis, IN: Bobbs-Merrill, 1938, 464; James M. Smith, *Freedom's Fetters: The Alien and Sedition Laws and American Civil Liberties* (Ithaca, NY: Cornell University Press, 1956), 376; *National Journal*, 26 March 1827; Liberty Hall & Cincinnati *Gazette*, 23 March 1828; Philadelphia *Daily Advertiser*, 17 July 1797; Boston *Daily Chronicle*, 25 September 1797; Richmond *Examiner*, 4 March 1800.

4. John C. Miller, *Toward a More Perfect Union* (Glenview, IL: Scott, Foresman and Company, 1970), 159-160.

5. Raleigh *Register*, 12 October 1824.

6. Various names were given to the political factions in the early Republic. Federalists were conservative, favored strong government support for commercial interests, a powerful central government, and rule by the elite, and were anti democratic. Republicans were more moderate, favored strong government support for the masses, a weak national government, and rule by the masses, and were democratic.

7. John C. Miller, *Crisis in Freedom* (Boston: Little, Brown and Company, 1931), 27-29; from a quote in the Federalist *Gazette of the United States*, 19 March 1801; *Columbian Centinel*, 17 October 1792; Philadelphia *Aurora*, 18 October 1796, 7 June 1800; *Independent Chronicle*, 31 August 1797; *American Minerva*, 21 August 1797; Albany *Gazette*, 10 April 1813.

8. See Frank Luther Mott's *American Journalism: A History: 1690-1960*, 3rd ed. (New York: Macmillan Company, 1962), 169.

9. New York *Journal*, 7 December 1793; Richmond *Recorder*, 17 November 1802; Sloan, "Scurrility and the Party Press, 1789-1816," 101; Miller, *Crisis in Freedom*, 25.

10. This was John Campbell's Boston *Newsletter*. It contained all the elements of

a newspaper, but the element that set it apart from earlier attempts was that it had continuity. Benjamin Harris's *Public Occurrences, Both Foreign and Domestick*, printed in 1690, was banned after a single issue. It looked like a newspaper and continued news. Likewise, *The Present State of the New-England Affairs*, printed in 1689, continued news and looked like a newspaper, but it, too, was published only once.

11. Donald H. Stewart, *The Opposition Press of the Federalist Period* (Albany: State University of New York Press, 1969), 4.

12. Ibid.

13. Ibid.

14. Donald R. Avery, "The Newspaper on the Eve of the War of 1812: Changes in Content Patterns, 1808-1812" (Ph. D. diss., Southern Illinois University, 1982), 46.

15. James Melvin Lee, *History of American Journalism*, new ed., rev. (Garden City, NY: Garden City Publishing, 1917, 1923), 143.

16. Edwin Emery and Michael Emery, *The Press and America*, 7 ed. (Englwood Cliffs, NJ: Prentice-Hall, 1954, 1993), 67.

17. Edwin Emery and Michael Emery, *The Press and America*, 4th ed. (Englewood Cliffs, NJ: Prentice-Hall, 1978), 95.

18. See generally, Stewart, *The Opposition Press of the Federalist Period*.

19. Lee, *History of American Journalism*, 143.

20. Ibid.

21. Sloan, "Scurrility and the Party Press," 99.

22. Ibid., 101.

23. Ibid., 100.

24. Edward P. Cheyney, *An Introduction to the Industrial and Social History of England* (New York: Macmillan, 1910), 201. See also E. H. Carter and R. A. F. Mears, *A History of Britain* (Oxford: Clarenden Press, 1960), 718-720.

25. Bradford Perkins, *Prologue to War* (Berkeley: University of California Press, 1961), 2. See also John Spencer Bassett, *A Short History of the United States*: 1492-1920 (New York: Macmillan, 1910), 306-307.

26. A. L. Burt, *The United States, Great Britain, and British North America from the Revolution to the Establishment of Peace after the War of 1812* (New Haven, CT: Yale University Press, 1940), 210-224.

27. Its purpose was to keep American goods at home and in the process coerce the English and French into permitting free access to European ports by American ships.

28. New Haven Connecticut *Journal*, 7 January 1808.

29. Washington *National Intelligencer*, 10 February 1808. The same quote appeared in the Worcester *National Aegis* six weeks later, 31 March 1808.

30. Roland G. Usher, *Pan-Americanism* (New York: Century, 1915), 54.

31. S. M. Hamilton, *The Writings of James Monroe* (New York: Columbia University Press, 1964), 23-24.

32. James F. immerman, *Impressment of American Seamen* (New York: Columbia University Press, 1925; reprint ed., Port Washington, NY: Kennikat Press, 1966), 11. During the colonial period, the impressment of American seamen occurred but was not regularly resorted to, as was the case in England. The intense opposition of the colonists can be seen in the case of the wholesale impressment of "sailors, ship-carpenters and labouring land-men" by Commodore Knowles in Boston

in 1747. immerman argues that the Americans were not accustomed to such treatment. This probably explains why three days of rioting followed the Boston impressments. The legal right to impress Americans rested on the same case as that for Englishmen. John Adams argued in 1769 that the impressment of Americans was illegal and that there were English statutes specifically exempting Americans from impressment. The judge agreed with Adams, but the victory was short-lived, for Parliament repealed the statute the same year.

33. New Haven Connecticut *Journal*, 10 December 1807.

34. Bradford Perkins, ed., *The Causes of the War of 1812* (New York: Holt, Rinehart & Winston, 1962), 4.

35. Leonard E. White, "The Embargo," in Perkins's *The Causes of the War of 1812*, 101.

36. Washington *National Intelligencer*, 28 December 1807.

37. New Haven Connecticut *Journal*, 14 January 1808.

38. Portland *Eastern Argus*, 4 June 1812.

39. New Haven Connecticut *Journal*, 9 April 1812.

40. Burt, "The Nature of the Maritime Issues," in Perkins's *The Causes of the War of 1812*, 14. See also Usher, *Pan-Americanism*, 50.

41. Burton Spivak, *Jefferson's English Crisis* (Charlottesville: University of Virginia, 1979), 70.

42. Ibid., 70-71.

43. See generally, Stewart, *The Opposition Press of the Federalist Period*; Jerry W. Knudson, "The Jefferson Years; Response by the Press, 1801-1809" (Ph.D. diss., University of Virginia, 1974); and William E. Ames and Gerald J. Baldasty, "The Washington, D.C., Political Press: A Developmental History of Functions" (Paper presented to the Association for Education in Journalism, University of Washington, Seattle, WA, 1978).

44. William David Sloan, "The Federalist-Republican Press: Newspaper Functions in America's First Party System, 1789-1816" (Paper presented to the Southwest Symposium for Mass Communication, Fort Worth, TX, 1981).

45. William David Sloan, "The Party Press 1783-1833," in *The Media in America*, 2nd ed., ed. William David Sloan, James G. Stovall, and James D. Startt (Scottsdale, AZ: Publishing Horions, 1993), 90.

46. See generally, Lee, *History of American Journalism*, 140-163. Lee called from 1812 to 1832 the party press period. Emery and Emery, *The Press and America*, consider only a single party press era and argue that it ended by 1800. Sloan, "The Party Press," argues forcibly that there were two periods of conflict divided by a single period of reduced rancor.

47. Samuel Eliot Morison, *The Oxford History of the American People* (New York: Oxford University Press, 1965), 400.

48. Sloan, "The Party Press," 79.

49. See generally, James, *The Life of Andrew Jackson*.

50. Sloan, "The Party Press," 70.

51. *Porcupine's Gazette and Daily Advertiser*, 5 March 1797.

52. Sloan, "The Party Press," 79.

53. Philadelphia *Censor*, December 1796, in Mary Eliabeth Clark's *Peter Porcupine in America: The Career of William Cobbett, 1792-1880* (Philadelphia, Beekman Publishers, 1939), 94.

54. Jim Allee Hart, *Views on the News: The Developing Editorial Syndrome 1500-1800* (Carbondale: Southern Illinois University Press, 1970), 67.

55. Philadelphia *Aurora*, 12 November 1796, as cited in Mott, *American Journalism*, 146.

56. Philadelphia *Aurora*, 1 April 1800, as cited in Mott, *American Journalism*, 146.

57. See Sloan, "Scurrility and the Party Press, 1789-1816," 97-98; William E. Ames, *A History of the National Intelligencer* (Chapel Hill: University of North Carolina Press, 1972), 10; Allan Nevins, *American Press Opinion, Washington to Collidge* (Boston: Ross Hargreaves, 1928), 11; Frank Luther Mott, *Jefferson and the Press* (Baton Rouge: Louisiana State University Press, 1943), 21; Smith, *Freedom's Fetters*, 278; Dumas Malone, *Thomas Jefferson and the Ordeal of Liberty* (Boston: 1962, 53-54; Lewis Leary, *That Rascal Freneau: A Study in Literary Failure* (New Brunswick, NJ: Rutgers University Press, 1941), 286.

58. Sloan, "Scurrility and the Party Press, 1789-1816," 98-99.

59. Ibid., 99.

60. See generally, Donald L. Shaw and Maxwell E. McCombs, *The Emergence of American Political Issues; the Agenda Setting Function of the Press* (St. Paul, MN: West Publishing Co., 1977).

61. James W. Tankard Jr., "The Theorists," in *Makers of the Media Mind*, ed. William David Sloan (Hillsdale, NJ: Lawrence Erlbaum Associates, 1990), 278-286, 331.

62. Body type sizes and faces varied. Generally, type size was five to six point (nearly unreadable without a magnifying glass); some newspapers, notably the New Haven Connecticut *Journal*, used body type sizes and faces that were similar to those used on the modern newspaper. However, most did not.

63. Avery, "The Newspaper on the Eve of the War of 1812," 60.

64. Frank Luther Mott, *American Journalism*, rev. ed. (New York: Russell & Russell, 1968), 200-201.

65. New Haven Connecticut *Journal*, 4 February 1808.

66. Richmond *Enquirer*, 12 January 1808.

67. Bernard A. Weisberger, *The American Newspaperman* (Chicago: University of Chicago Press, 1961), 69.

6. Mott, *American Journalism*. Newspapers were costly, with weeklies changing $1.50 to $2.50 per year, sometimes up to $5. Annual subscription rates for dailies usually ran from $8 to $10.

69. Letters to the editor were often signed "Hortensius," "Americanus," or "Civitus."

70. Mott, *American Journalism*, 203.

71. Although the newspaper was quite scathing in its attacks on anything Federalist or anti-French, Sloan, in *The Media in America*, argues that the newspaper was actually independent of the Republican party apparatus.

72. Miller, *Crisis in Freedom*, 26.

73. Ibid., 27.

74. Philadelphia *Aurora*, 23 December 1793, as cited in Mott, *American Journalism*, 128.

75. Quoted in the *Gazette of the United States*, 19 March 1801.

76. Emery and Emery, *The Press and America*, 66.

77. *The Wasp*, 6 January 1803, as cited in Mott, *American Journalism*, 149.

78. Sloan, "The Party Press," 77.

79. Ibid., 77-78.

80. See Lee's History of *American Journalism*, 123-124.

81. See generally, Clarence S. Brigham, "Bibliography of American Newspapers, 1690-1820," in *Proceedings of the American Antiquarian Society*, vols. 23-37 (Worcester, MA: new series).

82. Emery and Emery, *The Press and America*, 62-63.

83. Miller, *Crisis in Freedom*, 30.

84. Sloan, "The Party Press," 72.

85. Ibid., 73.

86. *Porcupine's Gazette*, 14 November 1797.

87. Sloan, "The Party Press, *The Media in America*, 73.

88. Cited by Willard G. Bleyer, *Main Currents in the History of American Journalism* (Boston: Houghton Mifflin, 1927), 133.

89. Brigham, "Bibliography of American Newspapers, 1690-1820."

90. James, *The Life of Andrew Jackson*, 456.

91. Ibid., 567.

92. Ibid., 567-568.

93. Sloan, "The Party Press," 82.

94. Lee, *History of American Journalism*, 157.

95. James, *The Life of Andrew Jackson*, 471.

3 🙥

THE LEGISLATION
OF PRIOR RESTRAINT

Donald Avery

He was no sailor, nor was he particularly wealthy. It was true that he was one of the lucky ones, part of the 20 percent of Haitians who had a paying job, working on the docks unloading the ships as they docked at Port-au-Prince. The job didn't pay all that great, but he made enough to keep his family from starving. He had even managed to save a few hundred dollars over the years. But now the embargo had stopped the ships from coming, and he had joined the rest of the unemployed.

As the economic and political situation in Haiti deteriorated, he found himself growing hopeless. Should he use his meager savings to join the others who were bailing out of Haiti, taking to the seas in hopes of reaching America, or should he remain, hoping for better times, while his savings were eaten by the needs of life? Still, he wondered about those who had been intercepted on the high seas by American warships and returned forcibly to Haiti. They certainly were worse off than he was. But what of those who made it through to Florida? They were illegal immigrants, but they were out of the degradation of their country. Finally, as his money dwindled, he decided to buy a piece of a small boat and with his family join the exodus.

The boaters were among the lucky. They managed to survive the treacherous Florida Straits, low supplies, overcrowding, and the warships. When they slipped ashore in the mangrove swamp, it didn't matter that he and his boat mates were illegal aliens. Like the millions of refugees who had come before, they had survived.

In 1994, it was the Haitians; throughout the 1980s and 1990s, it was the Mexicans and Cubans; in the 1970s, it was the Vietnamese; in the first quarter of the century, it was the eastern and southern Europeans, the Spanish, the Italians, the Albanians, the Greeks, the Turks, the Hungarians, the Lithuanians, the Russians; throughout the 19th century, it was the northern Europeans, the Swedes, the Dutch, the Germans; at the end of the 18th century, it was the French, the Irish, the British.

Revolution, along with political and economic hard times, and simple hope for a better life have always been the motivation for refugees to find a friendly port of call. For most of its existence the port of choice has been America. And for all its existence a substantial number of American citizens have opposed those refugees entering the country. All you have to do is read contemporary newspapers to see the political and economic opposition. At the heart of the problem has been the question of who to let in and who to keep out. Usually, the issue has been argued in public with the press acting only as a messenger boy. Only once, however, has the messenger boy become the target. In the first years of the Republic, the press met its first great challenge during the aptly named party press period.

The most important event of this period was the passage of the Alien and Sedition Acts. These were a direct result of the political maneuvering within the press, the voice of the two major political factions. At stake was freedom of the press, a relatively undefined concept not yet imbued into the fabric of the young nation. It was not surprising, then, that legislation "clarifying" rights be enacted. This legislative challenge came from the Federalists, the political party of George Washington and John Adams. Their gauntlet was the Alien and Sedition Acts of 1798, their primary targets Jeffersonian editors and vocal opposition supporters. The stakes were very high, both for the press and for the political parties: If the Federalists win, freedom of the press and expression is compromised; the viability of the two-party system is weakened, and the United States shifts dramatically toward a monarchical system instead of forging a democracy emphasizing states rights.

The Alien Act of 1798, approved for only two years, gave the president authority to expel aliens by executive order. Apparently urged by some in his administration, most notably Secretary of State Timothy Pickering, to use the law widely against aliens, President Adams actually only used it to expel two Irish writers. However, Frenchmen left America by the shipload, fearing reprisals from the Federalists in power. The overall effect was to put the fear of God in anyone who happened to disagree with Federalists and who also happened not to be native born or a naturalized citizen.

The Sedition Act of 1798 gave statutory authority to government to punish conspiracies against government and its officials. The effect was an attempt to silence critics of the administration, the Jeffersonians and the opposition Republican Party. Despite its attack on freedom of speech, the law was more liberal than similar laws in Europe. It required a jury trial and made truth a defense against libel. Badly executed, the law confused political opposition with sedition.[1] Opposition to the Federalists in general and the Adams administration in particular was invariably seen as sedition and thus a threat to the nation. For many Federalists, justice was simple: Oppose them and you qualify for prosecution under the Sedition Act.

Interestingly, most newspaper editors actually praised the Sedition Act and its limitations on freedom of speech. At least the Federalist newspapers did. In fact, no Federalist newspaper condemned the act, and nowhere was evidence to be found in the pages of the Federalist newspapers that they even recognized they could easily become the next victim. Here lies the irony, one not clearly enunciated until *Near v. Minnesota* in 1931 when the Supreme Court ruled prior restraint unconstitutional. What the Federalists more than a century and a quarter earlier didn't recognize was that prior restraint for some is, sooner or later, prior restraint for all.

The motivation behind the Sedition Act is quite clear. It would protect certain Federalist-dominated sections of government while excluding any control by Republicans, particularly Vice President Jefferson. The intent of the Federalists in pushing through the Alien and Sedition Laws was to brand Republicans as disloyal, at best, and treasonous, at worst. Clearly, this attempt at disarming the opposition, if successful, would give control of the national government to the Federalists.

While there were only 10 convictions during the law's two-year life, there were 25 arrests, 14 indictments, and 11 trials. Eight of the convictions were for the actions of editors. The primary targets of the law were Republican editors, several of whom found themselves either sitting in jail or paying a substantial fine. Thomas Adams of the Boston *Independent Chronicle* was arrested but never tried because of illness. However, his brother, Abijah Adams, was sentenced to 30 days in jail. Because he was found guilty of defaming the press, James Callender of the Richmond *Examiner* received the heaviest sentence, nine months in jail and a $200 fine. Thomas Cooper of the Northumberland *Gazette* was sentenced to six months and fined $400. William Duane of the Philadelphia *Aurora* and Philadelphia *General Advertiser* (in all later references called the *Aurora*) was indicted several times but succeeded in staying out of jail. David Frothingham of the New York *Argus* was found guilty by a jury that recommended mercy but was subsequently sentenced to four months in jail and fined $100. Charges against the owner of the newspaper, Ann Greenleaf, were dropped when she sold her newspaper. Charles Holt of the New London *Bee* was sentenced to three months in jail and fined $200 for urging men not to enlist in the army (some fifty years later Congress refunded the fine with interest). Anthony Haswell of the Vermont *Gazette* was sentenced to two months in jail and fined $200. None of the sentences were particularly harsh. While the Acts were national, the judges who heard the cases were local and often less enamored of the laws than local politicians.

One person charged under the act received the most outrageous penalty, considering the nature of the crime. Luther Baldwin, a resident of Newark, New Jersey, was found guilty of sedition for a comment he made while drinking in a pub. At the time, President Adams had just passed in an open carriage and cannons fired a salute. A patron at the same tavern said the cannons were firing at President Adams's arse. Baldwin, perhaps too long at the tavern, observed that he didn't care if they were firing through the president's arse. Unfortunately for Mr. Baldwin, his comment was deemed by the courts to be seditious to the tune of $150.

This was the new Republic's first excursion into the murky waters of prior restraint. Certainly, there had been other attempts during the colonial period to curtail the press, but the governing authority then had been England with its history of licensing and governmental control of commentary. Such an attack today would be met with swift and consistent opposition. After all, the press has had nearly 200 years of generally favorable treatment from government, a government that has by and large abhorred the idea of prior restraint. There was little such tradition in the early years of the Republic, which may go a long way toward explaining why some newspapers could accept the concept of prior restraint as long as it involved someone else's newspaper.

Ultimately, the fight was over both the ability of the press to criticize and the viability of the two-party system. From the perspective of the modern age, it is difficult to put a positive spin on the Alien and Sedition Acts, but, pragmatically, they provided the catalyst for a press free from prior restraint and a multiparty political system, no small feat for a nation with little history of either.

Because it had traditionally seen itself as a haven for the oppressed, Americans offered somewhat simple naturalization requirements following the Revolution. The residency requirement in 1790 was only 2 years. The requirement was raised to 14 years in the wake of the Naturalization Act of 1798. Four years later the residency requirement had been reduced to 5 years. Clearly, the extension of residency was designed to have specific targets among a range of French Jacobins, Irish radicals, Republicans and others who were seen as a threat to Federalists in general and the administration of John Adams specifically.

Federalist fears of the immigrants arose out of a general belief that only the elite—property owners, merchants, and professionals—were qualified to govern. Fundamentally, Federalists feared democracy with its government by the unwashed masses. Government for the people was fine; government by the people was just short of apocalyptic. For example, while referring to the Irish, one Federalist Congressman clearly expressed the Federalist fear of immigrants. Following a trip through Pennsylvania, he reported seeing many "United Irishmen, Free Masons, and the most God-provoking Democrats this side of hell."[2]

The United States has a history of responding to fears of immigrants. Twice in the 20th century such fear has led to legislation against foreigners, those of German descent during World War I and Japanese Americans in World War II. More recently, Americans have expressed their fears of Mexican, Cuban, and Haitian refugees, with conservatives in Congress pushing for limits.

The Revolution and the passage of the Bill of Rights were too recent for Americans to permit the government to infringe basic rights. The primary attack against the Alien and Sedition Laws came from the legislatures of two states, Kentucky and Virginia. At the heart of the Kentucky and Virginia Resolutions was that thorny issue, states' rights, which has haunted the Republic down to the present day. The position taken by Thomas Jefferson and James Madison and other Republicans was that the states were the final arbiters of the Constitution.[3]

Not since the constitutional convention had the differences between the political entities that came to be Federalists and Republicans been shown so glaringly. The Federalists, particularly Alexander Hamilton, wanted a powerful central government, while the Republicans, particularly Jefferson, wanted a loose confederation with power vested in the states. Had the language of the Kentucky and Virginia Resolutions been adopted widely, the federal government as we know it today could never have existed.[4] These were radical instruments recognized as such by the state legislatures that were asked to vote on them. In fact, no states ratified the resolutions, and even 40 percent of Virginia's delegates opposed the measures. The Philadelphia *Gazette* called the resolutions a cure worse than the disease.[5] Aaron Burr conceded that the resolutions had "in the honest love of Liberty" gone "a little too far."[6]

The overall effect of the resolutions was to focus attention on the Alien and Sedition Laws as threats to American freedom and to paint Federalists as opponents of freedom while establishing Republicans as champions of freedom. In addition to delivering the presidency into the hands of Jefferson and the Republicans in 1800, the Alien and Sedition Laws and the response of the Kentucky and Virginia legislatures drew into the open the issue of states' rights, which had bedeviled the young nation, ultimately leading to civil war and providing fertile ground for demagogues of various persuasions.

While all three of the laws were debated widely in the press, it was only the Sedition Act that was aimed at silencing a hostile press. The act was very broad, yet quite specific, as it provided punishments for those who would write or utter anything considered scandalous or malicious about the country, the Congress, or the president. In short, the pragmatic approach to the act was silence, a trait for which the Republicans exhibited little affection.

There is little in the record to suggest that Federalists were particularly dishonest in their beliefs concerning Republicans and those who would turn over government to the rabble. One Federalist newspaper thought there were more than enough "French apostles of Sedition" around "to burn all our cities and cut the throats of all the inhabitants."[7] There were wild rumors that seditious foreigners were attempting to obtain the plans of American fortifications, that they were planning rebellion in the West and, worst of all, preparing to murder American citizens in their beds.[8]

At the root of Federalist fears was the large foreign-born population of the country. They believed that this was the primary source of opposition to government, a breeding place for factions, and in short, the recruiting ground of the Republicans.[9]

Having made New England inhospitable to most immigrants, those staunch Federalists could only watch the growth of other areas of the nation as immigrants—Irish, Germans, French—moved to more comfortable environs. As has always been the case, established populations tend not to want immigrants; often their best bet for a new life lies in immigrating to the frontiers and other unsettled areas. Manufacturing had not yet grown to the point where New England industry needed large numbers of workers that could only be supplied by an immigrant labor pool. The loss of influence in national affairs became the major thrust for the passage of several naturalization laws, most notably the Naturalization Act of 1798. Between 1790 and 1798 the residency requirement increased from 2 years to 14. Because most immigrants were undesirable to conservative, and elitist, Federalists, immigrants gravitated to the Republican Party, where they represented a serious threat to Federalists' hopes. Solution: Reduce the threat; reduce the number of potential Republicans. How? Increase the alien residency requirements. Federalists believed that short residency requirements let in treasonable ingrates into the country.

The newspapers' role under the Alien and Sedition Laws seems to have been, as it was during the entire party press period, to represent and promote the programs of the political parties. In 1798 most newspapers in the United States were Federalist and could be counted on to support the laws.[10] Federalist newspapers seemed to see no threat to freedom of the press in the laws. After all, objectivity was not considered a virtue in the early 19th century. Newspaper editors were expected to be partisan in their treatment of the news and commentary. In fact, editors could expect scathing attacks when they were not partisan. In their attack on Republican newspapers, the Federalists were able to get indictments and convictions, but the real target, Jefferson, remained unreachable because of his policy of not writing for newspapers during the two years of the Sedition Act's existence.[11]

The object of Federalist attacks, Republican newspapers, simply continued to assail Federalists and the national government as they had before the passage of the laws. The federal judiciary interpreted the Sedition Act so broadly that even commentary was included. Because much of what was found in the newspapers of the early Republic could be classified as opinion, it is not surprising that virtually any newspaper could be the object of grand jury action under the Sedition Act.

The attacks on Republican editors and politicians continued throughout 1798 and 1799. However, the growing split within the Federalists found Adams more and more isolated from his cabinet, all Hamiltonians. Adams' secretary of state, Pickering, was the primary actor in a dump-Adams movement promoted by the Hamiltonian faction of the Federalist Party.[12] The split became so wide that there was talk of forming a new political party to consist of the disgusted and disgruntled of both political parties.[13] In the end, this "Constitutionalists" faction moved to the Republican camp.[14] The *Aurora* and the *Independent Chronicle*, both Republican newspapers, argued that because of the split within the Federalist camp, no one voting for the Federalists could know who actually would be president and, besides, one part of the Federalists didn't trust the other.[15]

The Federalist Party effectively ceased to exist following a rout by the Republicans in 1800. The split within the Federalists, peace with France, in-fighting among Federalists, and the election of Jefferson contributed to the collapse of the Federalist Party as a viable entity. In the end the party's demise grew out of the public shift from the Federalists with their narrow focus on commercial interests to the Republicans whose broader support for agricultural interests attracted voters not only from the agrarian South and West but from the Northeast as well.[16]

Although they might have liked to keep the Alien and Sedition Laws on the books, if only to harass opposition leaders and newspapers, Republicans had pushed so hard through their own newspapers to paint supporters of the measure as anti Bill of Rights that they permitted the Alien and Sedition Laws to expire with Jefferson's election in 1800. It would not be the last time government launched an attack on the freedoms guaranteed in the Bill of Rights, but it would be the last time newspapers themselves promoted the idea.

NOTES

1. Samuel Eliot Morison, *The Oxford History of the American People* (New York: Oxford University Press, 1965), 35.

2. Ibid.

3. John C. Miller, *Toward a More Perfect Union* (Glenview, IL: Scott, Foresman and Company, 1970), 151.

4. John C. Miller, *Crisis in Freedom* (Boston: Little, Brown and Company, 1931), 153.

5. Philadelphia *Gazette*, 6 May 1799.

6. *Gazette of the United States*, 29 April 1799.

7. Albany *Centinel*, 7 August 1798.

8. *Country Porcupine*, 12 November 1798.

9. Miller, *Crisis in Freedom*, 41.

10. William David Sloan, "Freedom of the Press," in *The Media in America*, 2nd ed., ed. William David Sloan, James G. Stovall, and James D. Startt, (Scottsdale, AZ: Publishing Horzions, 1993), 116.

11. Ibid.

12. Manning J. Dauer, *The Adams Federalists* (Baltimore, MD: The Johns Hopkins Press, 1953, 1968), 246. See also *Gazette of the United States*, 10 July 1799, 17 July 1779, 18 July 1799; and *Porcupine's Gazette*, 25 January 1798, 3 April 1798, 13 July 1798, 7 September 1798, 3 December 1798, 29 January 1799.

13. Boston *Gazette*, 21 July 1800.

14. Dauer, *The Adams Federalists*, 253.

15. See Philadelphia *Aurora*, 15 August 1800, 18 August 1800, 12 December 1800; and *Independent Chronicle*, 20 November 1800, 24 November 1800.

16. Dauer, *The Adams Federalists*, 263-264.

4

JOURNALISM FOR
GOD AND MAN

Bernell Tripp

From his hiding place beneath a pile of fresh-cut boards on the second floor of the carpenter's shop, *Liberator* editor William Lloyd Garrison could hear the well-dressed mob milling around on the streets below and swarming throughout the building. The cry for "Garrison! Garrison!" drowned out the sounds of the Anti-Slavery Office sign being splintered into a thousand pieces nearby.

"Mr. J. R. C.," an abolitionist friend and fellow fugitive from the mob of Boston's respected businessmen, was dragged from the carpenter's storeroom and displayed before the mob. "This is not Garrison, but Garrison's and Thompson's friend, and he says he knows where Garrison is, but won't tell," Garrison heard someone say. Further interrogation of "Mr. C." proved unnecessary. Suddenly, searchers pulled Garrison from his hiding place and attempted to hurl him to the street below, but other rioters intervened and, coiling a rope around his body, allowed him to descend a ladder to the street and into chaos. Mob members ripped pieces of clothing from his body. Others cried, "Lynch him! Kill him!" while two men conducted him down Wilson's Lane to State Street behind Boston City Hall.

In the confusion, police officers waded into the tangle of bodies, managing to rescue Garrison and take him to the mayor's office. There officers provided Garrison with clothes, along with a false charge of disturbing the peace in order to place him in protective custody. Guards escorted the "prisoner" to a waiting carriage for transport to jail. Not to be dissuaded, rioters clung to the wheels of the hack. They rattled the doors, swung on the horses' harnesses, and attempted to overturn the vehicle. The driver whipped at the horses, as well as at the rioters, as he dashed off toward the

Leverett Street jail, leaving angry men and dust in his wake.

The next morning, prior to his release from jail, Garrison inscribed the following words on his cell wall:

Wm. Lloyd Garrison was put into this cell on Wednesday afternoon, Oct. 21, 1835, to save him from the violence of a "respectable and influential" mob, who sought to destroy him for preaching the abominable and dangerous doctrine, that "all men are created equal," and that all oppression is odious in the sight of God.[1]

Like Garrison, many journalists operating newspapers and magazines during the antebellum period faced significant verbal and physical abuses. Presses and private homes were burned or vandalized. Editors were threatened or beaten. Frederick Douglass was pelted with rotten eggs and thrown down the stage steps at a lecture hall. Elijah Lovejoy was murdered protecting his presses for the fourth time. Before his death, his home had been attacked and his furniture destroyed. Mobs attacked the office of Gamaliel Bailey's newspaper, the *Philanthropist*, three times. The irony was that the violence and danger came not from a foreign or unknown enemy but from the journalists' neighbors and other United States citizens.

The cause of the conflict? The abolition of slavery.

By the 1820s the development of a press dominated by party loyalty was beginning to give way to a press concerned with its broader civic responsibilities. Editors and publishers still maintained their political ties, but the power of party rule within the confines of the newsroom was weakening. In addition, in the wake of the country's preoccupation with moral and ideological issues, many editors determined to break through the citizens' sense of apathy toward slavery and establish the basis for a reform movement that began with the antebellum press and continued well past the end of the Civil War.

Playing a pivotal role in this quest for human rights, newspapers and magazines served as platforms for self-expression, as well as for appeals to the masses for understanding and support against societal injustices. The written word became the backbone of the movement, and editors and publishers voiced their criticisms or stances on important issues such as discrimination in education, employment, and full-citizenship rights through editorials and published speeches usually presented on the first and second pages of their newspapers.

Historian Russel B. Nye concluded that the conflict over abolitionist press responsibilities and the slavery question marked a turning point in American journalism history. He explained that abolition became the first major issue in the struggle for a free press that the country had faced since the Revolution. In short, the abolitionist struggle was a two-pronged battle: to end slavery and to end press control by outside powers.

Nye reasoned that abolitionists were also devoted to "the struggle to define and to maintain the traditional American civil rights and liberties" such as "free speech, a free press, the rights of petition, assembly and trial by jury."[2] He determined that slaveholders and slavery supporters feared that antislavery editorials would incite blacks to violence, and local lawmakers wrote statutes aimed at restricting freedom of speech and of the press. Consequently, even the press was in disagreement over right and wrong and its own role in the dispute. Editors were forced to choose sides, along with every other individual and organization in a country battling against itself. It was a period that threatened not only the country but also the very roots of the development of the American press.

While traveling through the United States during this period, British author Harriet Martineau noted the passion and fervor of these editors and private citizens who pledged their lives to the cause of abolishing slavery. In her book *The Martyr Age of the United States*, she wrote:

There is a remarkable set of people now living and vigorously acting in the world, with a consonance of will and understanding which has perhaps never been witnessed among so large a number of individuals of such diversified powers, habits, opinions, tastes and circumstances. The body comprehends men and women of every shade of color, of every degree of education, of every variety of religious opinion, of every gradation of rank, bound together by no vow, no pledge, no stipulation but of each preserving his individual liberty; and yet they act as if they were of one heart and of one soul. Such union could be secured by no principle of worldly interest; nor, for a term of years, by the most stringent fanaticism. A well-grounded faith, directed towards a noble object, is the only principle which can account for such a spectacle as the world is now waking up to contemplate in the abolitionists of the United States.[3]

Abolitionist editors clearly became identified as reformers who faced a variety of obstacles, including slaveholders and big businessmen, in order to restore a sense of morality and democracy to the nation. On the one side were the forces of equality and reform, and on the other side were the wealthy and the politically influential. Newspapers of the time were generally independent of political influences, and growing dissension throughout the country forced editors to choose sides and to act as representatives for their causes. They, thus, recognized the importance of press freedom and an autonomous press, unhampered by outside influences.

However, slaveholders maintained control of the ideological structure of American society through their economic and political dominance. They possessed the greatest wealth among the property-owning classes prior to the war, and this economic dominance allowed them to control both political parties and, consequently, all branches of the federal government. This permitted them to dominate U.S. foreign and domestic policy.[4]

As a result, many abolitionists were reluctant to make stringent demands of the slaveowners. Antislavery activism prior to 1830 was characterized, with a few exceptions, by moderation in language as well as in actions. Some historians reasoned that this passive behavior almost trivialized the slaveowners' responsibilities toward the suffering of the slaves. Consequently, a message seemingly without convictions allowed those who acquired slaves to rationalize about their actions and to raise questions that would appear throughout the antislavery struggle: How could more than 3 million slaves be assimilated into American society, and how would they be able to support themselves?

Slavery supporters often defended their position by pointing out that enslavement offered blacks security—assurance of food, clothing, shelter, and protection against sickness and old age—far better than those many whites endured. If released into society without their benefactors, the ex-slaves would surely starve, slaveowners reasoned. Some prominent slaveholders, such as George Washington and Thomas Jefferson, who secretly abhorred the slavery system, assuaged their feelings of guilt by providing comfortable accommodations and working conditions, or by arranging for tenancy or apprenticeship situations for many of their slaves.

Other slaveholders stressed that Africans had been raised as heathens in their homeland, and slavery provided them with an opportunity to experience Christianity and a more civilized behavior. However, opponents of slavery were apt to stress the fundamental consideration the supporters frequently overlooked: The slaves were not *free*. They reasoned that no matter how benevolent the master, the slave did not possess the rights and privileges God intended.

Thus, the battle for enfranchisement became a religious one, particularly in the decade after 1825. This decade marked the beginning of a revolutionary spirit in American religion and the start of its most influential reform movement. Abolitionists before that time had been swayed by liberal religious teachings. Whether a moral wrong, a political travesty, or an economic exploitation, slavery was above all else a sin against God. Many slaveholders had used Christian benevolence as an excuse for retaining their human chattel. Therefore, abolitionists prior to 1830 had hoped to remove slavery gradually by appealing to the slaveowners' sense of Christianity and through their own benevolent efforts.[5]

However, this approach began to lose ground in the late 1820s and early 1830s. A radical spirit was beginning to infect many abolitionists, responding to the insurgent words of *Liberator* editor William Lloyd Garrison. These followers maintained little hope that moral suasion alone would convince slaveholders to part with millions of dollars in property. Moral or natural laws, they feared, were not strong enough to counteract economic interests, and they reconciled themselves with the knowledge that violence was inevitable, relying on the belief that this course of action was at least morally warranted.[6]

This point was apparently one of the few things upon which abolitionists could agree. Because of the many questions broached by slaveowners wishing to retain their property and their way of life, the struggle for emancipation developed into a divisive one. The dissimilarities among the abolitionists were obvious, and it was this disparity among the activists' backgrounds and opinions that caused disagreements over what changes were necessary and how those changes would be implemented to improve the condition of blacks.

Abolitionist editors represented liberty, civil reform, and equality. Consequently, the abolitionist movement was interrelated with other liberal crusades of the period—issues such as religion and political action. While the primary purpose of the movement was to end chattel slavery, individuals involved throughout the abolitionist campaign recognized the importance of such issues as racism and black inferiority, civil rights for blacks, freedom of speech, and the abandonment of Christian values.[7]

Activists within the movement argued that racism and the concept that whites were superior to blacks lay at the root of the slavery issue, and unless the abolitionist movement mounted an antiracism campaign, the problems between the races would continue to exist.[8] The Reverend Theodore S. Wright, a black abolitionist and contributor to numerous antebellum black newspapers, cautioned that slaveholders would never heed the words of an "abolitionist" who spoke of loving slaves when these same individuals enslaved them with prejudice.

Similarly, Nathaniel Peabody Rogers noted that racism barred antislavery lectures from the New Hampshire state house and allowed violations of the state constitution and Bill of Rights. Rogers, editor of the *Herald of Freedom*, the voice of the New Hampshire Anti-Slavery Society, also pointed out:

It [racism] sneers at human rights through the *free* press. It handed John B. Mahan over to the alligators of Kentucky. It shot Elijah P. Lovejoy at Alton. . . . Time would fail us to tell of its extent and depth in this free country, or the deeds it has done. Anti-slavery must cure it, or it must die out like the incurable drunkards.[9]

Another faction of the movement, led by Midwestern abolitionist and orator Theodore Dwight Weld and philanthropists Lewis and Arthur Tappan, insisted that freedom without rights as full citizens offered blacks little improvement over their present status. Those abolitionists who feared that full freedom would jeopardize the social order offered such solutions as gradual emancipation and colonization. Gradualism, or nonextension, seemed like the perfect solution: Slavery would ultimately become extinct within two or three generations; the South would not be fearful of the immediate loss of their valuable property; the unity of the country would not be jeopardized; and a mass of free blacks would not be thrust upon an unprepared social structure.[10]

This gradualism plan later became unacceptable to many activists after abolitionists began to doubt that the slaveowners would adhere to the plan. Colonization also lost supporters after William Lloyd Garrison's pamphlet *Thoughts on African Colonization* pointed out that plans to remove the slaves to colonies in Africa, Haiti, or the British West Indies upheld the proslavery argument that blacks were innately inferior. Abolitionist Lewis Tappan wrote that Garrison's constant interactions with blacks allowed him to regard colonization from their point of view. Tappan explained: "It was their united and strenuous opposition to the expatriation scheme that first induced Garrison and others to oppose it."[11]

Black abolitionists also opposed colonization because they felt that it was a plot by whites to deny the slave its most devoted ally, the free black, and to refuse blacks access to the land on which they had toiled and died. The colonization issue threatened to divide blacks at several points prior to the Civil War, but staunch opposition by such individuals as black newspaper editors Samuel Cornish and Frederick Douglass continued to sway public opinion.[12] Douglass warned blacks that the answer to equality was not to leave the country but to stay and work for a living. He explained:

The American Colonization Society tells you to go to Liberia. Mr. [Henry] Bibb tells you to go to Canada. Others tell you to go to school. We tell you to go to work; and to work you must go, or die.[13]

Other abolitionists in the movement demanded that the future development of the black race be considered in terms of education, financial stability, and self-improvement, in addition to slavery. The founders of the *Freedom's Journal*, the first black newspaper in the United States, were more than reforming abolitionists. The Rev. Samuel Cornish, a Presbyterian minister, and Bowdoin College graduate John Russwurm also tried to create guidelines for blacks' self-improvement, such as education and financial responsibility; to establish cohesiveness among blacks; and to provide black readers with a sense of their culture.[14] These goals were dictated by the problems and concerns of northern free blacks and ex-slaves, separate issues from the conditions of the slave.

Located in cities where black community life already existed, *Freedom's Journal* and most black antebellum newspapers and magazines provided antislavery news, as well as news items and information designed to benefit blacks in assimilating into U.S. society.

Disparity in purpose resulted in disparity in tactics and strategies. By the mid-1830s, moral suasion had become infeasible. New abolitionists under Garrison's leadership demanded immediate emancipation of all slaves, regardless of the consequences. This plan also virtually eliminated the concept of gradualism, which—while objectionable to early abolitionists—still offered a chance for peaceful compromise between the opponents.[15]

Genius of Universal Emancipation editor Benjamin Lundy was, likewise, reluctant to relinquish hope for the colonization plan. While Lundy, a proponent of the antislavery cause since about 1815, continued to urge the abolitionists to develop more efficient measures, he wrote of colonization, "I am clearly of the opinion that *every effort* that is made to exhibit to public view the deplorable condition of the colored race must have a *tendency* to mitigate it."[16]

Political action was also among the tactics employed by the abolitionists. Petitions were a particularly strong tool for the antislavery societies. Whether indifferent or hostile to the cause, no members of a representative governmental body could fail to be impressed by the sheer number of petitioners the activists were able to arouse.[17] Between December 1838 and March 1839 approximately 1,500 petitions with more than 163,000 signatures poured into the Capitol protesting interstate slave trade, territorial expansion of slavery, the admission of new slave states, and the existence of slavery in Washington, D.C.[18]

Inasmuch as the movement had no true focal point or any one leader, such detailed operations and tactics required careful organization. The hydralike body of the movement was organized along geographical, racial, gender, and age lines. The movement hierarchy included a national organization, the American Anti-Slavery Society (split for a relatively short time so that an American and Foreign Anti-Slavery Society appeared) and regional groups such as the New England Anti-Slavery Society. There were also statewide organizations such as the Massachusetts, the Rhode Island, the New York, the Ohio, and the Pennsylvania Anti-Slavery societies, as well as citywide groups like those in Boston, New York City, Providence, Philadelphia, Rochester, and Cincinnati.

Since American societal guidelines frowned upon mixing male and female audiences, societies were also maintained specifically for women activists, such as the Boston and the Philadelphia Female Anti-Slavery societies. For younger abolitionists, there were youth societies (also called juvenile antislavery societies) and societies in colleges, such as those at Amherst and Oberlin. In addition to these, which were black-white groups, there were organizations designated for black people alone, both secular and religious.[19]

Despite their divergence in leadership and rank-and-file members, abolitionists recognized the common thread that bound them together— eventual enfranchisement of slaves—despite varying opinions on what it meant to become an abolitionist. Historians have distinguished between those opposed to slavery in the abstract and those involved in the abolition movement.[20] This explained how some slaveholders, as antislavery proponents, could abhor the system of slavery but still retain ownership of their slaves. In an 1843 letter to the editor in the New York *Tribune*, Kentucky slaveholder and enthusiastic abolitionist Cassius M. Clay declared slavery to be "the greatest evil that ever cursed a nation." Like Thomas Jefferson, also a reluctant slaveholder, Clay concluded that slavery was subversive to Christianity, and he lamented that while it was necessary to the economic well-being of southern farmers, it would also lead to the moral and political degeneration of the South.[21]

Devotion to bringing about an end to slavery produced varying levels of commitment, ranging from spiritual to fanatical, and by many accounts the personalities of the participants often defined their cause. Historians of this period were unable to focus on the key issue of antislavery without also taking note of the individuals who made crucial contributions to the movement. Dubbed extremists by their antagonists, as well as by modern historians, abolitionists such as Garrison, Harvard attorney Wendell Phillips, and ex-seminary student Stephen Symonds Foster made public appearances that were often more memorable than the messages they attempted to convey.

Funereal in appearance with his black suit and black cravat, Garrison resembled a mild and benign minister, but his strong epithets and quick accusatory tones made him an inspiring and often volatile speaker. Phillips, who thrived on hecklers in his audiences, would plant admirers in the back row to hiss and motivate him to respond in witheringly contemptuous tones to opponents' criticisms. Not averse to using theatrics occasionally, Phillips would rinse out his mouth with water and spit on the floor whenever his speeches required him to use the name of fugitive slave commissioner George Ticknor Curtis.[22] Similarly, Foster often offended religious and civil authorities with his confrontational approach to attacking the slavery system. His work *Brotherhood of Thieves* (1843) denounced the influence of the clergy in perpetuating slavery.[23]

Because of the emotional nature of the subject, the abolitionists, pitted against ruling-class individuals or established institutions, struggled against various forms of repression, and they relied on the emotionalism resulting from these acts of violence and repression to gain sympathy and support for their cause. Many Americans who had not previously felt strongly about slavery began to believe that if abolitionists could be mobbed with impunity and denied access to congressional consideration, then the rights of all Americans were in jeopardy.[24]

The first martyr of the cause never considered himself to be an abolitionist. Puritan Elijah Parish Lovejoy, the eldest son of the Reverend Daniel and Elizabeth Lovejoy of Maine, had walked from Boston to Illinois, with almost no money, no job prospects, and no real interest in the antislavery movement. By 1833, when Lovejoy headed his own paper, the St. Louis *Observer*, he had spent time as a schoolmaster, an editor, and a preacher. The *Observer* was a reform paper, and Lovejoy angered numerous readers with his anti-Catholic editorials and eventually his items against slavery. Two years before his death at the hands of an angry mob in 1837 in Alton, Illinois, Lovejoy wrote of slavery:

God has not slumbered nor has his Justice been an indifferent spectator of the scene. The groans, and sighs, and tears, and blood of the poor slave have gone up as a memorial before the throne of Heaven. In due time they will descend in awful curses upon this land, unless averted by the speedy repentance of us all.[25]

Despite Lovejoy's admonitions that the term *abolitionist* did not fit him, his words against slavery marked him as one in the eyes of his slaveholding neighbors. Lovejoy was a gradualist but, nevertheless, insisted that something must be done on the subject of slavery.[26] By contrast, he demanded expediency when addressing the need to end unChristian treatment of slaves. He declared that "[h]ere the reform ought to be thorough and immediate. There is no possible plea which can afford an excuse for a moment's delay."[27]

Lovejoy was subsequently run out of Missouri by a mob that destroyed his office and $700 in printing materials. He later attempted to reestablish himself in Alton, where his press was damaged and thrown into the river immediately upon his arrival. Two more presses were destroyed before Lovejoy vowed to defend his right of free speech at all costs. At a public meeting days before his death he demanded protection under his rights as a citizen. He concluded his speech with the declaration: "If the civil authorities refuse to protect me, I must look to God; and if I die, I have determined to make my grave in Alton."[28]

On November 7, 1837, Lovejoy, having been shot five times outside the warehouse where his fourth press was located, dragged himself up the stairs to the second floor and died on the counting room floor before reaching his beloved machine. The press was then dropped from a third-floor window and the warehouse set ablaze.[29]

Lovejoy's murder provided the perfect opportunity for an ideological press to sway public thinking. Abolitionist editors wasted no time in playing on the sympathies of their readers and encouraging them either to accept an antislavery philosophy or at least to acknowledge the threat to free speech and a free press.

Abolitionists now possessed persuasive evidence that slave power threatened all of humanity. Unable to provide complete coverage of the recent murder, Garrison published the November 10, 1837, *Liberator* with a reprint of Lovejoy's letter to the editor of the *Emancipator* detailing his escape in October from the St. Charles mob that not only forced him out of Missouri after an antislavery lecture but also compelled him to reverse his pacifistic stance. His words were a warning, almost prophetic, of his eventual murder. After the mob had attacked his mother-in-law's home several times in the night, Lovejoy fled back to Alton with his wife. However, fearful that the mob would pursue them into Illinois, Lovejoy and his friends guarded his house, while Celia Lovejoy sank deeper into a state of hysteria and fear. Sitting by her bedside on the second night of their vigil in Alton, Lovejoy renounced his vow of nonresistance. He wrote:

A loaded musket is standing at my bed-side, while my two brothers are in an adjoining room, have three others, together with pistols, cartridges, & c. And this is the way we live in the city of Alton! I have had inexpressible reluctance to resort to this method of defence. But dear-bought experience has taught me that there is at present no safety for me, and no defence in this place, either in the laws or the protecting aegis of public sentiment. I feel that I do not walk the streets in safety, and every night when I lie down, it is with the deep settled conviction that there are those near me and around me who seek my life. I have resisted this conviction as long as I could, but it has been forced upon me.

Not content with the emotions undoubtedly stirred by Lovejoy's impassioned words of despair and resolve, Garrison published the *Liberator*'s subsequent issue in thick, black borders. Nearly the entire issue was devoted to Lovejoy's death. Headlines screamed: "Horrid Tragedy! Blood Crieth!" "The Riot and Murder at Alton!" "Voice of the Press! The First Martyr—Another Mob at Alton." Resolutions from antislavery societies and religious organizations throughout the North proclaimed Lovejoy a hero and decried the actions of apathetic city officials and savage proslavery champions.[30] The *Lyon Record* proclaimed that Lovejoy's blood "cries to you from the ground—'Sons of liberty, scorn to be slaves.' Rouse up, assert your rights and maintain them at all hazards. . . . He could not have died in a better cause."[31]

Other editors blamed officials and apathetic citizens for the murder. The New York *Evening Post* said Alton civil authorities "either shrunk like cowards, from a plain and imperative duty, or else they desired that the outrage meditated by the rioters might be committed." The *New Yorker* avowed that "[e]very one who attempts to gloss over or palliate the outrage by appeals to public prejudice against the cause in which Mr. Lovejoy was engaged, is an apologist for, if not accessary [sic] to foul murder, and an enemy to law and social order."[32]

Lovejoy's death became a symbol for the defense of all freedoms. The *Haverhill Gazette* announced that the "late attack upon the freedom of the press at Alton, Illinois, which has at length been consummated in blood and murder, should arouse every press and every voice in the country." The editorial also warned that if "our liberty of speech, and of the press, is confined to only such subjects as a lawless mob in the exercise of their omnipotent rascality, may see fit to license, we had better burn *up* our constitution, burn *down* our capitol, cease to pay taxes, and every one fight on his own hook."[33] The American Anti-Slavery Society also officially designated Lovejoy a martyr, issuing writing paper with a crest pronouncing "LOVEJOY the first MARTYR to American LIBERTY. MURDERED for asserting the FREEDOM of the PRESS. Alton Nov. 7, 1837."[34]

Slavery supporters could now be depicted as a bloodthirsty lot who would stop at nothing to preserve their way of life. Lovejoy's murder not only made an impression on antislavery followers, but it also persuaded others to join who probably had not considered that their own civil liberties might someday be in jeopardy. A grand jury indictment of 11 individuals who assisted Lovejoy in the warehouse incident served as additional fodder to fuel the campaign of righteous indignation against proslavery advocates.

A minority voice among the abolitionists criticized Lovejoy's physical defense of his press and the use of weapons and death to defend a cause. Among those voices was editor Benjamin Lundy.[35] Although one of the pioneers of the antislavery movement, Lundy had always maintained a moderate perspective on the slavery issue. Born in New Jersey, the only child of Quaker farmers Joseph and Elizabeth Shotwell Lundy, Benjamin Lundy developed a strong religious outlook at an early age. On his twenty-seventh birthday, he devised a plan for an antislavery association to be headquartered in Mount Pleasant, Ohio. The organization, dubbed the Union Humane Society, derived its operating principles from the "Golden Rule" and the Declaration of Independence. Its constitution stated that the members would use all legal means to end racial prejudice, to attain civil rights for blacks who were already free, and to secure the freedom of those blacks illegally enslaved.[36]

Lundy's personal plan for emancipation also called for action in which slavery would be abolished gradually and without malice, loss of life, or any other form of bloodshed.

Lundy espoused these ideas freely through his newspaper, the *Genius of Universal Emancipation*. Originally published in Mount Pleasant, Ohio, the *Genius* and Lundy moved to Greeneville, Tennessee, in 1822 to replace Elihu Embree's *Emancipator*, a paper devoted solely to abolishing slavery. Before his death in 1820, Embree and the *Emancipator* had elicited widespread hostility in its location so close to the enemy, and Lundy's *Genius* would not escape criticism. Considered tame by some standards in the late 1830s, the *Genius* nevertheless asserted the message that slavery was intolerable. In one of his more insulting passages, Lundy proclaimed the slaveholders "whoremongers" who dared to oppose emancipation on the grounds of their lust and greed:

[T]hey make a *business* of raising bastards and selling them for money;—they keep poor miserable degraded females for this identical purpose; they compel them to submit to their abominable avaricious, and brutal lusts.[37]

By the time Lundy moved the paper to Baltimore in 1824, a sense of growing impatience was pervading New England. By the 1830s, young men such as Wendell Phillips and Greensboro, North Carolina, *Patriot* editor William Swaim, participants who were less concerned with fears of disrupting the social structure, had begun to speak out for a less restrained approach to abolishing slavery. Demands for immediate action were beginning to be heard with increasing frequency from outspoken and zealot orators and writers such as school-teacher and *Liberator* contributor Maria Stewart and David Walker, author of the controversial *Walker's Appeal, in Four Articles, Together with a Preamble, to the Colored Citizens of the World.* The appeal was the first sustained written assault upon U.S. slavery and racism by a black man.[38]

Into this arena entered the abolitionist who would force the antislavery societies to adopt new philosophies and approaches and to develop a movement that would eventually lead to the destruction of the institution of slavery—William Lloyd Garrison. Perhaps the individual credited most with helping to define the abolitionist movement and its goals, Garrison joined Lundy at the *Genius* in 1829. The partnership should have been ideal. The two shared strong beliefs that slavery was wrong and should be abolished. With the exception of disagreements over gradualism versus immediatism, the only differences between the partners were in style and approach. Garrison was a master of fiery rhetoric, issuing pronouncements of his personal faith and commitment to the cause, while Lundy, having passed through that stage a decade earlier, preferred to examine more practical measures that he hoped would free some slaves immediately.[39]

However, Garrison's approach seemed to possess more appeal for the increasingly impatient abolitionists. Praised as a savior and criticized as a tyrant and agitator, Garrison maintained a love-hate relationship even with his fellow abolitionists. However, according to Oliver Johnson, temporary editor of the *Liberator* and Garrison's contemporary, Garrison wrote "not a word . . . from malice or the love of severity, or with the purpose of making men angry. He wounded only to heal."[40] Explaining his unorthodox approach to attacking slavery, Garrison wrote:

I am aware that many object to the severity of my language; but is there not cause for severity? I will be as harsh as truth, and as uncompromising as justice. On this subject, I do not wish to think, or speak, or write, with moderation. No! no! Tell a man, whose house is on fire, to give a moderate alarm; tell him to moderately rescue his wife from the hands of the ravisher; tell the mother to gradually extricate her babe from the fire into which it has fallen; but urge me not to use moderation in a cause like the present! I am in earnest. I will not equivocate—I will not excuse—I will not retreat a single inch—AND I WILL BE HEARD.[41]

Hearing Garrison's vow, blacks flocked to join the movement. Black physician and abolitionist J. McCune Smith noted in later years that it was difficult to discern whose love was greater—Garrison's for blacks or blacks' for Garrison.[42] This support was partially due to Garrison's attempts to meet with the free blacks and ex-slaves in the North and to ascertain their opinions on what would improve their condition. In a standard speech written for black audiences, Garrison vowed to devote his life to atoning for the wrongs inflicted upon the black race. Garrison's children later wrote that because of this passion many blacks assumed that Garrison must be a black man.[43] For the first three years of the *Liberator's* operation, the majority of the subscribers and supporters were black, and in April 1834, only one fourth of the 2,300 subscribers were white.[44]

However, others were not as fervent in their support of Garrison's activities and philosophies. The Garrisonians' single-mindedness toward antislavery forced many abolitionists to doubt the effectiveness of such policies of total opposition to all who supported slavery, or countenanced it by their inactivity—whether the individuals be of church, ministry, or government.[45] Unitarian minister Samuel J. May, a fellow abolitionist and close friend of Garrison's, often warned that the outspoken editor would "shake our nation to its center, but he will shake slavery out of it."

When Lundy and Garrison parted company in 1830, Lundy went to great lengths to assure his readers that Garrison's ostentatious speeches and editorials were not the cause of the breakup. He contended that financial difficulties had forced an end to the weekly paper, and he was returning to a monthly format.[46] Historians have speculated that the cause might have been the controversy of a libel suit resulting from a Garrison editorial that condemned Massachusetts ship owner Francis Todd and ship captain Nicholas Brown as participants in the slave trade. Both Garrison and Lundy were charged, but Lundy's charges were later dropped after the judge determined that his absence from the city at the time absolved him of all responsibility for the article. Garrison, however, was fined $50 and court costs, but he served six months in jail when neither he nor Lundy could raise the money.

Garrison later denied Lundy's statements and claimed that the dissolution of the partnership was based on his extremism in expressing his views and not because of financial complications.[47] However, Lundy admired Garrison's work. He once described Garrison's words as "warm, energetic and bold," stating that "[n]othing but this will reach the adamantine hearts of slavites."[48] Before the libel suit and his partnership with Garrison, Lundy had produced his own brand of fiery attacks against slavery supporters, particularly Maryland slave trader Austin Woolfolk. An August 5, 1826, editorial presented a sarcastic proposal to elect Woolfolk to the U.S. Senate "to represent the numerous class of citizens engaged in the *honorable* business of negro-chaining, man-driving, and soul-trafficking

in this 'happy land.' " Subsequent articles against the slave trader so enraged Woolfolk that on January 9, 1827, he accosted Lundy on a Baltimore
street and beat him severely on the head until bystanders intervened.
Lundy's injuries required two days of bed rest and a week of rest inside
his room.[49]

Almost as radical as Garrison and one of the greatest orators of the
movement was a former slave. As Lundy influenced Garrison, so did
Garrison's thinking manifest itself in Frederick Douglass. Douglass's slave
past gave him a distinctive place and special influence in the movement,
and the voices of Douglass and others who had escaped from bondage
became an essential weapon of the movement in the 1840s. Like Garrison,
Douglass pledged to stamp out slavery in all its forms, relying on fiery
rhetoric and harsh criticism of both blacks and whites who failed to support the cause or remained passive in the face of slavery's onslaught. One
such editorial in his newspaper in Rochester, New York, the North Star—
later known as Frederick Douglass' Paper—pointed out his resistance to colonization as a solution.

As with other black abolitionists and many white abolitionists after
1830, Douglass felt that the colonization issue was one designed to separate the slaves from their true allies.[50] Douglass also determined that only
one who had suffered racial discrimination could truly understand the
necessity of immediate and total emancipation, and a major purpose of
founding his newspaper was to serve as a voice for blacks, both free and
enslaved.

Like Garrison, Douglass fostered his own brand of hostility among
both proslavery advocates and abolitionists. His life was threatened many
times because of his harsh depiction of slavery and its supporters. For his
fellow abolitionists, however, he used some of his most acrimonious
words. In one instance, he accused black pastor and abolitionist
Charles W. Gardner of pastoring two slaveholding congregations in Tennessee.[51] He also accused abolitionist editor Stephen Myers of disregard-
ing the true needs of blacks because of his series of publishing ventures
that Douglass claimed served only to divide the race.[52]

Not all abolitionist editors were as flamboyant as Garrison and
Douglass or as inflexible in their attempts to bring about change in the
slavery system. These individuals, like Lundy, had logical and practical
reasons for the way they conducted their newspapers. They advocated
the idea that the press should work with the public and the government to
solve threats to national unity rather than emphasizing conflicts in order
to create divisions in society.

Less ostentatious and radical than Garrison, Gamaliel Bailey, editor of
the Philanthropist in Cincinnati and the National Era in Washington, D.C.,
was described by Garrison and abolitionist/philanthropist Gerrit Smith
as "a compromiser who modified anti-slavery principles for the sake of

popular approval." However, Bailey might also be considered a person who attempted to discover a balance between his moral principles and his conviction that only a powerful political movement could rescue the country from the detrimental effects of slavery.[53] In his first issue of the *Era*, Bailey reasoned that "a majority of the antislavery people of the free states without abating their zeal, or compromising their principles, clearly see that mere denunciation may inflame but not convince—may terrify the cowardly, but must arouse the indignation and resistance of men of courage and intelligence." He added that there were also southerners who realized that slavery could not survive and who were "willing to listen to discussion, so that they be treated as men whose peculiar circumstances should not be lost sight of and who have minds to be reasoned with, sensibilities to be respected."[54]

Consequently, Bailey might have adopted a more moderate style than that of abolitionists who chose to campaign further North because he hoped to extend his antislavery appeals into the lower North and the South. His moderate style allowed him to become a national leader at every stage of the expanding antislavery movement, utilizing a more effective strategy than that of other abolitionists as he sought a middle course between compromise and impractical or unpopular tactics.[55] Bailey believed that slavery could not survive without the support of the federal government and if abolitionists could remove slave power's control over the federal government by dismantling the proslavery tax structure, system of representation, fugitive slave law, and support for territorial expansion, southerners could be left to repeal their own state laws that supported slavery.[56]

The heart of Bailey's abolitionist outlook was the moral imperative that

[w]ell-being can never depend upon wrong-doing. The rights of one class are not to be secured by depriving another class of all rights. Equal justice to all men, of whatever race or color, grade or state, is the only foundation of solid prosperity.[57]

Bailey maintained that because slavery was a moral issue, no one could remain neutral in the struggle. At no other time in American history did so many individuals look for guidance in determining the path they should follow. Some looked to their neighbors and community leaders, others looked to God, and still others looked to their newspapers. Throughout the struggle, abolitionist editors continued to speak out against slavery and to awaken the conscience of America, convincing the people of the imperative need to abolish human bondage. In this way, they helped to mold the public opinion that ultimately resulted in the death of slavery.

Historians continue to debate whether the circumstances leading up to the Civil War forced antebellum editors into the role of attempting to correct the country's perceived moral and political mistakes, either as sincere abolitionists or as reluctant reformers. Whatever the motivation, the fact still remains that the circumstances either compelled or forced the press into a pivotal role in determining the future of the United States.

NOTES

1. Expecting to attack British abolitionist George Thompson for a $100 reward, proslavery supporters were angered by Thompson's failure to appear at a Boston Female Anti-Slavery Society meeting. Consequently, deprived of their intended prey, they sought Garrison as a new target upon which to vent their outrage. Taken from eyewitness C. C. Burleigh's and Garrison's accounts of the incident, appearing in the 24 October 1835 and 7 November 1835 issues of the *Liberator*.

2. Russel B. Nye, "Freedom of the Press and the Antislavery Controversy," *Journalism Quarterly* 22 (1945): 1.

3. Harriet Martineau, *The Martyr Age of the United States* (Boston: Weeks, Jordan and Co., 1839), 3.

4. Herbert Aptheker, *Abolitionism: A Revolutionary Movement* (Boston: Twayne Publishers, 1989), xii.

5. Merton L. Dillon, *Benjamin Lundy and the Struggle for Negro Freedom* (Urbana: University of Illinois Press, 1966), 152–153.

6. See, for example, Samuel J. May, *Some Recollections of Our Anti-Slavery Conflict* (Boston: Fields and Osgood, 1869), 27.

7. Aileen S. Kraditor, *Means and Ends in American Abolitionism: Garrison and His Critics on Strategy and Tactics, 1834–1850* (New York: Pantheon Books, 1967), 7.

8. Aptheker, *Abolitionism*, xiv–xv.

9. *Herald of Freedom*, 10 November 1838.

10. Martin Duberman, "The Northern Response," in *The Antislavery Vanguard: New Essays on the Abolitionists*, ed. Martin Duberman (Princeton, NJ: Princeton University Press, 1965), 402.

11. Lewis Tappan, *The Life of Arthur Tappan* (New York: Hurd and Houghton, 1870), 136.

12. See, for example, Bernell Tripp, "The Media and Community Cohesiveness: The Black Press and the Coloniation Issue" in *The Significance of the Media in American History*, ed. James D. Startt and William David Sloan (Northport, AL: Vision Press, 1993).

13. *Frederick Douglass' Paper*, 4 March 1853.

14. Kenneth D. Nordin, "In Search of Black Unity: An Interpretation of the Content and Function of *Freedom's Journal*," *Journalism History* 4 (Winter 1977–1978): 128.

15. Dillon, *Lundy*, 153–154.

16. *Genius of Universal Emancipation*, December 1830.

17. Aptheker, *Abolitionism*, 50–53.

18. C. Peter Ripley, ed., *The Black Abolitionist Papers, Vol. III, The United States, 1830–1846* (Chapel Hill: University of North Carolina Press, 1991), 326.

19. Aptheker, *Abolitionism*, 54.

20. Larry Gara, "Who Was An Abolitionist?" in *The Antislavery Vanguard: New Essays on the Abolitionists*, ed. Martin Duberman (Princeton, NJ: Princeton University Press, 1965), 33.

21. *National Anti-Slavery Standard*, 14 December 1843; and *Pennsylvania Freeman*, 18 April 1839.

22. Irving H. Bartlett, "The Persistence of Wendell Phillips," in *The Antislavery Vanguard: New Essays on the Abolitionists*, ed. Martin Duberman (Princeton, NJ: Princeton University Press, 1965), 109.

23. Ripley, *Black Abolitionist Papers*, 465–466.

24. Kraditor, *Means and Ends in American Abolitionism*, 7.

25. St. Louis *Observer*, 16 April 1835.

26. Merton L. Dillon, *Elijah P. Lovejoy, Abolitionist Editor* (Urbana: University of Illinois Press, 1961), 54-55.

27. St. Louis *Observer*, 30 April 1835.

28. Joseph C. Lovejoy and Owen Lovejoy, *Memoir of the Rev. Elijah P. Lovejoy; Who Was Murdered in Defence of the Liberty of the Press, at Alton, Illinois, Nov. 7, 1837* (New York: J. S. Taylor, 1838), 278-281.

29. Dillon, *Lovejoy*, 169-170.

30. *Liberator*, 24 November 1837.

31. Reprinted in *Liberator*, 1 December 1837.

32. Reprinted in *Liberator*, 24 November 1837 and 8 December 1837.

33. Reprinted in *Liberator*, 8 December 1837.

34. Dillon, *Lovejoy*, 177.

35. Philadelphia *National Enquirer*, 23 November 1837.

36. Dillon, *Lundy*, 18.

37. *Genius of Universal Emancipation*, June 1823.

38. Dillon, *Lundy*, 149.

39. Ibid., 146–147.

40. Oliver Johnson, *William Lloyd Garrison and His Times, or Sketches of the Anti-Slavery Movement in America, and of the Man Who Was Its Founder and Moral Leader* (Boston: B. B. Russell and Co., 1880), 54.

41. *Liberator*, 1 January 1831.

42. *Frederick Douglass' Paper*, 26 January 1854.

43. W. P. Garrison and F. J. Garrison, *William Lloyd Garrison, 1805-1879; The Story of his Life as told by his Children*, vol. 1 (New York: The Century Co., 1885–1889), 258.

44. Benjamin Quarles, *Black Abolitionists* (New York: Oxford University Press, 1969), 20.

45. See, for example, *Anti-Slavery Bugle*, 1 May 1846; and Philip S. Foner, *The Life and Writings of Frederick Douglass*, vol. 2 (New York: International Publishers, 1950–1955), 524.

46. *Genius of Universal Emancipation and Baltimore Courier*, 5 March 1830.

47. Dillon, *Lundy*, 159.

48. *Genius of Universal Emancipation and Baltimore Courier*, December 1830.

49. *Genius of Universal Emancipation and Baltimore Courier*, 9 January 1827.

50. *North Star*, 26 January 1849.

51. *Frederick Douglass' Paper*, 28 October 1853.

52. *Frederick Douglass' Paper*, 15 April 1852.

53. Stanley Harrold, *Gamaliel Bailey and Antislavery Union* (Kent, OH: Kent State University Press, 1986), x.

54. *National Era*, 7 January 1847.

55. Harrold, *Gamaliel Bailey*, xi.

56. *Philanthropist*, 30 December 1836.

57. *National Era*, 18 October 1857.

5 ⟳

OLD OSAWATOMIE BROWN:
MARTYR OR MADMAN?

Lloyd Chiasson Jr.

Saturday night. Spring in Kansas. A dampness fills the air and the wind blows across the dark prairie. All is quiet, then the thump thump thump of horses. The riders slow as they near the trees that edge Mosquito Creek. Then they lead their horses across the meandering stream. Downstream, some distance away, sits a cabin. It is there where the riders are headed.

At 11 p.m. the riders arrive at their destination. The leader of the small party dismounts. His skin is ruddy and sun-baked, and he looks older than his 56 years. He is five feet ten inches in height, but his angular frame makes him look taller. He has unkempt reddish-brown hair streaked with gray. His hawk nose is long and angular, and his lips are so thin that his mouth is no more than a slash. But it is his eyes that dominate his face. They are blue and clear and filled with fervor. They are eyes that burn with righteousness.

The leader walks to the cabin and knocks on the door. Inside, a man asks what the stranger wants. The leader asks for directions, and when the door is partially opened, he charges into the cabin, demanding that the owner, a settler named Doyle, surrender. The intruders separate Doyle and his three sons from his wife and daughter, and they are taken outside by the band of night riders. The wife asks for pity on the youngest son, a 14-year-old, and the leader shows mercy. Doyle and his eldest sons are less fortunate. They are hacked with broadswords, mercilessly slashed in the hands and arms as they try to protect themselves. Doyle and son William fall dead near one another. The other son, Drury, attempts to run, blood covering his face and both arms severed from his body. He falls near a ravine, and the leader walks to him. He takes out his gun and shoots Doyle's son in the forehead. The killing is far from over, however.

Two more die at the hands of the night riders this Saturday. Allen Wilkinson is found with his throat cut, William Sherman dead in the creek by a friend's cabin. His hand is nearly severed from his arm, and some of his brains have washed away.[1]

So went the massacres near Osawatomie, Kansas, in 1856. Five men died, and Kansas erupted into what was essentially a range war between pro and antislavery settlers. Bands of men roamed the territory, looting and killing across the southeast section of the state. Little was settled except the butchery near Pottawatomie Creek brought notoriety to the leader of the executioners, a man determined that Kansas be brought into the Union as a free state. In both the North and the South, people talked about the "executions" in the Kansas territory. Some people said the deaths were the doings of a madman. Others said it was the work of a religious zealot. Some fence-straddlers didn't know what to think about such a brutal raid. The man responsible, however, seems never to have doubted his motives—nor his actions. For John Brown, the issue was simple: His work was God's work.

The story of John Brown is one born of the antislavery movement and rooted in religious fervor. It began in Kansas, ended in Virginia, and played before a national audience. It held two regions hostage and either hastened, or made painfully clear, the approaching conflict between the North and the South.

In 1854, national attention focused on Kansas and Nebraska territories as the newest laboratories testing the volatile slavery issue.[2] After passage that year of the Kansas-Nebraska Bill, the way was paved for residents to decide if slavery would be legal in their territories. Free-state forces controlled Nebraska and tension was minimal there. Kansas' tranquil prairies, however, suddenly swarmed with Free-Soilers and proslavery settlers intent on inhabiting and claiming the territory as their own.[3]

In the early spring of 1855 John Brown's five sons headed west from New York to help the Free-Soilers seize control of Kansas. Several months later, their father left his home in the Adirondack Mountains to join them. Brown brought arms to aid the free-soil cause and make clear to everyone his fiery loyalties. Soon he became the leader of a small band of avid Free-Soilers.[4] Emotions ran high across the territory and occasional, small skirmishes occurred. Kansas was ready to boil over. Then in May 1856, Brown led a small force to Osawatomie, Kansas, where he ordered the execution of five proslavery settlers.[5] After this, he was known to the public as Old Osawatomie Brown.

In 1857, Brown began to recruit men for a bold mission leading to what he envisioned as an insurrection of the slaves and the establishment of a stronghold—probably in Virginia—where fugitive slaves and white friends could terrorize slaveholders and, at the same time, establish a free state within the South.[6] Within a year, President James Buchanan had labeled Brown an outlaw, and a reward for his capture was offered.[7] The fugitive remained free, however, moving across the North and into Canada.

In the summer of 1859, Brown returned and rented a farm about five miles from Harper's Ferry, Virginia, where he gathered arms for the slave rebellion he envisioned. On October 16, 1859, Brown and 21 men captured the town of Harper's Ferry, where the federal arsenal was located. By the next morning, Brown had control of both the U.S. armory and the bridges leading to the town. Besides taking some residents hostage, he killed several residents in capturing the small town. When no slave rebellion developed, however, Brown's disorganized plan would soon collapse.

By noon of the second day, the state militia arrived and shooting between the two forces resulted. The end neared, however, when during the night a company of United States Marines under the direction of the man who would later lead the Confederate army in the Civil War, Robert E. Lee, arrived. When Brown refused to surrender at dawn, Lee ordered the siege of the arsenal and captured Brown and four cohorts. In all, 12 of Brown's 22 men survived the battle. Brown was wounded, although not seriously.

Brown was taken to Charlestown, Virginia, and indicted a week later on charges of committing treason against the state of Virginia and of conspiring with slaves to commit treason and murder.[8] After being convicted of both charges, Brown was hanged on December 2, 1859. From the raid to execution, and during the period following the execution, Brown was a figure discussed in both the North and the South. The raid rekindled the already smoldering emotions concerning slavery in both southern and northern journals. Depending on the newspaper, Brown was reported as a martyr, a murderous maniac, or someone displaying qualities of each.[9]

From capture to execution, Brown was consistent in his reasoning for staging the raid: He wanted to right a societal wrong by freeing the slaves, and he saw himself an instrument of Providence, a man guided by God.[10]

Whether John Brown was guided by ego or Providence, insanity or abolitionist propaganda, remains conjecture.[11] What is clear, however, is Brown was major news—and fodder for editorial discussion in newspapers across the North and the South.[12]

Clearly, the period was a highly charged one, particularly in the South. According to historian Eric Foner, as far back as the Nat Turner uprising in 1831, the South "never again was . . . free from the fear . . . of a slave uprising, a fact potent in the history of the republic during the next thirty years."[13] Fear of another rebellion, one organized in the North, seems to have occupied southern minds to some extent.[14] As early as 1832, the Charleston (South Carolina) *Mercury* advocated secession,[15] largely over concern of violent northern intervention. The Turner rebellion, for instance, was widely considered by southerners to be a northern plot.[16] But fear of insurrection from within also lay dormant in many a southern mind. Simply put, the South was frightened of its own creation, and in 1859, John Brown's raid heightened that fear.

Abolitionist newspapers in the North continued to attack slavery during the next 30 years and, indirectly, the fears of the South. At that same time, other newspapers in the North represented decreasingly strong anti-slavery stands, depending on the publisher's personal position, the political situation of the time, or the overall emotional climate existing at the moment.[17] In New York City, for example, James Gordon Bennett's *Herald* and Horace Greeley's *Tribune* actively disagreed, the *Herald* often representing the Democratic Party on states' rights.[18] That southern stance was simple enough: Slavery was a regional issue, one that should be handled by the southern states that developed the institution.

In analyzing the raid and following events relating to Harper's Ferry, several points are worth mentioning. Without a competent southern press to distribute the news across the region, the South might have reacted in a totally different manner. According to the 1860 census, the 11 future Confederate states had 703 political journals. Although many readers imported northern newspapers, southerners preferred southern commentary.[19]

By 1860, four basic types of southern newspapers existed, two of which strongly supported southern rights, feared Abraham Lincoln and the Republican Party, and editorialized that a Republican victory in the 1860 presidential election warranted secession. The third type strongly supported states' rights and expressed conservatism on the secession issue, while the fourth disagreed with secession.[20]

Northern journals fell into broad categories also. Besides the abolitionist press, there were Black Republican and states' rights newspapers.[21] Although these broad categories do not represent every type of newspaper in each region, the papers categorized were probably the most active in covering the raid and subsequent events.

In both regions, however, the type of news the journals printed often included information concerning the possibility of co-conspirators who helped finance Brown's raid. The names were prominent—and exclusively northern: Horace Greeley, Congressman Garritt Smith of Ohio, and Senator William Seward of New York, the leading candidate for the Republican presidential nomination.[22] The naming of such well-known—and in some cases feared—persons, certainly promulgated southern anxiety over a possible conspiracy of large proportions in the North.[23]

If Brown had been killed at the raid, the immense newspaper coverage that followed probably would never have materialized. With Brown dead there would have been no trial to publicize and extend the coverage, nor much time for newspapers so inclined to garner public opinion for what they believed to be either his crime or heroism.[24] Brown seemed to be strongly aware of this. While waiting for execution in Charlestown, he observed that "I do not know that I ought to encourage any attempt to save my life. I am not sure that it would not be better for me to die at this time."[25] The poet and antislavery critic, Henry Ward Beecher, may have spoken the feelings of many when he said: "Let no man pray for that Brown be spared. Let Virginia make him a martyr." When this quote appeared October 31 in the New York *Herald*, Brown wrote the word good next to the story.[26]

An argument can be made that Brown never expected a successful rebellion—there were few slaves in that part of Virginia to even take part in an uprising[27]—but that he consciously was aware that an attack against the federal government at Harper's Ferry, where munitions and arms were stored, would get national attention, would let slaves know that support of their freedom could be had, and would create widespread concern throughout the South.[28]

As the trial neared, public interest grew, perhaps as much in the North as in the South. The short period—one week—between the raid and the trial created unfavorable public opinion in the North.[29] That Brown was still injured at the time of his trial also intensified feelings that Virginia authorities were guilty of unfair treatment,[30] as did the fact that two Virginia lawyers defended Brown.[31] The greatest outrage in the North, however, surfaced with the reportage that Brown might be insane, and sentencing probably would not display consideration of that possibility.[32]

In short, numerous elements existed prior to and after the raid that probably created greater coverage of the episode than might have developed otherwise. At the center of this national drama was the press, and how the story was covered became crucial in both regions.

Short of studying every newspaper in the country, there is no way to know exactly how the events surrounding John Brown were reported. Did readers in the North and the South get an untainted picture of events? Or were some informed of events as their local newspapers perceived, then shaped them to be? Two prominent newspapers, one from the South and one from the North, provide a sampling of what was printed from October 18 (two days after the capture of Brown) to December 10 (eight days after Brown's execution). What the New Orleans *Daily Picayune* and the New York *Tribune* wrote provides a good case study of what readers were told about this highly charged issue.

The New Orleans *Daily Picayune* first reported the raid on October 18 in a dispatch from Baltimore.[33] Although most of the early dispatches originated there, others eventually came from Harper's Ferry or Charlestown, as was the case with the *Tribune*. Unlike its northern counterpart, however, the *Daily Picayune* did not send a reporter to cover the trial, and all its news stories were wire service dispatches.

Stories about Brown were daily items in the newspaper. In only ten issues were stories on the raid or its aftermath omitted from the newspaper.

Early reports in the newspaper were sketchy, the purpose of the raid and the number of participants differing in the reports.[34] Initial wire service reports gave a figure of insurgents totaling 600 to 900 with an unknown number of blacks involved (the term Negro was used by the wire services). Any numerical discrepancies probably resulted from Brown's seizing of the town for about one day. In any case, the report placed the number of black participants at 600 and explained that the movement originated with a secret abolitionist group, its object being to free the blacks of Maryland and Virginia and to incite rebellion in the adjoining states. The newspaper also reported that John Brown and his sons were killed and that letters from prominent abolitionists (such as Garritt Smith and Frederick Douglass) had been found at Kennedy Farm.[35]

On October 20, the *Daily Picayune* reported that Brown was alive and that a search of Kennedy Farm revealed "an immense number of letters from all parts of the North."[36] In an editorial of October 22, the paper wrote that support of the raid by leading abolitionists proved them a "class whose humanity would prompt the desolation of our states by fire and sword, the kindling of civil war, and even the disruption of this confederacy, to accomplish their irrational ideas of philanthropy." Calling the entire plan insane, the newspaper continued: "We cannot but hope . . . that its lesson will be salutory upon the exposition of the humanity and love of those who lead a crusade of sectionalism."[37]

Another editorial advised slaveholders against giving monthly passes to "negroes," since the passes essentially set those slaves free. Readers were reminded that state policy was to reduce the number of free blacks in Louisiana.[38] Another editorial that day asked:

Are the thinking men of the North ready for civil war—a war of vengeance, embittered by the hottest fanaticism? Will they recognize the desperado, Osawatomie Brown, as a martyr in a good cause, deserving the respect of mankind? Unless we much mistake the people of the North, this futile attempt at treason . . . will produce among them a thrill of horror and will enable them to see a moral deformity of the pseudo philanthropy of the Abolition school.

The commentary also explained that the slaves would support the South in any insurrection but that "care and careless guardianship should be exercised over our servants which are devoted to our more immediate households."[39]

In another editorial published on October 24, the *Daily Picayune* wrote how the soldiers at Harper's Ferry wanted to lynch Brown. In the paper's view, he should be hanged.[40] The following day, another editorial suggested that the antislavery party of the North was much too smart to have ties with any such insurrection. Appearing to be writing for northern as much as for southern readers, the newspaper added that it had confidence that northerners would understand the horror of the act and that the South certainly had no fear of such types as Brown. Apparently concerned with public opinion, the newspaper called upon both the pro and antislavery press to help all people learn from "the idiocy" of the raid.[41]

On October 28, the *Daily Picayune* reported Brown's trial had begun in Charlestown, and that a captured mulatto had confessed that an insurrection in neighboring Kentucky had been planned.[42] Prominent northerners, such as the governor of Ohio and Senator William Seward, were reported to have been linked to the insurrection.[43]

Two days later the newspaper criticized northern journals for suggesting slavery was ripe for overthrow, adding that the lesson of Harper's Ferry was that the raid was not an insurrection but "an invasion of Virginia by a gang of abolitionists." It pointed out that the South was strong enough to prevent any intervention—just what type of intervention was vague—and that the slaves were loyal to the South. However, the previous calls for northern understanding of the southern position may have contained subtle uncertainty when the paper wrote: "The response thus far . . . is encouraging to the hope that the great body of the Northern people are awaking to the peril of the position into which they have been unwittingly drawn, by unprincipled and selfish men."[44]

On November 4, the paper expressed confidence that the raid had strengthened the South and then weighed the pros and cons of extradition of Garritt Smith from New York. This issue was addressed again the following day with the newspaper writing that the state of New York should have the "courtesy" to extradite Smith.[45]

Concern about the northern position surfaced again a few days later. In yet another editorial, the newspaper called on northerners to understand the southern position and to stop "hooligans" who were making trouble in the South. It asked northern readers to avoid turning Brown into a martyr, especially since he had been found guilty of both murder and treason. The editorial concluded by saluting the "conservatism" that had been aroused in the North. To the *Daily Picayune*, that reference to conservatism obviously meant an understanding of states' rights.[46]

A full column on the front page of the November 9 edition criticized "propagandist" journals in the North and South for printing abolitionist ideas. A week later another editorial argued against the free states' cries of mercy for Brown, and additionally tried to counteract what it apparently viewed as the possible martyrdom of Brown by many people, and by many newspapers, in the North.

If Brown is executed, we are warned that a great sympathy will grow up North; that he will be made a hero and martyr. His name will be the watchword with which to kindle a fire of indignation and hatred against the south . . . the blood of John Brown will be the cement of the Republican Church. . . . Perhaps this may be true in part, although we believe it greatly exaggerated.[47]

In another editorial, the *Daily Picayune* continued its condemnation of those who knew of Brown's plot but refused to act to stop it. It specifically named Senator Seward.[48]

The possibility of a northern plot to rescue Brown was also a concern.[49] Within a three-day span, the newspaper reported several rumors of rescue attempts.[50] Then the journal reported that although all was quiet in Charlestown, Governor Henry Wise had placed 1000 troops in the city with offers of more men from the South Carolina governor.[51] The following day's edition reported the offer of Pennsylvania and Virginia to prevent "the entrance into Virginia from the Northern states, of any abolitionists or bodies of men that come with the intent of rescuing Brown or his associate prisoners."[52] A second item also appeared reporting a possible abolitionist plot to help slaves on the Virginia coast escape their masters.[53]

On November 26 the offer by the Pennsylvania governor was printed again.[54] Later that week another editorial called on Governor Wise to be prepared for any rescue attempt. It appears clear that by this point the newspaper had begun to feel less certain of the general northern position on Brown and the raid. The newspaper wrote that because of the precautions taken against any rescue attempt, the abolitionists would now deny that a rescue effort had been planned and that the abolitionist press would claim Virginia and the governor were afraid of nonexistent enemies.

The prevalence of this taunting . . . is one of the worst signals yet of a debauched state of Northern mind in regard to the South. . . . To make a mockery of fear—if there were fear—is no trait of brotherhood. . . . The Philistines of old made sport of Samson.

The writer suggested that the North should remember the conclusion of that Biblical tale.[55]

The *Daily Picayune* on December 2 criticized those northerners who would make Brown a martyr, yet ended with the hopeful words: "We will not say that it is the ruling sentiment of the Northern people."[56]

The three-paragraph report of the execution of Brown came one day after the event, punctuated with the words: "Brown died easy."[57]

Front-page editorials on December 4, 6, 7, and 10 all expressed doubt for what the newspaper initially had expressed hope for: northern understanding of states' rights and a desire for peaceful coexistence. The *Daily Picayune* then criticized the editor of the New York *Tribune*, Horace Greeley, for supporting abolitionist propaganda, and called for the election of a Democrat in the next presidential election. On December 6, all of the southern governors were quoted concerning their attitudes about the prospect of friendship and understanding between the North and South. Emphasis was placed on the Alabama governor's feelings about the poor chances of preserving the Union in the light of Harper's Ferry and the growth of Black Republicanism.

Perhaps the strongest editorial concerning the future of relations appeared December 7 when the newspaper wrote that without cooperation between the two regions, "What will follow . . . is a question we prefer not to discuss, till the time arrives when we can see our way to the result."[58]

What the Daily Picayune viewed as a possible solution to the regional dilemma can be found in the December 10 issue, the final edition evaluated. That day a front-page editorial suggested the South begin to develop economic independence.[59]

In conclusion, the journal's wire reports were short, factual, and without opinion. Editorially, the Daily Picayune preached understanding of southern feelings concerning slavery, and did so often.

The news coverage and commentary in the New York Tribune differed from the New Orleans Daily Picayune in several ways. First, most of the editorials were on page four and the news on page five. This did not represent low news priority. Rather, the New York journal's first three pages were used for local announcements and advertising. Page four was the first news page.

Second, the Tribune sent a correspondent to Charlestown, his first correspondence appearing November 4 under the heading, "John Brown's Invasion." It had no heading defining it as news, as a column, or as editorial opinion, and its prime purpose appears to have been to discredit Virginians associated with the prosecution of Brown and those southerners who were not.[60]

Finally, in the span of one month, the Tribune ran 26 columns and 15 editorials dealing with Brown. In amount of news space and in numbers alone, this dwarfed the coverage by the southern journal.

Like the Daily Picayune, however, the Tribune first reported the raid on October 18 in a story that is consistent with the rest of the Tribune's treatment of the news: top placement of all the wire stories with an eye-catching seven-deck head. As did the Daily Picayune, the Tribune reported an incorrect number of insurgents.[61] The following day the 12 dispatches about the raid virtually took all the space on page four. The coverage appeared balanced, even to the point of mentioning that northern co-conspirators were probably involved.[62]

However, October 20 brought the first of many editorials, this one an attack on the Democrats and denial of Republican connection with "Old Brown's mad outbreak."[63] In the same issue, the Tribune retold the story of capture and described how the Harper's Ferry citizens had to be restrained from lynching Brown. "When the prisoners came out there were vocifer-

ous cries of 'Hang 'em' constantly repeated."[64] What was omitted, however, was Governor Wise's answer to the cries: "Oh, it would be cowardly
to do so now."[65] Later, the *Tribune* would use much space criticizing the
governor for many of his actions in the John Brown affair.

The next day an editorial entitled "Who Is Responsible" answered itself: those persons who encouraged "the pro-slavery war in Kansas." According to the *Tribune*, that did not include Brown. "John Brown, then a
peaceful and quiet citizen, went to Kansas with no intention to do anything against slavery . . . " except by peaceful means.[66]

On October 24, the *Tribune* once again defended the Republican Party
against claims that it had either been involved in or supportive of the raid.
The newspaper ran an editorial attacking an old foe, James Gordon
Bennett's New York *Herald*, for what the *Tribune* viewed as an attempt to
make Republicans responsible for the violence in Kansas as well as
Harper's Ferry with the goal being the election of a Democratic president
in 1860.[67]

The following day politics remained in the foreground with an editorial predicting that the trial would be a speedy one because "the prisoners
have no defense."[68] A second editorial attacked the Democrats for thinking of Harper's Ferry as "a windfall for the party."[69]

Another editorial in the following edition attacked slavery and informed readers that there was nothing for the South to be concerned
about.[70]

By the end of October, the *Tribune* abruptly reversed its earlier opinion
that the trial should proceed speedily. "In what marvelous hurry they are
in Charlestown Court!" In the strongest editorial to date, the *Tribune* un-
flinchingly claimed the South wanted revenge even if a trial delay were to
show Brown was insane.[71] A similar editorial was published October 31.[72]
Either the *Tribune* did not know or chose not to report that a Virginia statute clearly called for an immediate trial.[73]

The next edition brought a renewal of the attack on the Democratic
Party, plus a long, dramatic piece on the conviction of Brown.[74] The fol-
lowing day two editorials dealt with the same subject. First, the *Tribune*
asked that Republicans' names—apparently Giddings, Seward and
Greeley—be left out of the entire episode.[75] A second editorial praised the
New Orleans *Daily Picayune* for not playing up the news of the letters
Brown had received from prominent Republicans, quoting the *Daily
Picayune*'s comments that rational men wouldn't be connected with that
conspiracy.[76]

Then on November 3 the *Tribune* wrote:

Let the Democratic Party succeed, by hook or by crook, in carrying the next Presidential election, and we shall see immediately afterward the revival of the African
slave-trade brought forward as the policy of the party.[77]

The next day another editorial attacked the Democrats.[78] This issue also marked the first appearance of the *Tribune* correspondent—no byline was ever used—in Charlestown. His column typically ran much longer than the wire stories or the editorials.[79] This column may also have been the *Tribune*'s strongest weapon in trying to develop public opinion against Virginia, the South, the trial and its results, and the Democratic Party. Until December 5, when Brown's body reached New York, the correspondent was a daily fixture, writing assorted items such as:

—An attack on local Charlestown papers for being biased.[80]

—Apparent pro-Brown comments and quotes. For example: "Brown's cheerfulness never fails him."[81]

—Several attacks on the court trying Brown.[82] For example: "Jurors are qualified who do not understand the nature of the duties they assume."[83]

—A comparison of the North and South. For example: "Everything shows how far this region is behind the age, lingering sluggishly in the lap of idleness."[84]

—Attacks on the southern populace. For example: "They want a full five-act tragedy. . . . It is a pretty scheme—a scheme worthy of Virginia, I think."[85]

—An attack on the prosecutors, Andrew Hunter, whom he termed a dictator and a person who was prejudiced, and Charles Harding, who "carries the worst marks of intemperance. His face is a vindictive as well as a degraded one."[86] Also: "He has a way of expressing profound contempt by ejecting saliva aloft, and catching it on his chin, which he practices with great success."[87]

—Several attacks on Governor Wise.[88]

—An attack on Colonel Lusius Davis, the commander of the military in Charlestown. For example: "He is the incarnation of pompous dignity."[89]

—That Brown was pleased with the problems he had caused for Virginia and the South because "[h]e has seen the frightened fury which has spread."[90]

—Attacks on the southern accent.[91]

—Quotations, without name identification, of what southerners offhandedly told him. For example: "I would die content if I could see Greeley, Frederick Douglass, Emerson, Garrison and Beecher strung up alongside old Brown on next Friday." Also: "Sire, I would be glad to see the whole North sunk to the deepest depth of the bottomless pit!"[92]

The *Tribune*'s editorial page was more narrow in the range of its views. On November 5, another editorial was written about concern in the North over the spread of slavery territories.[93] A similar editorial arguing against that growth followed two days later.[94]

Not just editorials displayed Brown in a favorable light. On November 8, a letter was printed from a Maria Child, a noted abolitionist and the author of antislavery literature such as *Anti-Slavery Catechism*.[95] In part it read: "I think of you night and day, bleeding in prison, surrounded by hostile faces, sustained only by trust in God and your own strong heart."[96] This type of sentiment was consistent with that of the *Tribune* correspondent, who often wrote of Brown's courage and consideration of others. More stories about Mrs. Child were published as the execution drew near.[97]

In the November 18 and 19 editions, articles related a possible plot by insurgents in Memphis, Tennessee, as well as a possible rescue attempt of Brown in Charlestown.[98] Also in the November 19 issue was an editorial about how Virginia needed to relax and not be so terror-stricken concerning the raid.[99] On the following page, a story appeared about a fire four miles outside Harper's Ferry. Two days later the correspondent "supposed" that the fire was set by slaves.[100] Until the second week of December, the stories and editorials dealt principally with overreaction by the Virginia populace, while the news stories appeared under headlines that seemed to promote the very problems the editorials argued against. For example, the following headlines appeared within just one news story in the November 22 edition: "The Virginia Panic"; "Troops Under Arms"; "Another Arrest"; "Suspicious Signs"; "Effect of Slavery on White Men"; "Destroying Presses"; "Niger! Niger! [sic]"; "The Irrepressible Conflict."[101] This headline approach was consistent throughout November and in early December.

As Brown's execution date approached, editorials appeared on November 25, November 27 and December 2 that portrayed Brown as a sick man who should be given a new trial.[102] How much the newspaper wanted to promote favorable public opinion for its views about a stay of execution is impossible to say.

In summary, there seems little doubt that both newspapers tried to provide guidance in a period each perceived as critical for the country. It also appeared that one, the *Tribune*, propagandized in news reports in an attempt to mold public opinion.

Many of the newspapers of the period may have done just that with their reportage of John Brown since news and views are an essential part of the growth of public opinion.[103]

Unquestionably, both the *Daily Picayune* and the *Tribune* considered John Brown a major story, as the number of news stories and editorials written by each indicate. The newspapers, however, varied noticeably in presentation and quantity of news. During the period studied, the *Daily Picayune* printed 18 editorials and 34 news stories relating to John Brown and tangential events. Except for 14 news stories and 1 editorial, every article ran on the front page. Most of the news stories were short—usually two to four columns in length—and all were telegraphed dispatches. This means the *Daily Picayune* could be subjective only in story selection, and whether this was the case is not known.

The *Tribune* was much more active. It reported or editorialized on Brown every day of the period studied. Thirty-four commentaries and 28 editorials were printed. Telegraphed news stories appeared each day. In no way did the news columns, which appeared every day for over a month, appear to be anything but anti-South propaganda. The wire reports, however, were balanced and apparently objective news presentations. But the *Tribune* headlines used for these dispatches were not. Multidecked headlines told of a violent and, at times, a fearful South. This appears to have been the basic point the newspaper was intent on hammering home throughout its coverage of the raid and trial. Southern concerns about more violence were unfounded, wrote the *Tribune*, primarily because southern newspapers were reporting the entire incident out of proportion.

The *Daily Picayune* viewed Brown as an anarchist who had recklessly committed murder and treason. The *Tribune* disagreed and changed position over time. It first wrote that Brown was a sick man involved in a ridiculous plot, then it contended he was a strong, moral man who devised a sick plot, and finally the newspaper wrote of a martyr who represented a force against the southern evil of slavery. In presenting this view, the *Tribune* spared little news space. Its correspondent in Charlestown had more printed about Brown than the total coverage in the *Daily Picayune*. In all, the correspondent's daily column averaged more than two and a half columns in length. (The *Tribune* had a six-column format at the time.)

The New York *Tribune*'s opinions were squarely opposite those held by the *Daily Picayune*, and the *Tribune*'s intentions in reporting the John Brown episode appear clear: It wanted to lead public opinion, not follow it. In attempting to do so, the newspaper in large part relinquished its role as informer for one of antislavery propagandist.

The southern newspaper attempted through editorials to calm the fears of readers frightened of those persons in the North who might try to reduce southern rights through violence. If the *Daily Picayune* was indicative of the general attitude of the South, it appears to have been a threatened, insecure region, concerned as much with public opinion in the North as it was with creating any in the South.

The relatively soft approach taken by the *Daily Picayune* as compared to the *Tribune* may have resulted from the fact that it was the South being threatened. If the *Daily Picayune* editors felt the region was being challenged by outside forces that it could not control, reserved commentary may have been the result.

The end result of the coverage of these two newspapers was that the events surrounding John Brown may not have been as important as the possibilities offered to the newspapers to sway public opinion in a period of great anxiety and crisis.

The John Brown trial was a crisis of the first magnitude, one that many readers certainly attended with interest.[104] The raid and trial were engulfed in racial issues that surfaced in the news pages of newspapers from both regions. Newsmen from each region may have presented as fact only those happenings which, as representatives of their cultures, they believed to be true.[105] If this occurred with the coverage of John Brown, as may well have been the case, the gatekeepers became participants in shaping news beside just reporting it.[106]

The question still stands, however: Who was John Brown? Was he martyr or madman? Time seems to have changed little regarding "Old Osawatomie." Like the *Daily Picayune* and the *Tribune*, biographers have generally split in regard to Brown's frame of mind, as well as his motivation. The "who" may have been lost to the ages on the scaffold in Richmond, but the "what" was not. He brought the country to the precipice and the slaves would soon be emancipated the only way Brown believed they could be: through armed conflict.[107]

It would be problematical to hold that Brown helped clarify the issues for either the North or the South. However, through the immense news coverage of the raid and trial, a crystallization of the differences between the regions emerged. John Brown drew the line in the sand. Who he was becomes a historical footnote compared to what he accomplished, be it righteous or unholy.

NOTES

1. Richard O. Boyer, *The Legend of John Brown, a Biography and a History* (New York: Alfred A. Knopf, 1973), 64-66. Also see Stephen Oates, *To Purge This Land with Blood: A Biography of John Brown* (New York: Harper & Row, 1970), 132-135

2. Boyer, *The Legend of John Brown, a Biography and a History*, 462-513.

3. Robert Penn Warren, *John Brown, the Making of a Martyr* (New York: Payson and Clarke, Ltd., 1929), 135.

4. Ibid.

5. Oates, *To Purge This Land with Blood: A Biography of John Brown*, 135-137.

6. *Dictionary of American Biography* (New York: Scribner's Sons, 1929), 3: 133.

7. Ibid., 134.

8. Oates, *To Purge This Land with Blood: A Biography of John Brown*, 309.

9. Franklin Sanborn, *The Life and Letters of John Brown* (Boston: Roberts Brothers, 1891), 565.

10. Oswald Garrison Villard, *John Brown: A Biography Fifty Years After* (Gloucester, MA: Peter Smith, 1965), 140.

11. Ibid., 471-490.

12. Truman Nelson, *The Old Man: John Brown at Harper's Ferry* (New York: Holt, Rinehart and Winston, 1973), 152. See also *Dictionary of American Biography*, 19: 70.

13. Eric Foner, *Nat Turner* (Englewood Cliffs, NJ: Prentice-Hall, 1971), 471-490.

14. Edwin Emery and Michael Emery, *The Press and America: An Interpretive History of the Mass Media*, 5th ed. (Englewood Cliffs, NJ: Prentice-Hall, 1984) 155.

15. Foner, *Nat Turner*, 56.

16. Villard, *John Brown: A Biography Fifty Years After*, 476.

17. Ibid., 472.

18. Warren, *John Brown, The Making of a Martyr*, 89.

19. Donald Reynolds, *Editors Make War: Southern Newspapers in the Secession Crisis* (Nashville, TN: Vanderbilt University Press, 1970), 5.

20. Ibid., 24.

21. Villard, *John Brown: A Biography Fifty Years After*, 471-476, 480-481.

22. Steven Channing, *Crisis of Fear* (New York: Simon and Schuster, 1970), 129.

23. Gerald Johnson, *The Secession of the Southern States* (New York: G. P. Putnam's Sons, 1933), 129.

24. Villard, *John Brown: A Biography Fifty Years After*, 471.

25. Ibid., 518.

26. Ibid., 518-519.

27. Warren, *John Brown: the Making of a Martyr*, 331.

28. Ibid., 328.

29. Villard, *John Brown: A Biography Fifty Years After*, 479.

30. Ibid., 481.

31. Ibid., 483.

32. New York *Tribune*, 25 November 1859.

33. New Orleans *Daily Picayune*, 18 October 1859, 19 October 1859.

34. New Orleans *Daily Picayune*, 18 October 1859, 19 October 1859.

35. New Orleans *Daily Picayune*, 19 October 1859.

36. New Orleans *Daily Picayune*, 20 October 1859.

37. New Orleans *Daily Picayune*, 22 October 1859.

38. New Orleans *Daily Picayune*, 22 October 1859.

39. New Orleans *Daily Picayune*, 22 October 1859.

40. New Orleans *Daily Picayune*, 24 October 1859.

41. New Orleans *Daily Picayune*, 25 October 1859.

42. New Orleans *Daily Picayune*, 28 October 1859.

43. New Orleans *Daily Picayune*, 28 October 1859, 29 October 1859.

44. New Orleans *Daily Picayune*, 30 October 1859.

45. New Orleans *Daily Picayune*, 4 November 1859.

46. New Orleans *Daily Picayune*, 8 November 1859.

47. New Orleans *Daily Picayune*, 17 November 1859.

48. New Orleans *Daily Picayune*, 17 November 1859.

49. New Orleans *Daily Picayune*, 19 November 1859.

50. New Orleans *Daily Picayune*, 22 November 1859.

51. New Orleans *Daily Picayune*, 23 November 1859.

52. New Orleans *Daily Picayune*, 24 November 1859.

53. New Orleans *Daily Picayune*, 24 November 1859.

54. New Orleans *Daily Picayune*, 26 November 1859.

55. New Orleans *Daily Picayune*, 30 November 1859.

56. New Orleans *Daily Picayune*, 2 December 1859.

57. New Orleans *Daily Picayune*, 3 December 1859.

58. New Orleans *Daily Picayune*, 7 December 1859.

59. New Orleans *Daily Picayune*, 10 December 1859.

60. New York *Tribune*, 4 November 1859, 5 November 1859, 7 November 1859, 8 November 1859, 9 November 1859, 10 November 1859, 15 November 1859, 16 November 1859, 17 November 1859, 19 November 1859, 21 November 1859, 25 November 1859, 27 November 1859; 1 December 1859, 2 December 1859, 4 December 1859, 6 December 1859.

61. New York *Tribune*, 18 October 1859.

62. New York *Tribune*, 19 October 1859.

63. New York *Tribune*, 20 October 1859.

64. New York *Tribune*, 20 October 1859.

65. Warren, *John Brown, the Making of a Martyr*, 392.

66. New York *Tribune*, 21 October 1859.

67. New York *Tribune*, 24 October 1859.

68. New York *Tribune*, 25 October 1859.

69. New York *Tribune*, 25 October 1859.

70. New York *Tribune*, 26 October 1859.

71. New York *Tribune*, 28 October 1859.

72. New York *Tribune*, 31 October 1859.

73. Warren, *John Brown, the Making of a Martyr*, 393.

74. New York *Tribune*, 1 November 1859.

75. New York *Tribune*, 2 November 1859.

76. New York *Tribune*, 2 November 1859.

77. New York *Tribune*, 3 November 1859.

78. New York *Tribune*, 4 November 1859.

79. New York *Tribune*, 4 November 1859, 7 November 1859.

80. New York *Tribune*, 8 November 1859.

81. New York *Tribune*, 8 November 1859.

82. New York *Tribune*, 8 November 1859, 10 November 1859, 15 November 1859.

83. New York *Tribune*, 8 November 1859.

84. New York *Tribune*, 9 November 1859.

85. New York *Tribune*, 16 November 1859.

86. New York *Tribune*, 17 November 1859.

87. New York *Tribune*, 19 November 1859.

88. New York *Tribune*, 16 November 1859, 19 November 1859, 24 November 1859.

89. New York *Tribune*, 19 November 1859.

90. New York *Tribune*, 24 November 1859.

91. New York *Tribune*, 25 November 1859.

92. New York *Tribune*, 29 November 1859.

93. New York *Tribune*, 5 November 1859.

94. New York *Tribune*, 7 November 1859.

95. Lydia Maria Child, *Anti-Slavery Catechism* (Newburyport, MA: Whipple, 1836).

96. New York *Tribune*, 8 November 1859.

97. New York *Tribune*, 8 November 1859.

98. New York *Tribune*, 18, 19 November 1859.

99. New York *Tribune*, 19 November 1859.

100. New York *Tribune*, 21 November 1859.

101. New York *Tribune*, 22 November 1859

102. New York *Tribune*, 25 November 1859, 27 November 1859; 3 December 1859.

103. D. G. Boyce, "Public Opinion and Historians," *Journal of the Historical Association* 63 (September 1978): 222.

104. D. W. Harding, "General Conceptions in the Study of the Press and Public Opinion," *Sociological Review* 29 (October 1937): 390. See also *Dictionary of American Biography*, 19: 70.

105. David Manning White, "The Gatekeeper: A Case Study in the Selection of News," *Journalism Quarterly* 27 (Fall 1950): 389.

106. N. C. Rhoodie, *Intergroup Accommodation in Plural Societies* (London: St. Martin's Press, 1978), 236-237.

107. Albert Fried, *John Brown's Journey: Notes and Reflections on His America and Mine* (Garden City, NY: Anchor Press, 1978), 269-270.

6 〜

WORDS
FOR WAR

Donald Reynolds

General Ambrose E. Burnside was angry. The former commander of the Army of the Potomac had been banished to the Department of Ohio in early 1863 after suffering a humiliating defeat at Fredericksburg the previous December. Since the press had helped make him the scapegoat for that disaster, the volatile Burnside was understandably sensitive to the criticism he had continued to receive at the hands of Midwestern Democratic newspapers.

More recently, editors had scathed him for ordering the arrest and military trial of Democratic politician and leading Lincoln critic Clement L. Vallandigham of Ohio, and as the summer of 1863 approached, their railings against the administration over such issues as the draft became daily features of the opposition press. Enough was enough. On June 1, Burnside issued Order Number 84 indefinitely suppressing publication of the Chicago *Times*. The order, which also forbade circulation of the New York *World* in the Department of Ohio, might just as well have included a dozen other opposition papers, but Burnside apparently believed that making examples of a couple of the worst offenders would have the desired salutary effect. Instead, his action, like that against Vallandigham a month earlier, ignited considerable, and robust, protest. A chorus of editorials and petitions decrying the general's assault against the First Amendment reached a crescendo that was quickly heard in Washington. Lincoln, who ironically would take a similar action against the New York *World* the next year, now commanded Burnside to rescind his order.[1]

Burnside's skirmish with the press in 1863, together with Lincoln's intervention, is a fair representation of the frustration and confusion that characterized the Union government's policy toward newspapers during the Civil War. To a somewhat lesser degree, the same inconsistency plagued government-press relations in the Confederacy as well.

It is easy to understand why both the Union and the Confederacy found it difficult to develop a consistent approach to the issue of freedom of the press. To begin with, by the mid-19th century that portion of the First Amendment that stated "Congress shall make no law . . . abridging the freedom of speech, or of the press" had become virtually sacrosanct in the thinking of the American people. The only serious effort to suppress that cherished freedom—the Sedition Act of 1798—had sparked protest and was important in causing the downfall of the Federalist Party in the election of 1800. The Sedition Act expired in 1801, and from that point to the Civil War, no further efforts were made to legislate restrictions upon the press's freedom to print whatever it wanted.[2]

The Civil War inevitably brought with it new challenges to freedom of speech in general and of the press in particular. The challenges arose in part from changes that had occurred in the American press during the generation before the war and in part from the unique nature of the war itself. Newspapers were in a much more formidable position to affect public opinion by the beginning of the Civil War than they had ever been. For one thing, there were more of them; the nation's 1200 papers of 1833 had swelled to 3000 by 1860, a remarkable pattern of growth in less than 30 years.[3]

This expansion had been abetted by revolutionary improvements in technology that had given rise to the penny newspaper in the 1830s. Taking advantage of their ability to provide a less expensive product to a growing population, shrewd entrepreneur/publishers like James Gordon Bennett of the New York *Herald*, Benjamin Day of the New York *Sun*, and William M. Swain of the Philadelphia *Public Ledger*, had succeeded in building large circulations during the two decades that preceded the Civil War.[4] At the advent of the penny press in 1833, no American newspaper had a circulation of as many as 5000, but on the eve of the Civil War, Bennett's *Herald* listed 77,000 subscribers to its daily edition, and weeklies like the New York *Tribune* and New York *Ledger* boasted circulations of 200,000 and 400,000, respectively.[5]

Fierce battles for new subscribers inspired each publisher to attempt to outdo his competitors in providing the most thorough and sensational coverage of the Civil War. As a result, the Civil War was more thoroughly covered by the press than any previous war.[6] In fact, the Mexican War, fought only a little more than a decade earlier, was the first conflict in which correspondents actually had gone to the front and sent back dispatches describing what they had seen. There had been few restrictions on reporters during the Mexican War; they had moved freely with the armies and in fact often were indistinguishable from the troops. Their stories were no threat to national security, since they appeared in the newspapers long after the events themselves and revealed nothing that would be of use to the Mexican army.[7]

The Civil War press, however, was bound to pose a much more serious problem for both sides. The large circulations of the Civil War-era newspapers would enable editors—at least those of the more successful urban sheets—to send numerous correspondents to the key battle areas, and the extensive network of telegraph wires that crisscrossed the nation, north and south, provided these reporters with the potential for quickly sending descriptions of battles and reports of troop movements to their editors.

On the one hand, Union and Confederate leaders recognized that newspapers could be important instruments for informing the respective publics of important events both at home and at the front and for building morale. But they also knew that the ubiquitous correspondents were in a position to do an infinite amount of mischief. From the loyalist perspective of both sides, publication of military secrets and expressions of disloyalty amounted to nothing less than treason. In the view of those who held this opinion, offending journals should be suppressed and their correspondents and editors arrested and perhaps imprisoned. Nevertheless, the constitutions of both belligerents protected newspapers, and with some notable exceptions, both the northern and southern publics generally continued to support the principle of a free press. Consequently, neither Congress passed a sedition act, and although the exigencies of war led both governments to try varying degrees of censorship, a lack of consistency in application doomed their efforts to failure.

The nation's inexperience with censorship showed clearly in both the Lincoln and Davis administrations. Of the two presidents, Lincoln was the more ambiguous in his policy toward First Amendment freedoms. During the course of the war, he invoked his power to suspend the writ of habeas corpus to allow the imprisonment of thousands of individuals who were suspected of disloyalty. Yet almost all of these individuals were detained for only short periods of time, and many historians think that the president showed remarkable restraint in the degree to which he used his power to jail individuals suspected of treason. And he never used this power to punish his critics, regardless of how vicious or unfair they were. As one Lincoln scholar has observed, the president "suffered more abuse than any other president, despite having more power to stifle abuse than any other president."[8]

Lincoln also occasionally allowed the suppression of papers, although his interference in Burnside's vendetta against the Chicago *Times* and New York *World* demonstrated that he was not always consistent in such matters. Invariably, whenever the president interfered with a subordinate's suppression of a newspaper, it was because he felt that it would have adverse political effects that, on balance, would be more harmful to the war effort than the journal's indiscretions. James G. Randall lists some 21 papers suspended by the Union government. Most of these suspensions occurred for only short periods of time.[9] They were usually ordered by military commanders or by the War Department; however, there was one specific instance in which Lincoln took a direct hand. In May, 1864, the New York *World* published a forged presidential proclamation setting a day of humiliation and prayer and asking for 400,000 more troops. The bogus proclamation was printed also in the New York *Journal of Commerce*. Coming as it did on the heels of bad military news, this apparently desperate appeal by the president threw many in the war-weary North into a panic. On grounds that such irresponsibility amounted to treason, an angry Lincoln ordered the papers suppressed and the offending editors and publishers arrested and kept in jail until they could be tried by a military court. After only two days, however, amidst growing howls among Democratic leaders in New York, political acumen replaced anger and Lincoln lifted the suspension of the papers and released the jailed newspapermen.[10]

Lincoln's suppression of the *World* and *Journal of Commerce* was uncharacteristic of his usual approach to the press. He preferred to leave newspapers as free as possible, even when they printed views that were potentially harmful to the war effort, not so much because he feared newsmen but because he did not wish to make martyrs of them. For this same reason, whenever suppressions did occur, they usually were of very brief duration.[11] His policy of restraint was perhaps best summed up in advice he wrote to General John M. Scholfield, commander of the Department of Missouri:

You will only arrest individuals and suppress assemblies or newspapers when they may be working palpable injury to the military in your charge, and in no other case will you interfere with the expression of opinion in any form or allow it to be interfered with violently by others. In this you have a discretion to exercise with great caution, calmness and forbearance.[12]

The president's subordinates, both in and out of uniform, often lacked their commander-in-chief's remarkable ability to tolerate the excesses of the press, as the Burnside incident demonstrated. Those members of the administration who were charged with supervision of the military effort, for example, often found themselves at odds with the press. Reporters disliked Secretary of the Navy Gideon Welles and Secretary of War Edwin M. Stanton, neither of whom made much effort to disguise his contempt for the press. They especially despised Stanton, whose manner, wrote one, "has made him offensive to everyone who approaches him." The Washington correspondents dubbed him "Marie Antoinette," after one of their number thought he perceived a resemblance between Stanton and the wife of Louis XVI.[13]

Stanton became a lightning rod for the administration's policies, because on February 25, 1862, the responsibility for censorship was placed with the War Department.[14] Even before this step had been taken, Stanton had helped gain passage of legislation empowering the president to place all telegraph lines under government supervision. Using this new authority, Lincoln had announced that all telegraphic dispatches dealing with military matters must be approved either by a representative of the War Department or by the commanding officer of a military district. Stanton promptly appointed the president of the American Telegraph Company to the post of "Military Supervisor of Telegraphs" and made him responsible for employing trustworthy agents who essentially would act as censors for the government. Theoretically, this order might have placed a stranglehold upon the rapid distribution of news dispatches, but in effect it was more of an aggravation and an inconvenience; there never were sufficient numbers of trained personnel to provide effective censorship.[15]

Even when telegraphic censorship was effectively imposed, however, correspondents found alternative ways to send their dispatches, most commonly through the mails.[16] Only rarely were the mails censored, and even when they were, newsmen showed great ingenuity in finding other ways to get their reports to their editors. For example, when Postmaster General Montgomery Blair purposely delayed mails from northern Virginia during the Wilderness Campaign—presumably to delay publication of the terrible losses being experienced by the Army of the Potomac—Bennett's *Herald* resorted to sending messengers by steamer from City Point, Virginia, each morning at 10. In this way, packages arrived in New York on the evening of the next day. Other papers followed the *Herald*'s example, and the news from the front continued to be printed on schedule.[17] Once the dispatches had arrived at the various newspaper offices, there was little, short of the unusual step of confiscation and suppression, to prevent them from reaching their readers. Few authorities went to such lengths as the provost marshal in New York, who sent agents to tear down bulletins describing the disaster at Second Bull Run that had been posted outside newspaper offices in the city.[18]

Early in the war, northern officials apparently hoped that newsmen could be convinced to withhold publication of information that might compromise the war effort. For example, after the defeat at First Bull Run, the army's new commander, George B. McClellan, met with representatives of the press and dictated to them the so-called Gentlemen's Agreement. In exchange for their promise that they would not publish any material "that may furnish aid and comfort to the enemy," McClellan promised to provide "facilities for obtaining and immediately transmitting all information suitable for publication, particularly touching engagements with the enemy."[19] Although signed by the general and the dozen reporters who were present, the agreement lasted only five days. Numerous correspondents who were not in attendance at the meeting felt unbound by the agreement, and besides, the competition between newspapers was too intense to allow compliance to last long.   The collapse of the Gentlemen's Agreement was followed on August 10, 1861, by a stern order from McClellan forbidding newsmen from sending any reports "reflecting operations of the Army or military movements on land or water, or respecting the troops, camps, arsenals, intrenchments, or military affairs within the several districts."[20]   Demonstrating the administration's support of McClellan's order, Secretary of War Simon Cameron, with Lincoln's approval, invoked the 57th Article of War, which meant that individuals "convicted of holding correspondence with, or giving intelligence to the enemy, either directly or indirectly," could be tried by court-martial and, if found guilty, sentenced to imprisonment or even death.[21]

Newsmen were unintimidated. Spurred on by intense competition, correspondents outdid one another in ferreting out sensitive information and including it in the dispatches that they sent to their editors. Whether their reports revealed military secrets, damaged morale, or libeled military commanders was not so important to most of them as whether their contributions sold papers. There is no question that northern journalists were responsible for the transmission through their papers of key information to the Confederates. For example, General Braxton Bragg learned of Union General Rosecrans's risky plan to divide his army east of Chattanooga from the Chicago *Times*.

In other examples, southern generals found General William T. Sherman's plans for his Georgia campaign detailed in the New York *Times*, and during the Wilderness Campaign in 1864, Lee was apprised of Grant's planned movements, expected reinforcements, and even of his "secret" meeting with other generals by the New York *Daily News*. And when an amphibious expedition departed Fort Monroe, Virginia, to launch a surprise attack on the port of Wilmington, North Carolina, in December 1864, several New York papers combined to publish not only the destination of the task force but also a complete list of participating vessels, an identification of the army and naval commanders. Although the assault on Wilmington was eventually successful, the element of surprise had been lost, resulting in a larger number of casualties than otherwise would have been the case.[22] Little wonder that Confederate generals eagerly examined northern journals for information concerning Yankee troop movements. Lee, in particular, avidly scanned such papers when he could get them. One of his favorite sources of information was the Philadelphia *Inquirer*, from which he learned of McClellan's impending departure from Harrison's Landing in August 1862. This news helped him determine to launch his highly successful attack against General John Pope at Second Manassas.[23]

Such indiscretions on the part of the press clearly damaged the Union war effort, and since they violated orders issued by the authorities, they might well have resulted in severe penalties against those responsible. Nevertheless, there were surprisingly few such repercussions. Since no sedition laws were on the books, the legal system was not well suited to prosecute offending newsmen. There were a few efforts to prosecute editors on various charges, but no convictions resulted.[24] Although correspondents traveling with the armies were covered by military law, relatively few of them were subjected to courts martial. The dearth of such prosecutions and total absence of executions were remarkable in view of the contempt in which correspondents and newspapers in general were held by many of the army's generals. General Winfield Scott told one reporter that his kind were doing an excellent job keeping the enemy informed of Union military activities, adding that he would rather have a hundred spies in camp than one reporter. After a paper in New Hampshire revealed an elaborate plan by General Ben Butler to trap a Confederate tugboat in the James River, the general fumed that not much would be accomplished until the Union had hanged a half dozen spies and "at least one reporter."[25] And General Sherman was supposed to have responded to a report that three reporters had been killed during an engagement with the enemy: "Good! Now we shall have news from Hell before breakfast."[26] Although the quote may be apocryphal, it accurately sums up the acerbic Sherman's view of the press.

In 1862, General Henry Halleck proposed expelling reporters from all the field armies. Lincoln apparently opposed such a drastic measure, however, on grounds that it would be unfair to punish all correspondents for the indiscretions of a few.[27] Nevertheless, the War Department—with the President's approval—authorized all army commanders in the field to expel from their lines those individuals whose dispatches violated secrecy or in some way undermined the morale of the army. Acting on this authority, Union generals frequently ordered reporters to leave their jurisdictions, often on short notice. For example, when George Williams, a reporter for the New York *Times*, published an erroneous report of Federal losses in one of General Phil Sheridan's battles in northern Virginia, Sheridan gave the newsman 24 hours to leave his department. When Williams protested that his home newspaper also was technically in the general's jurisdiction, the exasperated Sheridan blurted: "Oh, go to the devil if you like!" "Alright [*sic*] General," retorted the newsman, "but I am afraid I shall not be out of your district even with his Satanic majesty."[28]

Although expulsion was the usual penalty for publishing sensitive military information, various generals did occasionally order the arrest and military trial of a newsman. More often than not in such instances, the journalist escaped prosecution by fleeing from the general's jurisdiction.[29] The most famous example of a case that actually went to trial not surprisingly occurred in the jurisdiction of General Sherman. Convinced that newspapers seriously compromised the war effort, Sherman believed that the First Amendment guarantee of freedom of the press should be suspended for the duration of the war. Notorious among correspondents for his harsh treatment of the press, Sherman often peremptorily ordered journalists out of his lines for seemingly trivial offenses. To those who argued that the public had a right to know what was going on at the front, he answered that all needful information could be gleaned from soldiers' letters and official communiqués.[30]

In late December 1862, Sherman led an abortive assault against Chickasaw Bluffs, north of Vicksburg. Before leaving Memphis, he had issued General Order Number 8, explicitly forbidding newspapermen from accompanying the army; anyone who published an account of the campaign was to be arrested and tried as a spy. After failing to get exemptions, a number of journalists managed to accompany the army anyway. Several versions of the disastrous assault were later published, most of them full of errors. Sherman was furious. His wrath fell primarily upon Thomas W. Knox, a reporter for the New York *Herald*, who wrote an extremely critical account that made Sherman look especially bad. The general had Knox arrested and tried by court-martial on several charges, including that of spying. The court exonerated Knox of the most serious charges, finding him guilty only of violating Sherman's General Order Number 8, to which the court attached no criminality. Knox was banished from Sherman's jurisdiction but suffered no other penalties.[31]

Knox was lucky. On other occasions, Sherman and other generals, as well as the War Department, jailed newspapermen, sometimes for several months, without ever bringing formal charges against them. Thus, on General Ulysses S. Grant's order, Sherman arrested Warren P. Isham of the Chicago *Times* for indiscretions that were never very clear. Although he was not brought to trial, Isham was kept in jail for three months before he was released.[32] B. S. Osbon, a correspondent of the New York *Daily News*, apparently spent several months in jail in 1865 after Secretary of the Navy Gideon Welles determined that it was he who had revealed the target and date of the attack at Wilmington, North Carolina, the previous December.[33] In February 1862, Malcolm Ives, a reporter assigned to set up a Washington Bureau for the New York *Herald*, was ordered arrested by Secretary of War Stanton, because he persisted in eavesdropping in the War Department's offices after being warned to leave. Imprisoned in Fort McHenry, Ives was not released until the following June.[34] Occasionally, a reporter escaped even harsher treatment. General Burnside, having rejoined the Army of the Potomac as a corps commander during the Wilderness Campaign of 1864, took offense at the criticism leveled at him by New York *Times* correspondent William Swinton. He not only had the newsman arrested but ordered him shot that day. Fortunately, Grant intervened and commuted Swinton's "sentence" to expulsion from the army's lines.[35]

Perhaps, as James G. Randall has suggested, it is surprising that journalists were not tried more often under the military code to which they were legally subjected.[36] On the other hand, newsmen had significant weapons of their own in resisting the heavy hand of the government and the military. The political influence of the press had grown enormously in the North during the generation before the Civil War, and politicians could not afford to tamper too freely with the First Amendment. We have already seen that Lincoln's circumspect approach to the press was due in large measure to his concern for the political implications. The Congress was similarly sensitive to the power of the press. It not only refused to pass a sedition law that would have made prosecutions of newsmen easier, but it demonstrated its sensitivity to journalistic pressure when, at the urging of several newspapers, the House leadership ordered an investigation of censorship of the press in December 1861. The House Judiciary Committee ultimately passed a resolution stating that the government should not "interfere with free transmission of intelligence by telegraph" when the information transmitted did not aid the Confederates by giving them information that would compromise the Union war effort. The full House of Representatives concurred, and although the resolution had no practical effect—it was still up to the War Department to decide what was damaging and what was not—it nevertheless illustrated the power of the press to influence the Congress.[37]

It may be that the most powerful weapon of correspondents in resisting censorship and the wrath of the government and the generals was their pens. What they published not only gave politicians pause but also led many generals to treat them with more deference than they would otherwise have done. Those generals who were considered uncooperative (such as Grant) or abusive (such as Sherman) were often "written down" by the journalists covering their campaigns, while second-raters who cultivated the press (such as John McClernand) were given far more credit than they deserved.[38]

Although a Grant or a Sherman could survive a bad press because their achievements enabled them to please the president, other targets of the press were not so fortunate. After the Army of the Potomac was badly bloodied by Lee at the Battle of the Wilderness in early May 1864, Edward Crapsey, a correspondent of the Philadelphia *Inquirer*, wrote an account alleging that General-in-Chief U.S. Grant's presence with the army had saved the campaign against Richmond. The reporter implied that General George Meade, commander of the Army of the Potomac, would have retreated back to the North had not General-in-Chief Grant been on the scene. The infuriated Meade not only expelled Crapsey from his lines; he humiliated him by parading him past the ranks, mounted backwards on a mule with a sign attached to his chest and back that read: "Libeler of the Press"—all to the tune of the "Rogue's March." After returning to Philadelphia, Crapsey convened a meeting of correspondents, all of whom agreed that Meade's name would not be mentioned again during the campaign, except in connection with defeats; all future credit for victories would go to Grant. As a result, the press almost totally ignored Meade for the next six months. This "blackout," denying Meade his share of the credit for the final defeat of Lee, may well have done serious damage to that general's future political prospects.[39]

Although a more or less constant tension existed between Confederate government and military leaders, on the one hand, and the press, on the other, there was never an adversarial relationship such as the North experienced. There were several reasons for this. To begin with, southern newspapers were more amenable to controls on their freedom than northern papers. For a generation before the war, a fierce battle had raged, especially in the lower South, over freedom of thought and expression. The rise of abolitionism had fueled the controversy, but the issue of freedom of speech had spilled over into other social realms as well. One casualty had been the liberalism of the sort that Thomas Jefferson and other sons of the Enlightenment had nurtured in the late 18th century. The rise of orthodoxy in southern thought was intensified during the secession movement; as the war approached, it became dangerous to defend the Union too strongly in certain areas of the South. As a result of these developments, most southern editors were used to accepting limitations upon their right to speak freely.[40]

Of more immediate concern, southern editors generally recognized that the Confederacy faced large odds in its struggle against a more numerous, richer adversary; and since a great majority of them supported Confederate independence, they were more willing than many northern editors to work hand in hand with the government to achieve the desired goal. The relative weakness of the southern press also worked to minimize the conflict between newspapers and the Confederate government. In the first flush of southern patriotism that followed the attack on Fort Sumter, scores of journalists had deserted their papers to enlist in the army, leaving such a shortage of professional help that some papers barely had the staffs to continue publishing, let alone to cover the battlefields. Even when qualified individuals were available, however, many Confederate papers, given their relatively modest circulations, could not afford to send correspondents into the field like their northern counterparts (the New York *Herald* had as many as 40 paid correspondents reporting the war). Thus, from the standpoint of numbers alone, there were not as many opportunities for friction between reporters and the military as there were in the North.[41]

Other problems not faced by northern journals seriously weakened the ability of Confederate newspapers to report the war adequately to the southern people. Shortages of paper and printer's ink plagued editors almost from the beginning and became increasingly problematical as the war progressed. Runaway inflation soon forced publishers to raise their prices to such heights that their already relatively small readerships diminished even further.[42]

Some southern journalists, such as Samuel C. Reid Jr., and Felix de Fontaine, achieved a degree of distinction as battlefield reporters, but they were few in number compared to the legions of northern correspondents who regularly attached themselves to northern armies. For the most part, the stories from the Confederate lines were filed by visiting editors or were received in the form of letters from amateurs, many of whom were soldiers.[43]

It was in large measure to make up for the inability of each southern journal to maintain its own correspondents in the field that the Confederate Press Association (PA) was created in 1862. Consisting primarily of the Confederacy's 43 dailies, the PA's members chose John S. Thrasher as general manager. Working from his headquarters in Atlanta, Thrasher recruited professional newsmen and sent them to the various theatres of action. By the spring of 1863, the PA had some 20 agents spread out from the Potomac to the Mississippi. Their reports were relayed on to the member newspapers. As a part of his job of gathering news for the PA's members, Thrasher also worked to resist unreasonable censorship of the news. His visits with Confederate generals, such as Bragg, Pemberton, and Johnston, who had made it difficult for the PA's agents to transmit their dispatches, were at least partially successful.[44]

As in the North, censorship policy was slow to develop in the Confederacy. Although it was clear to members of the government and to the military that certain information should not be published, there was uncertainty over the extent to which restrictive regulations should go. On one point, however, the Confederate leaders were apparently in agreement with their northern counterparts: It was essential to establish control over the telegraph, the primary means of rapid communication. Less than a month after Fort Sumter was fired upon, the Provisional Congress of the Confederacy passed a law giving president Jefferson Davis sweeping power to censor the telegraph lines. The president was authorized to assign to telegraph offices special agents who were to read and censor messages. The law made it a crime, punishable by fine and imprisonment, to transmit information harmful to the Confederacy.[45] In January 1862, the Confederate Congress also passed a law making it a crime to publish information about "the numbers, disposition, movements, or destination" of Rebel armies or naval units.[46] The Congress effectively censored its own proceedings by the simple expedient of going into secret session whenever it considered military matters.[47] Nevertheless, the southern congressmen were anxious to avoid any appearance of tampering with freedom of the press, and whenever proposals were made to suppress newspapers for publishing material that seemed damaging to Confederate arms, loud protests, both from the press and from within the Congress, defeated them.[48]

President Jefferson Davis's benign approach to the South's newspapers echoed the views of a majority of the Congress. It is ironic that Davis, who could be petty and quarrelsome in responding to critics, should have been more generous in his dealing with the press than Abraham Lincoln. We need to remember, however, that Davis faced nothing resembling the bloc of subversive Copperhead papers that Lincoln had to contend with. Moreover, the absence of an opposition political party in the Confederacy meant that there were relatively few papers in the South that were consistently antigovernment or anti-Davis. Although individual journalists, like E. A. Pollard of the Richmond *Examiner* and Robert Barnwell Rhett Jr., of the Charleston *Mercury*, frequently leveled vicious attacks against the president for his war leadership, Davis usually ignored them.

Why would Davis—normally so sensitive to criticism—be determined to maintain freedom of the press, even in the face of intemperate and unfair criticism? In part, the answer lay in the very rationale for the southern revolution: The federal government, under the Republican Party, had allegedly violated the constitutional rights of southerners, causing 11 southern states to leave the Union and form a new government that would presumably restore and guard those lost freedoms. Therefore, consistency of argument required that the new government place a high priority on maintaining freedom of speech and of the press. It was probably for this reason that Davis, in 1862, said in a speech to Congress that the government had been scrupulous in guarding the right to free expression, and why he could later boast that the war had been managed "without the suppression of one single newspaper."[49]

The cabinet member charged with implementing censorship in the South was Secretary of War Leroy P. Walker. Taking a less aggressive approach than his northern counterpart Stanton, Walker's early approach was consonant with that of Davis. In an open letter to newspapermen, published in the Richmond *Examiner*, July 1, 1861, the secretary asked for their cooperation in refraining from publishing any reports of the strengths or weaknesses of military units "at any points in the vicinity of the enemy" or any other information that might aid the Yankee armies.[50] Most southern journals were agreeable and dutifully complied with the administration's wishes, but a vocal minority was not. Responding to Walker's request, Rhett's Charleston *Mercury* argued that its readers "have a right to know everything which transpires in the operations of the government, or the conduct of the war, that they might approve, support, condemn or rectify."[51] Exasperated perhaps by the refusal of such papers as the *Mercury* to voluntarily suppress information that might help the enemy, Walker ordered "commanders of regiments and detachments [to] use their best exertions to prevent this foolish and pernicious itching for newspaper notoriety."[52]

Confederate military commanders hardly needed Walker's prompting to convince them that they should crack down on the press. Generals Joe Johnston, P. G. T. Beauregard, Thomas J. "Stonewall" Jackson, Earl Van Dorn, and Braxton Bragg were just some of the more prominent army commanders who at one time or another excluded correspondents from their lines. Usually these actions were taken as preemptive measures to prevent leaks that might tip northern generals about Confederate strategy, or they were provoked by the publication of some military information that the commanders thought might help the Union army. The usual punishment for publishing sensitive information was expulsion of the offending newsman; however, stronger steps were occasionally attempted. For example, Bragg, who was to southern journalists what Sherman was to those in the North, arrested a reporter of the Montgomery *Advertiser* for publishing some references to the army's movements. After strong protests from the *Advertiser*'s influential editor, however, Bragg released the incarcerated correspondent.[53] On another occasion, General Earl Van Dorn announced that he was suspending the writ of habeas corpus for portions of Mississippi and Louisiana and that he would imprison any reporter or editor who revealed troop movements or who wrote anything that undermined public confidence in the commanding officer of the army. After many southern editors protested this measure, many congressmen expressed their opposition, and Van Dorn rescinded his order.[54]

Southern editors frequently complained about what they considered to be unreasonable restrictions by the military. Although their reporters were not abused or arrested as often as those of the Union, news from the front was more effectively censored than in the North.[55] Not only were reporters sometimes excluded entirely from army lines during a campaign, but even when they were not, commanding generals often refused to allow them to send their reports of battles over the telegraph. And when such dispatches were allowed, they often were so mangled by censors that it was impossible to tell what had actually occurred.

The Press Association's general manager, J. S. Thrasher, protested the restrictions placed on his agents, but although his efforts helped somewhat, the veil of secrecy that covered many military encounters kept the people of the Confederacy confused as to the real state of the war. But the Confederate newspapers themselves were at least partly responsible for the distortions that appeared in their accounts of battles. With few exceptions, they wanted to put the best "spin" possible on the military events they reported so that morale would remain high among the people. Thus, they were quick to accept uncritically the initial official rosy battle reports and to report battles that turned out to be defeats as great victories for

Confederate arms. They distorted casualty lists, so that the Yankee armies always appeared to suffer more. The danger of such patriotic reporting, of course, was that when the real result of a Shiloh or a Murfreesboro or a Peachtree Creek became known, the press lost credibility with the public. By war's end, few southerners believed what they read in the newspapers.[56] One man in Georgia demonstrated this lack of faith in talking with some of Sherman's officers in 1864 during the famous march to the sea:

They say that you are retreating, but it is the strangest sort of retreat I ever saw. Why, dog bite 'em, the newspapers have been lying in this way all along. They allers are whipping the Federal armies, and they allers fall back after the battle is over. Our army was allers whipping the Feds, and we allers fall back.[57]

The inaccurate, Pollyannaish versions that appeared frequently in Confederate newspapers were in part the result of the overall poor quality of southern journalism, at least when it was compared with that in the North.[58] The shortages of men and supplies had made it difficult for Confederate editors to publish any sort of paper, much less one of good quality.[59] But the overoptimistic picture painted by Confederate newspapers was also the result of a conscious desperate effort to buttress the sagging morale of a people who were losing faith. In the final analysis, censorship may have been less important in denying southerners a true picture of the state of Confederate arms than these other factors.

Neither the Union nor the Confederacy succeeded in their efforts to establish a truly effective system of censorship. It would be surprising had it been otherwise. Given the high regard that both sides had for the principle of freedom of the press, the failure of either to pass sedition laws that might have effectively controlled the press, the nation's historical lack of practical experience in censorship, the newness of war reporting, and the existence of a vigorous, competitive press (at least in the North), it was perhaps inevitable that efforts to control that which the papers published about military matters and governmental leaders would largely fail. The primary concentration of both North and South was upon censoring telegraphic dispatches. Effective control of the telegraph wires depended on local commanders and telegraph agents, however, and success was always sporadic. Moreover, when the telegraph was closed to them, correspondents found other methods of filing their stories—most notably, the uncensored mails. Also, since soldiers' letters were not censored, the men in blue and gray often sent lengthy accounts of military matters home, and these often ended up in the local newspaper. In effect, such men in uniform were acting as correspondents. In spite of all the leaks and inconsistencies, however, it is doubtful that any important battle's outcome was altered by the premature publication of sensitive material. Nor can it be shown that the war's duration was extended one minute by the newspapers' numerous violations of the rules of censorship.

The failure of both the Union and Confederacy to censor the press consistently does not mean that their efforts were of no consequence. The political and military leaders of America's future international wars would learn much from the halting and often inconsistent attempts of both sides in this brothers' conflict to control the dissemination of information. Of course, it would be much easier to regulate the movement of correspondents in modern wars, since all would be fought on foreign soil. Although reporters would often be allowed to accompany troops to the front in later conflicts, they could do so only under carefully controlled conditions, and the stories that they filed would have to be cleared by military censors before they could be sent to their papers back home. Often, the modern correspondent would have to depend upon official government communiqués—"invented" by Secretary of War Stanton in 1864 when he began issuing short news bulletins to the press as a means of providing the public with news from the front.[60] Moreover, the mails, which had provided one of the loopholes for correspondents in the Civil War, would fall under close scrutiny in the great wars of the 20th century. The Civil War experience had revealed the difficulties inherent in maintaining democratic freedoms in wartime. Although neither side solved the problem in that greatest of American wars, the efforts of both pointed the way to more effective solutions for future generations.

NOTES

1. James G. Randall, *Constitutional Problems Under Lincoln* (Urbana: University of Illinois Press, 1951), 493-496; William Marvel, *Burnside* (Chapel Hill: University of North Carolina Press, 1991), 245-246; Lincoln to Edwin M. Stanton, 4 June 1863, in Roy P. Basler, ed., *The Collected Works of Abraham Lincoln*, vol. 6 (New Brunswick, NJ: Rutgers University Press, 1953), 248.

2. Randall, *Constitutional Problems Under Lincoln*, 478-480.

3. Frank L. Mott, *American Journalism: A History of Newspapers in the United States Through 250 Years, 1690 to 1940* (New York: Macmillan Co., 1941), 216.

4. Ibid., 228-252.

5. Ibid., 303.

6. Ibid., 329.

7. Joseph J. Matthews, *Reporting the Wars* (Minneapolis: University of Minnesota Press, 1957), 54-58.

8. Don E. Fehrenbacher, "Lincoln and the Paradoxes of Freedom," in *Freedom in America: A 200-Year Perspective*, ed. Norman A. Graebner (University Park: Pennsylvania State University Press, 1977), 95.

9. Randall, *Constitutional Problems Under Lincoln*, 500-502. It should be noted that many of these papers were located in the South and were suspended because they continued publishing pro-Confederate views after occupation by Union

forces.

10. Ibid., 496-499.

11. Bernard Weisberger, *Reporters for the Union* (Boston: Little, Brown and Co., 1953), 256.

12. Lincoln to Scholfield, 1 October 1863, in Basler, *The Collected Works of Abraham Lincoln*, 6: 492.

13. J. Cutler Andrews, *The North Reports the Civil War* (Pittsburgh, PA: University of Pittsburgh Press, 1955), 56.

14. Censorship responsibility had originally been given to the War Department, but subsequently it moved to the Treasury and then to State before finally settling again in Stanton's department—all within less than a year's duration. Robert S. Harper, *Lincoln and the Press* (New York: McGraw-Hill, 1951), 129.

15. Louis M. Starr, *Bohemian Brigade: Civil War Newsmen in Action* (New York: Alfred A. Knopf, 1954), 84.

16. James G. Randall, "The Newspaper Problem in Its Bearing upon Military Secrecy During the Civil War," *American Historical Review* 33 (January 1918): 304.

17. Andrews, *The North Reports the Civil War*, 649; Randall, *Constitutional Problems Under Lincoln*, 481-483.

18. Weisberger, *Reporters for the Union*, 106.

19. Quoted in Emmett Croier, *Yankee Reporters, 1861-65* (New York: Oxford University Press, 1956), 131-136. See also Harper, *Lincoln and the Press*, 130-131.

20. Quoted in Andrews, *The North Reports the Civil War*, 151.

21. Starr, *Bohemian Brigade*, 67; Randall, *Constitutional Problems Under Lincoln*, 489-490.

22. Randall, *Constitutional Problems Under Lincoln*, 484-485; idem, "The Newspaper Problem," 310-313.

23. Ibid., "The Newspaper Problem," 311.

24. Ibid., 320.

25. Weisberger, *Reporters for the Union*, 78-79.

26. Matthews, *Reporting the Wars*, 86.

27. Andrews, *The North Reports the Civil War*, 267-268.

28. Quoted in John F. Marsalek, *Sherman's Other War: The General and the Civil War Press* (Memphis, TN: Memphis State University Press, 1981), 43.

29. For examples, see Andrews, *The North Reports the Civil War*, 551-553.

30. For a thorough explanation of Sherman's views on freedom of the press, see Marsalek, *Sherman's Other War*, 17-18, 105, 211.

31. Ibid., 117-138; Croier, *Yankee Reporters*, 291-305; Andrews, *The North Reports the Civil War*; Weisberger, *Reporters for the Union*, 112-114.

32. Marsalek, *Sherman's Other War*, 103-104.

33. Harper, *Lincoln and the Press*, 136-137.

34. Ibid., 132-133.

35. Ibid., 140. Burnside's biographer says that the threat "was all bluff, designed to frighten the columnist." Apparently, the bluff was successful; after Grant's intervention, Swinton wasted no time in leaving the army's lines. Marvel, *Burnside*, 381.

36. Randall, *Constitutional Problems Under Lincoln*, 506-507.

37. Harper, *Lincoln and the Press*, 130-132.

38. Randall, *Constitutional Problems Under Lincoln*, 485.

39. Andrews, *The North Reports the Civil War*, 545.

40. J. Cutler Andrews, *The South Reports the Civil War* (Princeton, NJ: Princeton University Press, 1970), 528. For a fuller discussion of the generation-long conflict, see Clement Eaton, *The Freedom-of-Thought Struggle in the Old South*, rev. ed. (New York: Harper Torchbooks, 1964), 196-215, 398-402. For pressures brought to bear on recalcitrant editors during the secession crisis, see Donald E. Reynolds, *Editors Make War: Southern Newspapers in the Secession Crisis* (Nashville, TN: Vanderbilt University Press, 1970), 118-160.

41. Starr, *Bohemian Bridgade*, viii-ix.

42. Mott, *American Journalism*, 362-363; Matthews, *Reporting the Wars*, 94-95.

43. Matthews, *Reporting the Wars*, 93.

44. Quintas C. Wilson, "A Study and Evaluation of Military Censorship in the Civil War," Master's thesis, University of Minnesota, 1945), 215-229; Andrews, The *South Reports the Civil War*, 45, 532; Edwin Emery and Michael Emery, *The Press and America*, 5th ed. (Englewood Cliffs, NJ: Prentice-Hall, 1984), 200-201.

45. Senate Doc. No. 234, 58 Cong., 2d Sess., *Journal of the Confederate States of America, 1861-1865*, vol. 25 (Washington, DC: 1904-1905): 202-203.

46. Mott, *American Journalism*, 365.

47. Andrews, *The South Reports the Civil War*, 530-531.

48. Robert N. Mathis, "Freedom of the Press in the Confederacy: A Reality," *Historian* (August, 1975): 633-648; Andrews, *The South Reports the Civil War*, 531.

49. Mathis, "Freedom of the Press in the Confederacy: A Reality," 634-635. In 1864, Davis did consider using his power to suspend the writ of habeas corpus to suppress William Woods Holden's Raleigh (North Carolina) *Standard*, which was a leading advocate of the peace movement, calling for mediated negotiations to end the war. Political opposition apparently caused the president to change his mind. John B. Robbins, "The Confederacy and the Writ of Habeas Corpus," *Georgia Historical Quarterly*, 55 (Spring, 1971): 91.

50. Andrews, *The South Reports the Civil War*, 76; also see Starr, *Bohemian Brigade*, 41.

51. Quoted in Patricia Towery, "Censorship of South Carolina Newspapers, 1861-1865," in *South Carolina Journals and Journalists*, ed. James B. Meriwether (Spartenburg, SC: The Reprint Col., 1975), 148-149.

52. Ibid., 149.

53. Andrews, *The South Reports the Civil War*, 236-237.

54. Ibid., 246-247; Mathis, "Freedom of the Press in the Confederacy: A Reality," 638.

55. On this point of comparative effectiveness of censorship, see Matthews, *Reporting the Wars*, 94; and Andrews, *The South Reports the Civil War*, 533.

56. J. Cutler Andrews, "The Confederate Press and Public Morale," *Journal of Southern History* 32 (November 1966): 445-465.

57. Quoted in Wilson, "A Study and Evaluation of Military Censorship in the Civil War," 230.

58. Mott, *American Journalism*, 365.

59. During the first year of the war, 40 papers suspended publication in Virginia alone; 50 of Texas's 60 journals gave up the ghost during the same period, and by war's end, the 43 dailies that had been published throughout the Confederacy in 1863 had been cut in half. Andrews, "The Confederate Press and Public Morale," 463-464.

60. Matthews, *Reporting the Wars*, 88, 91-92.

7

JOURNEY TO CUBA:
THE YELLOW CRISIS

Gene Wiggins

Shortly before 9 p.m. on February 15, 1898, Walter Scott Meriwether sent a telegram from Havana, Cuba, to his newspaper, the New York *Herald*. The telegram was a one-word message—*tranquillo*. It was tranquil in the Cuban city and Meriwether and other American newspaper correspondents were enjoying the quiet after several incidents, including a riot by Spanish officers, had threatened the strained relationships between the United States and Spain.

George Rea of the New York *Herald* and Sylvester Scovel of the New York *World* were dining in a cafe in central Havana. Near the harbor, Clara Barton, the famed founder and head of the American Red Cross, was working late on paperwork. Barton had arrived a week earlier to help with the thousands of sick and dying Cubans who had been herded into *reconcentrado* camps around the city by Spanish authorities.

Captain Charles Sigsbee was sitting in his cabin aboard the U.S. battleship *Maine*, anchored in Havana Harbor. Sigsbee, after listening to the mournful sound of taps being blown, returned to the letter he was writing to his wife. In a few short minutes, Sigsbee's tranquil daily routine, as well as that of Barton, Scovel, and Rea, would end abruptly. The sleepy languor enveloping Havana would be shattered. At 9:40 p.m. a tremendous explosion rocked the battleship, followed shortly by another horrific blast. Sigsbee found his way through the darkness to the main deck and began directing evacuation of the sinking ship and a rescue of the wounded on the ship and in the water.

Barton reported to a hospital where she and her staff quickly went to work helping the wounded and dying sailors and marines. The American reporters hurried to the harbor. Rea and Scovel told police on the dock they were officers from the *Maine*. At the end of the dock the police chief invited them into his boat to hurry out to the *Maine*.

The Havana telegraph office had closed at nine but reopened on orders from a Spanish officer. Sigsbee, under the watchful eye of censors, was allowed to send a message to Key West and then on to Washington, informing American officials of the disaster. In New York, William Randolph Hearst, owner of the New York *Journal*, arrived home to find a messenger from the *Journal*, who told him to call his editor immediately. Upon being informed of the incident, Hearst asked the editor what he had put on the front page. The editor replied that the front page contained news about the *Maine* as well as the other big news of the day.

Hearst replied that there was no other big news and instructed the editor to fill the front page with the news of the *Maine*, adding, "This means war."[1]

Hearst was not only right about war but, no doubt, was pleased. Along with many other editors of the "yellow" journals in New York and across the country, he had pushed, cajoled, and screamed for just such a war in Cuba for three years. Now Hearst's wish was coming true.

Certainly the great editor of the New York *Evening Post*, E. L. Godkin, knew better than most editors of his day of the method and madness of "yellow journals." Godkin, a rare voice of reason in New York City in the years prior to the Spanish-American War, was witness to one of the great media spectacles of history—powerful newspapers in America's great cities playing the major role in creating the national crisis that led to war with Spain.

While newspapers like the New York *World*, New York *Journal*, Chicago *Tribune*, and others were referring to the sensationalistic journals' style of reporting and publishing as "new journalism" (a term that seems all too familiar today), Godkin and a few other conservative newspaper editors and publishers quickly labeled the work as "yellow journalism," "sensationalism," and occasionally even worse. Godkin felt much of the work of these newspapers was self-serving:

Every one who knows anything about "yellow journals" knows that everything they do and say is intended to promote sales, or, in other words, is meant to be an advertisement of the paper and show the power of "Journalism." No one–absolutely no one–supposes a yellow journal cares five cents about the Cubans, the Maine victims, or any one else. A yellow journal is probably the nearest approach, in atmosphere, to hell existing in any Christian state.[2]

Unlike most wars in which the United States has fought, the Spanish-American War was a popular one with the public, with the press, and with most members of the federal and state governments. Also unlike most other wars, this one was precipitated by a large amount of publicity from the press as well as a tremendous amount of posturing by Congress and the Cleveland and McKinley administrations. In short, expansionist attitudes prior to the Spanish-American War were common, and the country's major institutions generally supported intervention in those parts of the world that could best serve America's economic interests.[3]

According to J. E. Wisan, from March 1895 to April 1898, "there were fewer than a score of days in which Cuba did not appear in the day's news. . . . The effect was cumulative. . . . Little wonder that the 'average reader,' indoctrinated with these opinions, called on his Government for War."[4] This three-year period provides a remarkable example of how the press of the late 19th century exerted tremendous influence with the general citizenry, especially when this near-rabid cry for war was combined with the voices of government leaders and Cuban Americans.

If the press was guilty of being the primary instigator of a major war, then the two publishers generally credited with doing most of the instigating were Hearst, owner of the New York *Journal*, and Joseph Pulitzer, owner of the New York *World*, with the former getting the lion's share of the credit. Indeed, Hearst did much to inflame the American people and Congress. Even though it wasn't reported until several years after the war, Hearst supposedly cabled his famed artist, Frederic Remington, who had requested to return to America from Cuba: "Please remain. You furnish the pictures and I'll furnish the war."[5]

However, to place all the guilt of the press on Hearst would be to overlook the jingoistic activities of many other newspapers of the period. The "*Journal*'s voice was merely the loudest, seconded by the *World*'s," writes historian John Tebbel, "in a journalistic outcry emanating from most of the nation's newspapers."[6] Because the newspapers of the nation utilized one or more news services, they published much of what the New York and Chicago newspapers were dispensing through their news services. Regardless of the editorial policy of a particular newspaper, its news pages were filled with reports of Spanish atrocities in Cuba and Spanish aggression against American ships. Additional "news" also was furnished by the Cuba junta based in the United States.

If Godkin's assessment of the yellow journals is even partially correct, then the Cuban rebellion that began in 1895 was just more fodder for newspapers such as the *World* and *Journal* to build tremendous circulation so common to the period. Of course, newspapers in other cities—Chicago, Philadelphia, and Boston are but a few—used the same sensationalist tactics to build circulation. Newspapers often took on the yellow hue for economic reasons, although, as historian Sidney Kobre points out, "the daring editors . . . readjusted pre-Civil War journalism to the new industrial and urban age."[7]

There is little doubt, however, that the competition of the *World* and *Journal* in New York exemplified yellow journalism at its worst. The Cuban situation was an ideal and timely event that both newspapers latched onto during the three years between the beginning of the Cuban insurrection and the U.S. declaration of war upon Spain. Three years of sensational, and often inaccurate, news stories. Three years of banner headlines. Three years of unmatched circulation growth.

Pulitzer directed the activities of the *World* from afar, but Hearst maintained a hands-on approach and personally directed most of the coverage of the prewar incidents. While Hearst personally wrote little or nothing, he possessed the genius to hire the right people for the type of newspaper he wanted. As Ambrose Bierce commented, Hearst "could not write an advertisement for a lost dog," adding, however, that "if a man of brains is one who knows how to use the brains of others this amusing demagogue is nobody's dunce."[8] Regarding Pulitzer, considered one of the great journalists in American history, biographer and fellow journalist Oswald Villard wrote that the publisher was willing to outdo Hearst in "shameless and unwarranted sensationalism lest Hearst inflict on his papers irrevocable injury."[9]

Newspaper treatment of five incidents during this three-year period demonstrates how the press helped create a national crisis that pushed the United States into war with Spain. These incidents include Spanish aggression toward American ships near Cuba, the atrocities (both real and imagined) committed by Spanish authorities in Cuba, the Cisneros affair, the de Lome letter incident, and the sinking of the American battleship *Maine*.

At times, truth seemed to run a distant third to profits and circulation since many newspapers, especially the *World* and *Journal*, sought any information about Cuba that would arouse the interest and indignation of their readers. Hundreds of thousands of dollars were spent on correspondents to cover the events in Cuba and to equip ships to enhance that coverage. In spite of all the money spent, and perhaps because of it, a litany of rumors about Spanish atrocities inflicted upon the Cubans was printed. This included the number of Cubans who died during the period, as well as the incidents mentioned above.

It is true that Spanish ships were stopping and boarding ships leaving American ports bound for Cuba. However, most of these incidents were efforts by the Spanish to counter the filibustering activities of Americans and Cubans. Filibustering involved sending private expeditions to another country to assist in revolution. Many private ships were outfitted in the United States and transported men and supplies for the Cuban rebels during this three-year period. Cuban leaders had organized the junta in the United States, an organization dedicated to raising funds for filibustering activities and to arouse American sympathy for the Cuban cause.

One incident after another received banner headlines in the American press as the Spanish stopped ships, arrested American citizens, and sentenced some to death. President Grover Cleveland also sent ships to southern coasts to prevent these private expeditions from sailing to Cuba. Both the activities of the Spanish navy and the American authorities garnered immense amounts of news coverage, including condemnation by the newspapers who supported the Cuban cause and U.S. intervention.

American newspapers actively encouraged filibustering expeditions by carrying many stories of these ventures during the three-year period. The New York *Journal* went so far as to claim that one ship was sunk by a traitor even though it was apparently overloaded and went down off the Florida coast.[10] The *Journal* also claimed, without proof, that Enrique Dupuy de Lome, the Spanish minister in Washington, was spending over $15,000 per month for information that would help stop the filibustering expeditions.[11]

News of Spanish cruelties on the Caribbean island were carried on virtually every front page in America for months. When Spain sent Captain-General Valeriano Weyler to take command of the growing problem in Cuba, newspaper accounts of his exploits became fresh fodder for the press. Weyler immediately put into effect the infamous *reconcentrado* plan of moving all Cubans into prison camps near Spanish bases. Cubans who refused to move into these camps were considered enemies and were to be eliminated. Problems with food supplies began immediately, and many Cubans were in desperate straits. In addition, Cuban rebels destroyed many of the crops that would have fed these people in the camps, making the Spanish look even more brutal. During the course of these and other repressive measures taken by the Spanish, the sensationalist newspapers reported death counts in Cuba in excess of 400,000, while a more accurate count was approximately 110,000 deaths. Even the conservative press was obliged to carry such reports on their front pages.

As reports of the suffering and mistreatment occurring in Cuba aroused the indignation of the American public, the New York newspapers were among the first to send reporters and artists to the scene. Hearst dispatched Richard Harding Davis and Frederic Remington.[12] James Creelman, Sylvester Scovel, and others were sent by the *World* to match the *Journal*'s coverage. The Associated Press sent reporters and also used dispatches of its member newspapers. Newspapers from across the country sent correspondents to Cuba or the Florida coast to cover the events of the revolution, including the treatment of the Cuban population by the Spanish army.

Cuban rebel leaders were among the first to appreciate the sea of news coverage by the American press and to recognize the residue of propaganda from it. For example, when Cuban General Maximo Gomez cut off a large amount of the food supply to the cities, it forced Cubans into his ranks or into the reconcentration camps to starve. American editors simply did not understand the strategy and blamed the starvation entirely on the Spaniards. Which is what Gomez hoped would happen. Gomez felt confident that the American press would again side with his forces, condemning the Spanish for starving the Cubans who entered the reconcentration camps. "Without a press," Gomez commented, "we shall get nowhere."[13]

The correspondents who flooded into Havana and other Cuban cities almost uniformly utilized interpreters who were naturalized American citizens, virtually all of whom were in sympathy with the revolutionaries. One correspondent in Havana who was not sympathetic to the insurrection noted that many of these journalists would obtain their "news" from these sources without any evidence as to the truth of the information. Such journalists would fill their notebooks "with the stock stories of atrocities, battles, rapes and other horrors attributed to the Spanish troops by interested parties."[14] Daily, the American public was treated to fresh sensations, each newspaper correspondent seeking to be the first to report some battle or personal atrocity that he or she was given "first-hand" information by the local Cuban population.

Faking stories was commonplace, too. Historian Walter Millis recounted two incidents involving unidentified reporters. A woman correspondent, thinking she heard shots from the direction of Cabanas fortress, later informed her readers that the Spaniards butchered captives inside the fort daily.[15] Another reporter "discovered" the new capital city established by the rebels from his hotel room in Havana.[16]

Hearst, of course, was not about to be beat out of any stories, be they real or imagined. He bought a yacht, the *Vamoose*, and used it to transport his reporters and artists to the island and return dispatches when needed. By the time Weyler had taken command of the Spanish troops in 1896, four New York newspapers—the *Journal*, *World*, *Herald*, and *Sun*—had reporters in Cuba, sending back stories and drawings "of mutilation of mothers and killing of babes, of the execution of suspects, of imprisonment in filthy and fever-charged stockades."[17] Some reporters wrote their "eye-witness" accounts of these horrors sitting in their rooms in Key West, Florida.[18]

Weyler did attempt to stop such reporting by deporting several correspondents and arresting a few. One of the *World*'s best reporters, Scovel, was jailed after being caught in rebel territory and was released only after his newspaper had stirred up sympathy for Scovel all over the United States. Two other *World* reporters, one of whom was James Creelman, were expelled by Weyler in 1896, along with Frederick Lawrence of the *Journal* and artist Thomas Hawley Jr. Shortly thereafter, Creelman jumped to Hearst's *Journal* and continued his coverage of the war.[19] In 1897, reporters for the *Journal* and the *Sun* received the boot from Weyler. During the same year, the U.S. State Department intervened to secure the release of Ona Melton, arrested with the other crewmen aboard the *Competitor*.[20] The *Journal* virtually ignored the arrest of Scovel but dedicated hundreds of inches of space to "freeing Melton," a writer for the *World* who had switched to the *Journal* during his imprisonment.

Weyler never succeeded in controlling news coverage of the revolt. His efforts did result in many inaccurate stories being published since the correspondents had to depend upon unreliable or biased sources for much of their information. Seeking to top one another in news coverage, stories of Spanish atrocities continued to command banner headlines in the United States. These stories pushed the American public's sympathies further into the Cuban revolutionaries' camp.

The death of Ricardo Ruiz, a Cuban dentist who had become a naturalized American citizen, in a Spanish prison cell provided Hearst's newspaper with ample ammunition for another series of sensational stories. The influence of the *Journal* on other American newspapers in 1897 can be found in the number of publications that picked up stories from the *Journal* concerning the incident and subsequently called for revenge upon the Spanish oppressors. With *Journal* headlines screaming about an American brutally murdered in prison, other newspapers began criticizing the administration's lack of action in the matter and demanding some kind of military response to such horrible occurrences. The Chicago *Tribune* asserted that newspaper correspondents had evidence that Ruiz was tortured for days before being murdered.[21] The New York *Sun* said the suspicious death of Ruiz had brought about deep feeling in the United States; the New Orleans *Times-Democrat* lambasted the administration for failing to protect American citizens in Cuba; the Boston *Herald* demanded that a warship settle the matter of the murder of Ruiz.[22]

In mid-1897, the Cisneros affair showed the extent to which Hearst was willing to go to build his circulation and to keep alive the public's outrage at Spain for its Cuban policies and actions. Evangelina Cisneros was the niece of the Cuban revolutionary president. Her father had been imprisoned on the Isle of Pines, charged with complicity with the insurgents. The young senorita voluntarily accompanied her father to the Isle but later was arrested and returned as a prisoner to Havana. While charged with treason, the newspapers in the United States contended that her only crime was resisting the advances of a Spanish officer.[23] The story struck home immediately with the American public.

The *Journal* seized the opportunity and enlisted the support of America's women. Mrs. Jefferson Davis, widow of the president of the Confederacy, wrote the Queen Regent in Spain, seeking to save the young Evangelina from a "fate worse than death," while Mrs. Julia Ward Howe was persuaded to write Pope Leo III, appealing for his support in obtaining the release of the beautiful Cuban aristocrat.[24] Other American women enlisted by the *Journal* for the fight to release Miss Cisneros included Mrs. John Sherman, wife of the secretary of state; Clara Barton; Mrs. John D. Logan; Mrs. Mark Hanna; Mrs. E. D. E. N. Southworth, the novelist; Mrs. William C. Whitney, wife of the former secretary of the navy; Mrs. John G. Carlisle, wife of the former Secretary of the Treasury; Miss Eugenia Washington, grandniece of George Washington; and Mrs. Letitia Tyler Simple, daughter of President Tyler. These ladies were part of an "honor roll" of women who had agreed to aid in seeking the fair Evangelina's release.[25] Even the first lady, Mrs. Nancy McKinley, signed the list of 20,000 signatures collected by the *Journal*.[26]

Labeling the young Evangelina as the "most beautiful girl in all Cuba," the *Journal* proclaimed her innocent of assisting in murdering the military governor of the Isles. According to the newspaper, she was but a harmless girl whose beauty had "excited the lust" of the governor, the nephew of Spain's prime minister.[27] When hearing that Miss Cisneros could receive a 20-year sentence, possibly in Spain's penal colonies in Africa, the *Journal* began one of the most aggressive campaigns in newspaper history. The newspaper devoted an eye-popping 375 columns to the affair, compared to only 12.5 columns in the *World*, 10 in the *Times*, 3.5 in the *Tribune* and 1 column in the *Sun* and the *Herald*.[28] However, the story resulted in many, many columns being printed in the nation's newspapers and brought about a daily demand for some kind of intervention, either political or military.

Day after day, week after week, from late August through mid-October, 1897, the *Journal* kept the pressure on Weyler and Spain, demanding the immediate release of Miss Cisneros. Interviews with Miss Cisneros and drawings of an emaciated young lady languishing in the "vilest prison in Cuba" were published in the *Journal* and disseminated throughout the country by the Associated Press. At the same time, the *Journal* saw the events of the day as signals of imminent war with Spain, claiming that plans were under way for such a war.[29] No evidence existed to support these claims. General Weyler no doubt would have paid any price to get rid of the young maiden he was allegedly mistreating in prison. The *World* even published a statement from Weyler denying the *Journal*'s charges against him. Hearst immediately printed a severe rebuke of the *World*'s actions and declared that Miss Cisneros would be saved "in spite of Weyler and the *World*."[30]

As it turned out, the *Journal*'s declaration was no idle boast. Plans

were under way to rescue Miss Cisneros. Hearst dispatched reporter
Karl Decker to Cuba with orders to free the young woman "at any hazard."[31] Decker reached Cuba in late August and took a month to set his
plans in motion. When time for the rescue came, Decker simply climbed
to a roof of a house adjoining the prison, pried loose a bar, and helped
Evangelina out the window. P. T. Barnum couldn't have orchestrated
the events that followed any better. On October 10, 1897, the *Journal* ran
a banner headline followed by a seven-column bank headline:
"Evangelina Cisneros Rescued by the *Journal*; An American Newspaper
Accomplishes at a Single Stroke What the Red Tape of Diplomacy Failed
Utterly to Bring About in Many Months."[32]

News of the rescue swept the nation. The Associated Press picked
up the *Journal* story and sent it to member newspapers. Other news
services dispatched the story across the country. Meanwhile, Hearst
used the two weeks following the announcement of the rescue to generate a fantastic amount of news coverage about Miss Cisneros. Following a public reception in New York City and another reception at the
Journal offices, the rescued maiden was packed off to Washington, D.C.,
with much fanfare by the *Journal*. A meeting with President McKinley
received a page spread with accompanying drawings.

The Cisneros incident heightened the American public's opposition
to Spanish control of Cuba at a time when the U.S. State Department
was working hard to bring about a peaceful settlement of the Cuban
problem. Spain, however, proved as inept at diplomacy as it was in
putting down the Cuban rebellion. The result: more unfavorable press
in America as well as in Europe. A riot of Spanish soldiers on January
12, 1898, in Havana created a furor in the American press, especially
when it was reported that the targets of the rioters were four newspapers that supported the recently announced autonomy for Cuba. Of
course, the Cuban rebels had rejected autonomy and sought total independence. But the two incidents in 1898 that seemed to solidify the
American public, the administration, and the press against Spain were
a letter written by the Spanish ambassador in Washington to a friend in
Havana and the destruction of the battleship *Maine* in Havana harbor.

The Spanish minister, Enrique Dupuy de Lome, wrote a personal
letter to his friend, José Canalejas y Mendez, editor of the *El Heraldo de
Madrid*. The letter was stolen by a member of the Cuban junta in Havana, smuggled out of the country, and presented to the *Journal*. No one
knew the letter had been purloined from Canalejas' desk until the letter
and numerous accompanying stories filled most of pages one and two
of the *Journal* on February 9, 1898. The letter, written sometime in December 1897, was critical of the autonomy status granted Cuba and of
President McKinley's address to Congress on December 6, in which
McKinley discussed the situation in Cuba. Dupuy de Lome referred to

McKinley as being "weak and catering to the rabble, and, besides a low politician."[33]

De Lome also attacked the *Journal* reporter in Havana for his jingoistic stories. This was just what the *Journal* needed. Under the banner headline "The Worst Insult to the United States in Its History," the *Journal* printed the contents of the letter and roundly criticized the Spanish authorities for its actions and the McKinley administration for doing nothing.[34] With headlines screaming for his dismissal, the *Journal* published numerous stories during the next few weeks concerning the affair. *Journal* editors were unaware that Dupuy de Lome had cabled his resignation to Madrid the very day the letter became public.

Following the *Journal*'s lead, the *World* immediately published cartoons and editorials calling for the Spanish ambassador's dismissal. The *World* termed Dupuy de Lome's words "outrageous and insulting to the country."[35] Both newspapers criticized the Spanish minister for disparaging remarks about American women he allegedly made in a book written earlier in his career.[36] American newspapers received the news dispatches from the Associated Press, most of which were taken from the *Journal*, and provided the American public with another taste of Spain's supposed disdain for Americans. The New York *Sun*, which had only recently lost its great editor, Charles Dana, jumped into the fray when it called for Dupuy de Lome's expulsion from the country,[37] and the Chicago *Times-Herald* said the incident was just another incident that showed the "Machiavelian hypocrisy of Spain" in her relationships with other nations.[38] Rather than dismiss the Spanish minister, the Madrid government accepted his resignation amid much heated debate in Congress and expectations of war by the press, especially the *Journal*. The Hearst paper began a "war scare" crusade by printing more about the Dupuy de Lome affair, atrocities in Cuba, and the debates in Washington concerning war.[39]

Madrid officially notified Washington two days prior to the Dupuy de Lome incident that it could make no further concessions in its Cuban policy without risking its own downfall.[40] Other than issuing an official apology for the Spanish minister's personal letter, for which it really had no responsibility, Spain was willing to concede nothing further to the United States' continuing pressure to settle the Cuban affair.

While Dupuy de Lome was in New York awaiting a ship to carry him to Spain, he was awakened in the middle of the night by reporters seeking his comments on the latest news—the American battleship *Maine* had been blown up in the harbor at Havana.[41] Led as always by Hearst's *Journal*, the American press fed the public's appetite for news of the incident with inciting and sometimes outrageously erroneous information.

The cause of the *Maine*'s destruction has never been pinpointed, but the sensationalistic press aimed its fingers of blame directly at Spain. War fever in the United States reached epidemic proportions as news of the loss of 266 American lives spread. The *Journal* posted a $50,000 reward for any information that would lead to the arrest and conviction of the culprits responsible for the tragedy. A banner headline in the *Journal* read like pulp fiction: "The Whole Country Thrills with War Fever."[42] Congress passed a huge defense bill, and members of the administration used quotes from the *Journal* and other newspapers to justify war preparations. Pulitzer's paper at first urged caution, then called for a quick and decisive war.[43]

The battleship *Maine* had arrived in Havana at the request of the consul general in Havana, Fitzhugh Lee, after he determined that American lives and property were endangered by the riots and threats. A threat had been made to bomb the *Journal*'s offices in that city. When Senator Henry Cabot Lodge predicted that an explosion could occur in Havana at any time, he certainly wasn't expecting the explosion to be aboard the *Maine*.[44] News of Cuban events were quiet on the night of February 15, 1898, and even the *World* and *Journal* staffs were thinking of running their Cuban stories on inside pages. The New York *Tribune* carried a strong editorial urging settlement of the Cuban question.[45] Then news of the explosion was received.

President McKinley and his staff faced the monstrous problem of mitigating the damage. Some officials told reporters the explosion could have been accidental. The New York *Tribune* argued that the horrors of war would be worse than the horror of the *Maine*.[46] But the *Journal*, the *World*, and many other newspapers wanted a U.S. declaration of war.

The result was even bolder, louder headlines. Newspapers had been using striking headlines for months, but the sinking of the *Maine* instigated most American newspapers' practice of using heavy type across several columns. The ensuing war refined the practice.[47]

The *Journal*'s accounts of the *Maine* disaster claimed to have information from a secret cable sent by the captain of the sunken battleship to the secretary of the navy. According to the *Journal*, the cable claimed the destruction was not an accident. Hearst's paper also asserted that a team of divers had evidence that the explosion was external. Other newspapers, including the New Orleans *Times-Democrat*, recognized such claims for what they were—false.[48] However, the Associated Press carried stories about the team of divers, undoubtedly picked up from the *Journal*, and numerous newspapers across the nation ran the stories. Even normally conservative newspapers, including many which backed the administration, were soon calling for war and criticizing McKinley for lack of action. The *Times-Democrat* claimed:

Mr. McKinley may not have sufficient backbone even to resent an offense so gross as this, but war in this country is declared by Congress and no explanation of the Spanish Government, no offer to make reparation, could prevent a declaration of war.[49]

The New York *Tribune*, a strong administration supporter, published an editorial stating that the president was "prudently" preparing for an emergency. While the *Journal* and *World* printed several "war extras," Godkin seemed alone in his cautious approach to war and his caustic criticism of the sensational press tactics. He wrote that he had never seen anything as disgraceful as the behavior of the *Journal* and the *World* in the history of journalism. He lamented that there was a gross misrepresentation of facts and deliberate falsehoods printed to excite the American public.

As to the appearance of such papers, Godkin commented that type resources had been exhausted, even red ink had been used for an attraction of terror. He added that if a real war came along, the sensationalists could print their papers in red, white, and blue. "In that case, real lunatics instead of imitation lunatics should be employed as editors and contributors."[50]

Undeterred by the rhetoric of Godkin and others, Hearst immediately set up a fund to build a monument to the victims of the *Maine*, and many famous and respected men were enlisted to join the fund-raising committee. Former President Cleveland declined the request, saying he would not allow his "sorrow for those who died on the *Maine* to be perverted to an advertising scheme for the New York *Journal*."[51]

While calmer heads in Washington, D.C., deliberated about foreign policy, while many newsrooms waited for an official verdict on the *Maine* disaster, the *World* and *Journal* stood still for no one. For Pulitzer and Hearst, it was head-to-head combat to sell newspapers. And they did. The circulation of the *World* reached 5 million in one week, and the *Journal*'s circulation soon reached more than a million copies per day.[52] If streamer headlines and scare tactics sway public opinion, Hearst and Pulitzer, aided by many, many American newspapers who carried news generated by the two New York newspapers, had become the conductors for a national war symphony.

The *Journal* continued to publish "extras," and Hearst hired a special train to rush them to Washington as they were printed.[53] The *Journal* had two ships and an army of reporters in Cuba, while the *World* sent reporters plus a tugboat with divers to search the Havana harbor. Both newspapers printed "surveys" of congressmen, as did the Chicago *Tribune*. Not surprisingly, the surveys revealed a strong demand for immediate action. The New York *Sun* called for swift congressional action and a general strengthening of the coastal defenses. The Boston

Herald and San Francisco *Chronicle* ran news stories that implied that treachery resulted in the *Maine*'s destruction, but on their editorial pages each called for caution on swift judgment until the official investigation was concluded. This contradiction between news and views was probably due to the fact that these newspapers used news services from New York, much of which pointed to some form of skullduggery in the sinking of the *Maine*.[54]

Theodore Roosevelt, an assistant secretary of the navy, repudiated an "interview" with the *Journal* that quoted him as being pleased with the newspaper's policy. Roosevelt labeled the story as "an invention from beginning to end. It is difficult to understand the kind of infamy that resorts to such methods."[55] In the spirit of yellow one-up-manship, the *World* gave a great amount of coverage to Roosevelt's denial, printing it on the front page, and commented that Hearst's war news was "written by fools for fools."[56]

As the media frenzy continued, demands by Congress and the public for intervention in Cuba grew. War became inevitable despite the best efforts of McKinley's administration and the Spanish government. In New York, the *Journal*, the *World* and the *Sun* demanded immediate action. The Chicago *Tribune*, New Orleans *Times-Democrat*, Atlanta *Constitution*, and Indianapolis *Journal* did likewise. The New York *Herald*, Chicago *Times-Herald*, Boston *Herald*, San Francisco *Chronicle*, and Milwaukee *Journal* opposed intervention, but carried much of the sensational news coverage. Other New York papers, such as the *Evening Post*, *Times*, and *Tribune*, along with the Chicago *Daily News* and Boston *Transcript* urged caution and calm heads. Only Godkin's *Evening Post* opposed intervention right up to the declaration of war.[57]

When the conflict, later to be termed "Hearst's War,"[58] finally began, the American press was ready. Particularly Mr. Hearst. With several boats and a platoon of more than 20 writers and artists, and even a motion picture photographer, the publisher sailed for Cuba. Expense was no consideration as boats raced to Key West to cable news to New York, and then across the nation. By the end of April, the *World* was selling over 1.3 million copies per day, and on May 2, 1898, when Admiral Dewey captured Manila in the Philippines, the *Journal* sold over 1.6 million copies.[59] Both newspapers averaged 1.5 million copies daily for the remainder of the war. Just as circulations grew, so did the headlines. On May 2, for example, the *Journal* ran the headline "Manila Ours" with a deck underneath that proclaimed "Dewey's Guns Shell the City." Headline and deck filled half the front page.[60]

The *Journal* didn't rank first in every journalism category, however. Pulitzer's *World* scooped the *Journal* in Manila when the paper got the first cable back to New York by paying a phenomenal $9.90 per word. Unfortunately, the *World*'s circulation department couldn't handle a 4 a.m. "extra" and lost the news advantage, although many of the *World* news service subscribers took advantage of the early news.[61]

Man-made news embodied the very spirit of the news coverage. Hearst even waded ashore to "capture" a handful of Spanish sailors in Cuba about to surrender to a waiting American flagship. Of course, Hearst's "exploits" were recounted with much fanfare in the *Journal*.

While Hearst was making news himself, there were many competent journalists in Cuba reporting the news for a number of newspapers at once. Richard Harding Davis, now reporting for the New York *Herald* and the London *Times*, was fortunate enough to be in several locations to get the stories early. Creelman was churning out copy for the *Journal*, even leading a charge in one battle in which he was seriously wounded. He reported that he awoke to find Hearst leaning over him with a pencil and notebook, ready to take down his story for the *Journal*. "I'm sorry you're hurt," Creelman reported Hearst as saying, "but wasn't it a splendid fight? We must beat every paper in the world."[62]

News coverage of the war by the sensational press was merely a reflection of the three previous years' coverage, pushed forward to high gear. Actually, news coverage of the war was more accurate than the coverage of the major incidents that precipitated the conflict. Little fabrication was needed to make the American victories look glamorous.

While Pulitzer, Hearst, Dana, and a few other publishers and editors of the period might be justifiably blamed for playing a major role in creating the national crisis that resulted in war with Spain, certainly these men could not have done so without a "cadre of reporters" who shared their publishers' philosophy of expansive journalism.[63] Many of these editors and reporters felt they had a calling to perform public service for the people. Such enthusiastic fervor certainly paved the way to journalistic excesses and misrepresentations as the reporters, ever loyal to their publishers' ideals, pressed on for the good of the people—whether Cuban or American. Utilizing the zeal and energy of their correspondents, newspapers like the *World* and *Journal*, locked in a life-and-death circulation battle, pushed journalism—and ethics—to its limits during the period from 1895 to the beginning of the war in 1898.

It is conjecture whether the New York *Journal* simply leapt upon the wave of popular sentiment to rise to its heights of popularity or whether Hearst's paper was largely responsible for pushing the United States to the position where war with Spain was inevitable. Hearst critics have declared he caused the war.[64] Hearst did little to dissuade this opinion, publishing in the ears each day during the conflict, "How do you like the *Journal*'s war?"[65]

A determined drive for higher circulation and profits was the primary purpose behind the methods of the "yellow press." At times, there was little regard for journalistic ethics, and objectivity certainly took a backseat to circulation and profits. The conservative press found it could not compete for two reasons: the sensationalism of the "yellow press" and the influence of the wire services.

Sensationalism sold newspapers, and the cause was a popular one. The conservative press was forced at times to carry stories about the war to satisfy the interests of its readers. At the same time, the wire services used by the conservative press were, for the most part, owned by those newspapers that supported war. Thus, front pages of the members of the conservative press frequently resembled those of the "yellow press," while their editorial pages urged caution and restraint.

The sensational press in America played a significant role in creating an atmosphere of crisis and war fever. It kept the American public inflamed while boosting circulation in virtually every yellow journal. Between events, during the infrequent slow times, the press keep the war engine warm and running. Led by the *Journal* and the *World*, by Hearst and Pulitzer, the yellow press attained three highly sought after goals: higher circulation, increased profits, and war.

NOTES

1. G.J.A. O'Toole, *The Spanish War* (New York: W.W. Norton & Company, 1937), 34.

2. New York *Evening Post*, 17 March 1898.

3. I. Dementyev, *USA: Imperialists and Anti-Imperialists* (Moscow: Progress Publishers, 1979), 120-123.

4. J.E. Wisan, *The Cuban Crisis as Reflected in the New York Press*, as quoted in Alfred M. Lee, *The Daily Newspaper in America* (New York: MacMillan Company, 1937), 637.

5. O'Toole, *The Spanish War*, 82.

6. John Tebbel, *The Compact History of the American Newspaper* (New York: Hawthorne Books, 1966), 202.

7. Sidney Kobre, *The Yellow Press and Gilded Age Journalism* (Tallahassee: Florida State University Press, 1964), p. iii. See also Edwin Emery and Michael Emery's *The Press and America*, 6th ed. (Englewood Cliffs, NJ: Prentice-Hall, 1988), 227.

8. Oswald Garrison Villard, *The Disappearing Daily* (New York: Alfred A. Knopf, 1944), 205.

9. Ibid., 255.

10. New York *Journal*, 3 January 1897.

11. New York *Journal*, 2 December 1897.

12. Emery and Emery, *Press in America*, 236.

13. Walter Millis, *The Martial Spirit* (Boston: Houghton Mifflin Company, 1931), 41.

14. Ibid., 42.

15. Ibid.

16. Ibid.

17. Frank Luther Mott, *American Journalism:: A History of Newspapers in the U.S. Through 250 Years, 1690 to 1940* (New York: MacMillan Company, 1941), 528.

18. Ibid.

19. Emery and Emery, *Press in America*, 236.

20. Marcus W. Wilkerson, *Public Opinion and the Spanish-American War* (Baton Rouge: Louisiana State University Press, 1932), 12.

21. Ibid., 86.

22. Ibid.

23. Millis, *Martial Spirit*, 82.

24. Willard Grosvenor Bleyer, *Main Currents in the History of American Journalism* (Boston: Houghton Mifflin Company, 1927), 370.

25. Wilkerson, *Public Opinion*, 87, 89.

26. Millis, *Martial Spirit*, 83.

27. Wilkerson, *Public Opinion*, 87.

28. Emery and Emery, *Press in America*, 237.

29. New York *Journal*, 14 September 1897.

30. New York *Journal*, 23 August 1897.

31. Millis, *Martial Spirit*, 84.

32. Bleyer, *Main Currents*, 370.

33. O'Toole, *The Spanish War*, 122.

34. New York *Journal*, 9 February 1898.

35. New York *World*, 10 February 1898.

36. Wilkerson, *Public Opinion*, 93-94.

37. New York *Sun*, 17 February 1898, p. 6.

38. Wilkerson, *Public Opinion*, 95.

39. Ibid., 96.

40. O'Toole, *The Spanish War*, 122.

41. Ibid., 123.

42. Emery and Emery, *Press in America*, 237.

43. Ibid., 237-238.

44. Allan Nevins, *Henry White: Thirty Years of American Diplomacy*, quoted in Wilkerson, *Public Opinion*, 100.

45. Millis, *Martial Spirit*, 101.

46. Ibid., 107-108.

47. Wilkerson, *Public Opinion*, 101.

48. Ibid.

49. Millis, *Martial Spirit*, 110.

50. Bleyer, *Main Currents*, 377.

51. Mott, *American Journalism*, 531.

52. Millis, *Martial Spirit*, 110.

53. Wilkerson, *Public Opinion*, 103.

54. Ibid., 106.

55. Robert W. Jones, *Journalism in the United States* (New York: E. P. Dutton & Company, 1947), 435.

56. Ibid.

57. Emery and Emery, *Press in America*, 238.

58. Wilkerson, *Public Opinion*, 131.

59. Bleyer, *Main Currents,* 378.

60. Ibid.

61. Mott, *American Journalism,* 536.

62. Ibid., 535.

63. Gerald F. Linderman, *The Mirror of War* (Ann Arbor: University of Michigan Press, 1974), 166.

64. Jones, *Journalism in the United States,* 435.

65. Emery and Emery, *Press in America,* 231.

8

DESCENT INTO HELL:
THE RED CRISIS

Joseph McKerns

Darkness fell on American civil liberties the night of January 2, 1920. Swiftly and without warning, federal agents, state and local police, and vigilantes in 33 major cities in 23 states unleashed a dragnet that swept up more than 4,000 persons in a few hours. Without legal warrants, police entered bowling alleys, pool halls, cafes, club rooms, meeting halls, and private homes and seized everyone in sight. Families were separated, and prisoners were held incommunicado without legal counsel. These "hapless victims" were guilty of nothing more than the exercise of free speech and the right of association. However, they held views and espoused ideas contrary to the national consensus. Most were working-class people, aliens or naturalized citizens from eastern and southern Europe, Catholic, and Jewish. They were feared and arrested for who they were, and what they believed in, but not for anything they had done.[1]

The arrests were masterminded by Attorney General A. Mitchell Palmer, whose objective was to break the back of radicalism in the United States with one powerful blow. His primary targets were the Communist Party and Communist Labor Party and any radical organization or individual he felt posed a threat to the stability of American government. However, this "threat" may have existed only in the minds of the attorney general and the general public.

It was a bad time to be a stranger in America, a status that included anyone not a white, native-born Protestant of Anglo-Saxon ancestry. An "atmosphere of hate" created a national hysteria that engulfed the nation.[2] Anti-Semitism, anti-Catholicism, racism, prejudice, and intolerance of differences were at a crest. The Ku Klux Klan had terrorized African Americans but now also turned its ire on Jewish and Catholic immigrants. The ruthless Palmer Raids climaxed a year of growing alarm and dread that the "Bolshevik" contagion that had consumed Russia in the revolution of 1917 would sweep across Europe to the United States. In the minds of native-born Americans, all foreigners were bewhiskered, bomb-throwing radicals.

Evangelist Billy Sunday described a Bolshevik as "a guy with a face like a porcupine and breath that would scare a pole cat."[3] Sunday was among many public figures and officials who fanned the population's fear during 1919. The daily press of the country reported their messages of hate and paranoia. Exhibiting a disregard for basic American civil liberties, the press, with few exceptions, conveyed an image of a crumbling social order through sensational coverage of labor unrest, social turmoil, and race riots. Utilizing scare headlines, shrill language, and inflammatory editorials, the press helped create a context within which extreme measures would appear acceptable. A Massachusetts judge said that Palmer raids were "carried out on the theory of hang first and try afterwards."[4]

What is most disturbing about the Red Scare of 1919–1920 is that it was not a sudden eruption of hysteria, nor was it an aberration. The roots of the scare run far deeper than a fear of revolution,and the wartime belief in the need for national unity with little breathing space for differences of opinion. The roots lie with America's growing uneasiness with the tide of immigration from eastern and southern Europe and the Orient, which many native-born citizens feared would overwhelm American customs and traditions and alter the national character. Nativism emerged as early as the 1820s. Samuel F. B. Morse, inventor of the telegraph, authored pamphlets in 1829 that linked immigration, which had been thought beneficial to the country, with Catholicism, which most Americans saw as a threat. In the 1830s, nativists attacked Catholic immigration by asserting that a republican form of government could not be sustained with a large Catholic population. Protestants believed that republicanism required a virtuous and independent electorate, and they saw Catholics as superstitious, ignorant, and dominated by their priests. When the Irish arrived, they were greeted with signs that read "No Vacancies, No Irish" and "No Irish Need Apply."[5]

From 1865 to 1917, more than 27 million immigrants came to the United States, a total that exceeded the entire population of the country in 1850. Between 1900 and 1910, 6 million immigrants arrived from Italy, Russia, and Austria-Hungary alone. The tide of immigration reached its zenith between 1905 and 1914, when the number of immigrants surpassed 1 million in six different years. In 1914, the peak year, 73.4 percent of the immigrants were from eastern and southern Europe.[6] In 1891, Josiah Strong likened immigration to the barbarian conquest of the ancient Roman Empire: "We have suffered a peaceful invasion by an army four times as vast as the estimated numbers of Goths and Vandals that swept over Southern Europe and overwhelmed Rome."[7]   Americans believed they needed special laws to protect them from the deluge of Catholics and Jews.

The beginning of attempts to curb the political activity of aliens and radicals was a 1902 New York law that punished the preaching, publishing, and distributing of anarchist literature. In 1903, Congress passed legislation banning alien anarchists from entering the country. Laws requiring immigrants to pass literacy tests were an attempt to block immigration, but contrary to stereotypes, most immigrants were literate. In California, Japanese and Chinese immigration was stopped. Federal legislation created a quota system for immigration that was weighted against Eastern and Southern Europeans.[8] Americans saw immigrants as unfit to vote; temperance advocates condemned their saloons, and urban reformers denigrated their living habits. By the time of the Palmer Raids in 1920, Americans justified their concerns with racial theories that categorized the immigrants as genetically inferior "dirty little dark people" who were mongrelizing the population.[9] The same rationale was used to justify racism and the segregation of African Americans.

Immigrants were scapegoats for economic and political woes in America. President William McKinley's assassination in 1901 by an anarchist in Buffalo, New York, cast blame on all immigrants. Agitation for better wages and better working conditions by organized labor was considered the fault of alien radicals. Americans felt that immigrants flooded the labor market, lowered the standard of living, and helped create economic depressions in the 1880s and 1890s. Most immigrants worked 12-hour days, seven days a week, in steel mills, coal mines, and dress and shirt factories. They earned wages so low that several families shared a house, and boarders took turns sleeping in a single bed.[10]

The outbreak of war in Europe in 1914 stemmed the tide of immigrants but exacerbated concerns about the presence of so many "foreigners" with divided loyalties. While most native-born Americans favored England in the war, immigrants from Germany and eastern Europe did not. When the United States declared war in 1917 as an ally of England, the fear that divided loyalties in the population threatened national security and the ability to conduct a successful war and led federal and state governments to adopt measures aimed at guaranteeing unity.[11] President Woodrow Wilson, who referred to the immigrants as "hyphenated Americans," declared, "This is no time either for divided counsels or for divided leadership."[12] Congress passed the Espionage Act on June 15, 1917, which gave the federal government authority to punish false statements or reports that could interfere with the war effort, promote disloyalty in the armed forces, or obstruct recruitment efforts. It empowered the postmaster general to declare "unmailable" any publication that violated the act.[13] Under this act, if a pacifist publication called for peace, it broke the law.

Fearing the Espionage Act was not enough, Congress passed the Sedition Act on May 16, 1918, which permitted prosecution for criticism of the government. The two laws constituted the gravest assault on First Amendment freedoms by the federal government since the infamous Alien and Sedition Acts of 1798. In addition, between 1917 and 1921, two thirds of the states passed their own sedition laws. This onslaught of legislation resulted in more than 1900 prosecutions and 800 convictions. The postmaster general interfered with the distribution of more than 100 publications. It became criminal to advocate heavier taxation in lieu of bond issues; to assert that conscription was unconstitutional; to say the sinking of merchant ships was legal during war; to state that war was contrary to Christ's teachings; or to criticize the Red Cross.[14]

Paranoia about anything German or "un-American" spilled over into daily life and language. German words were discouraged, so hamburgers became "liberty sandwiches," sauerkraut became "liberty cabbage," and the name of the popular comic strip "Katzenjammer Kids" was changed to "Shenanigan Kids." Playing German music and teaching or speaking German were prohibited in many cities and schools. A statute of Frederick the Great that was a gift from the kaiser in 1904 was removed from the grounds of the Army War College in Washington when war was declared. The statue was not returned to its pedestal until 1927.[15]

The response of mainstream journalism to the trampling of civil liberties during the war was more of a whimper than a roar. Most publications either remained silent about the repression of unpopular opinions or openly condoned it as a necessity of war. The Washington *Post* called for all "enemy aliens" to be excluded from the District of Columbia until after the war. On November 17, 1917, the Wilson administration ordered 1000 resident German males over the age of 14 out of the city. In September 1918, the *Post* reported erroneous charges by Attorney General Palmer that the Washington *Times* had been bought by the German brewers Hamm, Pabst, Miller and Ruppert. The brewers felt they had to buy a full-page ad in the *Post* to declare their loyalty and point out that 95 percent of their families were born in the United States. *The New Republic* and Oswald Garrison Villard's *The Nation* and New York *Evening Post* were among the few mainstream journals to criticize government actions. An issue of *The Nation* was held up in the New York post office because of an editorial entitled "Civil Liberty Dead." In 1918, Villard sold the *Evening Post* because his pacifist views and defense of civil liberties caused revenue to drop.[16]

Wartime repression had a devastating impact on the labor, radical, and ethnic press of the nation. More than 400 German-language newspapers folded during the war. In St. Louis, the Westliche *Post*, an old and respected newspaper, saw its circulation drop from 28,000 to 18,000 in 1917–1918. At least 75 newspapers either lost their second-class mailing privi-

leges or were able to retain them only after agreeing not to publish anything about the war. Among those banned from the mails were the *American Socialist*; *Solidarity*, an Industrial Workers of the World (IWW) paper;
Bull, a pro–Irish Republican Army paper; the *Masses*, because of its antiwar cartoons and a poem defending Emma Goldman and Alexander
Berkman; and two socialist dailies, the New York *Call* and the Milwaukee
Leader, whose editor, Victor Berger, was twice denied the seat in the House
of Representatives he was legally elected to. Even the Irish-American
press suffered repression when newspapers, such as the *Gaelic American*,
the *Freeman's Journal* and *Catholic Register*, the *Irish World*, the *American Industrial Liberator*, and the San Francisco *Leader* criticized British policy in
Ireland or advocated Irish-American solidarity with the struggle for self-
determination.[17] Any criticism of Great Britain was considered pro-German propaganda.

Progressive Americans had believed that the world war was a "war to
end wars" and a harbinger of peace and progress. However, when fighting ended in 1918, the nation sank into disillusion at its outcome. The
"Great War" was the birthing of global turmoil, not its dying convulsions.
Americans saw the Russian Revolution as an omen of ill. Despite their
own revolutionary tradition, Americans saw the Russian Revolution as a
vast social upheaval that espoused a collectivist ideology and was the an-
tithesis of capitalist democracy. The nation's response to it was twofold:
(1) the landing of troops in Murmansk and Vladivostok in August 1918 in
an attempt to strengthen counterrevolutionary forces and (2) the tendency
at home to see "Reds" everywhere. Immigrants from eastern and southern Europe replaced pro-German propagandists as the focus of America's
fears, paranoia, and intolerance of dissent.[18]

Federal and state governments acted to combat the perceived threat of
a Bolshevik-led uprising in the United States. In 1919, Attorney General
Palmer created an intelligence division within the Justice Department,
which became the Federal Bureau of Investigation, to concentrate on subversive activities. It produced a list of 60,000 names within its first 100
days, and 450,000 in 18 months, including 625 newspapers. The Lusk
Committee was created by the New York assembly to investigate radical
activity. It staged raids on radical headquarters to seize files and publications thought to be subversive.[19] Vigilante groups pledged to maintain
American public safety and ethnic purity. Among them were the National
Security League, the American Defense Society, and the National Civic
Federation. The Ku Klux Klan was revived during the war years and grew
to 4 million membership by 1924. A Klansman in North Carolina said,
"All the Catholic gold in the universe can't buy our manhood and our
liberty." Klan national spokesmen supported every government campaign
against radicals and immigrants. Evangelist Billy Sunday would proudly
declare that "America is not a country for a dissenter to live in."[20]

The Red Scare of 1919–1920 was a logical extension of the hysteria that gripped the nation at the close of World War I. Fed by the alarmist statements of public officials, such as Attorney General A. Mitchell Palmer, the Red Scare enveloped the nation. The mainstream press must share the blame for fanning the flames of the hysteria. Most disheartening is the fact that respected newspapers like the New York *Times* were among the worst offenders. The press reported the alarmist statements of officials, and goaded the government and the public with sensational coverage of labor strikes, disorder, and police action. Thundering editorials demanded that government act swiftly to eradicate any threat to American stability but ignored the trampling of civil liberties such action entailed. If government suppression of radicalism interfered with basic American freedoms, the press considered that an acceptable price to pay for stability.[21]

The Washington *Post* declared that the District of Columbia was unsurpassed in its Americanism because of the relatively few immigrants living there. "Some cities we could mention are more conspicuous for numbers than for quality, " the *Post* bragged. "As for Washington, it does not suffer from the indigestibility of foreign masses."[22] On February 2, 1919, the *Post* reported on a meeting of dissidents in Washington under the headline "Urge Red America." The story said speakers interspersed descriptions of conditions in Russia and praise for the Soviet leaders with frequent attacks on the American system of government. The article warned, "Within the shadow of the Washington monument, bolshevism has shown its reptile head and desecrated a beautiful and peaceful Sabbath." It declared that all anarchistic speech and action were treasonable. The article quoted the pastor of the city's First Congregational Church, who described Bolshevism as "anti-home, anti-marriage, anti-morality, anti-property, anti-civilization, and anti-Christ." The *Post* sneered at those who would "whine" about free speech and liberty while the Soviet leader, Lenin, had "set a covetous eye upon America and is attempting to direct the tide of Bolshevism in this direction."[23]

The Denver *Post* used lurid red ink for the banner headlines of its Red Scare stories. It eagerly publicized Attorney General Palmer's predictions about a May Day revolution in 1920. Most newspapers published a letter by Palmer in which he stated that his "[o]ne desire is to acquaint people like you with a real menace of evil-thinking which is the foundation of the Red movement."[24] Palmer pushed Congress to pass peacetime sedition legislation and received the support of the mainstream press. Palmer wanted the authority to suppress left-wing publications and stop the "continual spread of the seeds of evil thought, the continual inoculation of the poison virus of social sedition." He wondered why there was no government authority in peacetime to "stand effectively for social sanitation."[25] However, when Palmer criticized some measures aimed at radicals that Congress was considering, the New York *Times* editorialized that he "expressed ancient and outworn views on immigration; . . . here is the Attorney General of the United States, whose official duty it is to have these alien seditionaries, anarchists, plotters . . . arrested, punished, deported, talking this pre-Adamite sentimentality."[26]

Irresponsible press coverage of the Red Scare fed the atmosphere of fear and hate that thickened as the days of 1919 rolled toward the January raids of 1920. In such an atmosphere, any person who dissented could be subject to severe retaliation. Some examples: In February 1919, a jury in Hammond, Indiana, took two minutes to acquit the murderer of an alien who yelled, "To hell with the United States!" In May 1919, in Washington, D.C., a man who refused to rise for the "Star Spangled Banner" was shot three times in the back by an enraged sailor. Onlookers applauded and cheered. In early 1920, a man was sentenced to six months in jail in Connecticut for saying Lenin was one of the "brainiest" leaders in the world. At the end of 1919, Lincoln Steffens, the muckraker, said, "It all looks to me as if our people were trying to imitate what they think Bolshevik Russia is." When Steffens returned from Russia, the Sacramento *Bee* said he was "a Radical and a Red of the deepest dye. The proper place for Lincoln Steffens is in jail."[27]

Events of 1919 seemed like bad tidings to the American press and its readers. Strikes, riots, and disorder strengthened the belief that revolution was imminent unless drastic measures were taken. Alarmist press coverage made it impossible to weigh the events in a calm and rational manner. What must have seemed like cataclysmic events followed one another in rapid succession: In January, a strike by 35,000 shipyard workers in Seattle; in March, the Overman Senate Committee issued an ominous report on subversive activities in the country; in May, a mob of 400 soldiers and sailors sacked the offices of the socialist New York *Call* and beat up the staff.

In May and June, bombs were sent to government officials and industrials, such as Attorney General Palmer and oil baron John D. Rockefeller; in the summer, race riots erupted in 25 cities, with the worst in Chicago where 38 people were killed and more than 500 injured; in the fall, a strike by Boston police resulted in a wave of looting and theft until businessmen and Harvard students restored order. Also, 350,000 steelworkers went on strike for an eight-hour day. Coal miners also declared a strike; in November, a mob in Centralia, Washington, dragged an IWW agitator from jail and castrated him before hanging him. That same month, FBI agents raided the office of the Union of Russian Workers and arrested 300; in December, Labor Department agents arrested 249 Russian Communists and deported them to Finland aboard the U.S.S. *Buford*, which was dubbed the "Soviet Ark."[28]

Press coverage of these events had the tone of a clanging tocsin bell, but the warning it sounded was based on excessive claims and charges, misinterpretation of fact, and a gross exaggeration of a threat that existed more in the minds of overzealous and publicity-hungry politicians than it did in reality. The Seattle strike was treated with shrill headlines and dire predictions across the country. The Los Angeles *Times* printed: "Reds Directing Seattle Strike—To Test Chance for Revolution." In Denver, the Rocky Mountain *News* said, "The Seattle Strike Is Marxian" and warned of a "revolutionary movement aimed at existing government." The Washington *Post* saw the strike as a "stepping stone to a bolshevized America," while the Cleveland *Plain Dealer* declared that in Seattle the Bolshevik "beast comes into the open." To the Chicago *Tribune*, the strike was "only a middling step from Petrograd to Seattle." The Overman Committee findings were reported with alarm. The New York *Times* shouted, "Red Peril Here"; in Boston, the *Evening Transcript* said, "Plan Bloody Revolution"; and the Atlanta *Constitution* reported that radicals "Want Washington Government Overturned."[29]

Prior to the bombings in May and June, the press reported that the Justice Department uncovered a plot against the government and confiscated a quantity of bombs in New Jersey. The Chicago *Tribune* announced in March that a radical plan for planting bombs in the city had been uncovered, but details in the story were sketchy. The *Tribune* issued a warning to every one of its readers: "Beware Box If It Comes Through the Mail—Do Not Open It—Call the Police Bomb Squad."[30] However, subsequent raids only netted three pistols. No explosives were found. When a bomb exploded outside the home of Attorney General Palmer, the Washington *Post* headlined: "'Red' Blown to Bits As He Dynamites Palmer's House: Bombs in Seven Other Cities Spread Nation-Wide Terror." In an editorial, the *Post* hammered at the "red assassins" and declared that there is such a thing as "treason of the tongue as well as of the head."[31] Bombs that exploded on May Day 1919 were greeted with a *Post* editorial that said, "Silence the incendiary advocates of force. . . . Bring the law's hand down upon the violent and the inciter of violence. Do It Now!" The Salt Lake *Tribune* editorialized, "Free speech has been carried to the point where it is an unrestrained menace."[32]

When a mob raided its offices in May, the New York *Call* described the event as "orgies of brutality" and reported that police stood by because they were sympathetic to the raiders. The mainstream press of the city maintained an editorial silence as if to condone the raid. The intolerance bred during the Red Scare spilled over into and melded with racism. The press seemed certain that Bolshevik agents were behind the riots of the summer. The New York *Times* headlined its riot coverage, "Reds Try to Stir Negroes to Revolt." An editorial noted that it was "no use in shutting our eyes to facts. . . . Bolshevist agitation has been extended among the Negroes." To the Cincinnati *Enquirer* it was clear that "[t]here may be, as is intimated, insidious and sinister agitation of revolutionary character back of these phenomena."[33]

Strikes by steel workers, coal miners, and Boston police in the autumn were reported in an apocalyptic manner: "Police Strike: Riots in Boston—Gangs Range Boston Streets, Women Are Attacked, Stores Are Robbed, Shots Are Fired"; "Troops Turn Machine Guns on Boston Mobs"; "Terror Reigns in City."[34] The Boston *Herald* described it as a "Bolshevist nightmare," and the Boston *Globe* told of "lawlessness, disorder, looting . . . as never was known in this city." The Boston *Evening Transcript* said the steel strike was evidence of the "extraordinary hold which 'Red' principles have upon the foreign born population in the steel districts."[35] Fear that radicals were poisoning the minds of children haunted the nations' schools. The Portland *Oregonian* asserted that children were "the prey of theoretical propagandists in our institutes of education"; and the Toledo *Blade* found college professors who "spill flapdoodle" as guilty as radical labor agitators in stirring up unrest.[36] The few publications to remain calm during these events were the St. Louis *Post-Dispatch*, the New York *World*, *The Nation*, and *The New Republic*. *The Nation* examined the hysteria sweeping the country and concluded that President Wilson and his advisers "have lost their moral balance."[37]

An abyss opened on January 2, 1920, into which the nation's government, its people and the press plunged. In a flurry of midnight arrests, mass jailings, interrogations, beatings, and deportations, thousands of eastern and southern European immigrants felt the wrath of a nation consumed by a hysteria that had reached a climax. Most native-born Americans and much of the press applauded the swift action. However, by spring the Red Scare began to subside, and the press raised doubts about the attorney general's tactics—and his sanity. By summer, memory of the raids had faded for those who were not victims of it. However, the Red Scare left a scar on the country and the press that will remain vivid as long as the documents recording the events are in existence.

The American press, as a whole, acted in a dismal and unconscionable manner in the days and weeks following the Palmer Raids. Among the worst offenders were newspapers respected for reliability, accuracy, and rational judgment, for example, the New York *Times*, the New York *Tribune*, and the Boston *Evening Transcript*. The press failed to defend the plight of the immigrants, which is not surprising, given the long-standing American tradition of intolerance and fear of aliens. But it also failed to see in the raids any permanent damage to American civil liberties.

Immigrants who left their homes on January 2 literally disappeared into the night. Many were arrested and deported without seeing their families again. Others were held incommunicado in jails for days. Most of the 4000 people swept up in the Palmer Raids were attending meetings sponsored by labor unions, ethnic associations, or political groups. Federal agents who infiltrated the immigrants' organizations had risen to leadership positions and had called the meetings. These agents also had written the position papers and party platforms the government used as evidence to prosecute the immigrants.[38] The raids occurred without legal warrants. The arrested were lined up against walls of meeting halls, searched, handcuffed, and chained together for transportation. Citizens were taken to central "stations" to be processed and jailed. Aliens were delivered to immigration authorities who conducted swift deportation hearings. An immigration service rule that an attorney must be present to provide legal counsel was ignored, because, as a Justice Department officer said, it "got us nowhere."[39]

In Detroit, more than 100 men were kept for a week in a 24 by 30 foot "bull pen" that the city's mayor called "intolerable in a civilized city." In New England, 5 women were put into a cell with no mattress. A mother of three was arrested with her 13-year-old daughter. The girl was sent home alone at midnight, and her mother was placed in a "dirty toilet room" with another woman. Thirty-nine people were arrested in Massachusetts at a meeting to discuss a co-op bakery. A naturalized citizen was awakened at his home at 6 a.m. and told to get dressed. He was arrested and his house was searched for subversive literature. Persons who went to a Hartford jail to see friends who were arrested were themselves locked up. Their inquiring was considered evidence of affiliation with the Communist Party. Most of the 4000 arrested were peaceful and did what they were told to by agents. The New York *Times* commented that they were "a tame, unterroristic looking crowd, and their appearance bore out the statements of operatives that not a man had tried to put up a fight."[40]

In the days following the raids, the majority of the nation's newspapers supported the government's actions. Press support was based on the premise that drastic measures were necessary because the revolution was imminent. A New York *Times* editorial said, "The more of these dangerous anarchists are arrested, the more of them are sent back to Europe, the better for the United States." The stance of the *Times* in the Red Scare is perplexing, given that its publisher, Adolph S. Ochs, was the son of a Jewish family that immigrated from Germany. *Times* coverage included photographs published in its "Mid-Week Pictorial" section. Headlines and captions read: "Radical Agitators Under Arrest at Ellis Island"; and "revolutionaries with foreign faces" in which "the foreign aspect of most of the faces is evident.[41]

The Washington *Evening Star* warned that the threat of revolution was "no mere scare, no phantom of heated imagination—it is a cold, hard, plain fact." The Washington *Post* felt there was " no time to waste on hairsplitting over infringement of liberty." A Denver *Times* editorial entitled "Stern Rule for Anarchists" called for their immediate deportation. The Hartford *Times* said "[T]hose who listen tolerantly to the tirades of soap box orators should join the departing Reds." The St. Louis *Globe-Democrat* wrote that free speech was open to the immigrants: "But these strangers, these unin-vited intruders . . . are a public menace, an intolerable nuisance, and our self-respect, as well as the safety of our people, demands their expulsion from the country." The Rocky Mountain *News* saw lasting benefits in the raids, such as "the awakening of the nation to the necessity of guarding against . . . the snapping of our American ideals in favor of exotic doc-trines, discontent with the orderly process of government and political truckling to the alien vote."[42]

Vigorous condemnation of the raids came from liberal church leaders, professionals, and some well-known journalists. By March, public reac-tion had turned hostile enough that Attorney General Palmer felt com-pelled to assert his commitment to freedom of speech and the press. The Baltimore *Sun* was among the first to express an uneasiness about the im-plications of the raids: "In these circumstances it is perhaps more impor-tant than ever before . . . that the constitutional right of freedom of speech should not be abridged." Walter Lippmann said that not since the admin-istration of John Adams had government made "so determined and so dangerous an attack" on constitutional liberties. *The Nation's* Villard wrote that "[t]o let loose an idea upon the world is often a terrible thing, but still more terrible is the effort to combat ideas by force and by incarceration." Other publications that saw the raids as a dangerous infringement of rights included the New Orleans *Times-Picayune*, the Philadelphia *Inquirer*, the St. Louis *Post-Dispatch*, the Richmond *Times-Union*, and the New York *World*. These newspapers felt that the raids signified weakness rather than strength and that indications of radical activity were insufficient to justify such extreme action. *The New Republic* charged that the government's claim of imminent revolution was so "utterly silly" that not even Attorney General Palmer could believe it.[43]

The ultimate undoing of the Red Scare may have had less to do with press criticism of the raids than with the behavior of the attorney general himself. Palmer, who had presidential ambitions, tried to keep public emotions a fever pitch when the hysteria began to wane in the spring of 1920. He predicted a May Day Bolshevik uprising that would plunge the nation into revolution and chaos. But the uprising never materialized, and Palmer's reputation was mortally wounded. On May 2, the New York *Times* called the scare a "mare's nest hatched in the Attorney General's brain." Other caustic comments portrayed Palmer as "full of hot air," "a national menace," and a "Little Red Riding Hood with a cry of Wolf." The *Times* printed comments from others newspapers that indicated they thought the attorney general was subject to hallucinations. On May 4, a Chicago *Tribune* cartoon depicted Palmer walking down a street on a warm day, wearing a winter coat. Parents and children at play appeared to him as wild-eyed, bomb-throwing anarchists. An editorial in the Indianapolis *News* called Palmer "an alarmist."[44]

Americans slowly realized there never was a real cause for alarm, and that the number of Bolsheviks was exaggerated. By mid-1920, when Germany, Italy, and France failed to be swept up by Communist revolutions, it seemed all the less likely that the United States would be overwhelmed. Republican presidential candidate Warren Harding's pledge to "Return to Normalcy" signaled a desire to leave behind the temper of the war years. The new medium of radio and the onset of Prohibition supplanted communism as topics of conversation and press coverage. In the late 1920s the *Saturday Evening Post* said that the Red Scare was "nothing but the last symptom of war fever."[45]

The short-term impact of the Red Scare was devastating. The IWW was rendered ineffective as a force in the organized labor movement. Labor union membership dropped from a peak of 5 million in 1920, to 3.6 million by 1923, and morale was damaged far more than statistics could show. Membership in the two Communist parties dropped from 70,000 to 10,000 by the time the scare was over, and the American Left was crippled for decades. Nicola Sacco and Bartolomeo Vanzetti, two anarchists, were convicted of murder in a 1921 trial filled with antiradical rhetoric. Between 1916 and 1920, 137 daily newspapers and 2268 weeklies folded. Many ceased publication because of wartime shortages and economic trends, but a large number were Left-leaning papers that stood a greater chance of failing because of wartime and Red Scare repercussions. The most disheartening short-term impact fell on freedom of expression. After the Red Scare, 35 states passed criminal syndicalism laws. And in a line of cases extending from *Schenck v. United States* in 1919 to *Whitney v. California* in 1927, the U.S. Supreme Court failed to uphold First Amendment rights.[46]

The lingering effects of the Red Scare are felt down to the present day. Fear of alien subversion led to the passing of the Smith Act and the creation of the House Un-American Activities Committee (HUAC) in the World War II era. HUAC and the Senate committee chaired by Joseph R. McCarthy terrorized the motion picture industry, broadcasting, the print media, and the American Left during the 1950s in another "Red Scare." In challenging McCarthy on his CBS program *See It Now* in 1954, Edward R. Murrow described an American tendency to associate "dissent with disloyalty." In the 1960s, federal agents harassed college students and anti–Vietnam War and civil rights activists for expressing their opposition to the status quo. And in the 1988 presidential campaign, the Democratic candidate, Michael Dukakis, an American of Greek descent, was put on the defensive by a Republican campaign strategy that associated George Bush with patriotism in political commercials depicting him pledging allegiance to the flag, implying that to oppose Bush was un-American.

Criticism of coverage of the Red Scare may have hastened the development of objective news values in the 1920s, but the news media has remained prone to news management by political leaders. Its performance in similar circumstances in the past 70 years oftentimes has been as dismal as in the Red Scare.

NOTES

1. The best source on the Red Scare is Robert K. Murray, *Red Scare: A Study of National Hysteria, 1919-1920* (New York: McGraw-Hill, 1955), 213; see also Irving Brant, *The Bill of Rights: Its Origin and Meaning* (New York: Bobbs-Merrill, 1965; Signet Classics, 1967), 31; John Lofton, *Justice and the Press* (Boston: Beacon Press, 1966; Beacon Paperbacks, 1968), 27; Dorothy Bowles, "Newspaper Support for Free Expression in Times of Alarm, 1920 and 1940," *Journalism Quarterly* 54 (Summer 1977): 272.

2. William Preston, Jr., *Aliens and Dissenters: Federal Suppression of Radicals, 1903-1933* (New York: Harper & Row, 1963), 236.

3. Seattle *Post-Intelligencer*, 3 May 1919, quoted in Murray, *Red Scare*, 83.

4. Quoted in Oswald Garrison Villard, *Fighting Years: Memoirs of a Liberal Editor* (New York: Harcourt, Brace and Co., 1939), 464.

5. Eric Foner and John A. Garraty, eds., *The Reader's Companion to American History* (New York: Houghton Mifflin Co., 1991), 779-780.

6. Ibid., p. 360; Arthur M. Schlesinger, *Paths to the Present*, rev. ed. (Cambridge: Riverside Press, 1964), 75; Richard B. Morris, ed., *Encyclopedia of American History*, 5th ed., Bicentennial ed. (New York: Harper & Row, 1976), 656-657.

7. Schlesinger, *Paths to the Present*, 75.

8. Frederick D. Buchstein, "The Anarchist Press in American Journalism," *Journalism History* 1 (Summer 1974): 44; Morris, *Encyclopedia*, 656-657.

9. Bernard Bailyn, David Brion Davis, David Herbert Donald, John L. Thomas, Robert H. Wiebe, and Gordon S. Wood, *The Great Republic: A History of the American People* (Boston: Little Brown & Co., 1977), 1059; Schlesinger, *Paths to the Present*, 74.

10. John Nerone, *Violence Against the Press: Policing the Public Sphere in U.S. History* (New York: Oxford University Press, 1994), 170; Preston, *Aliens and Dissenters*, 1-7, 21-26; Peter N. Carroll and David W. Noble, *The Restless Centuries: A History of the American People*, 2nd ed. (Minneapolis, MN: Burgess Publishing Co., 1979), 407.

11. Carroll and Noble, *The Restless Centuries*, 394-396.

12. Peter N. Carroll and David W. Noble, *The Free and the Unfree: A New History of the United States*, 2nd ed. (New York: Penguin, 1988), 312.

13. Edwin Emery,*The Press and America: An Interpretative History of the Mass Media*, 3rd ed. (Englewood Cliffs, NJ: Prentice-Hall, 1972), 515: Foner and Garraty, *The Reader's Companion*, 215.

14. John Lofton, *The Press as Guardian of the First Amendment* (Columbia: University of South Carolina Press, 1980), 169; Thomas I. Emerson, The *System of Freedom of Expression* (New York: Random House, 1970; Vintage Books, 1971), 63, 101.

15. Foner and Garraty, *The Reader's Companion*, 1172; Chalmers M. Roberts, *The Washington Post: The First 100 Years* (Boston: Houghton Mifflin, 1977), 155.

16. Roberts, *The Washington Post*, 155; Emery, *The Press and America*, 516; Lofton, *The Press as Guardian*, 171.

17. Harvey Saalberg, "The Westliche Post of St. Louis: German Language Daily, 1857-1938," *Journalism Quarterly* 45 (Autumn 1968): 456; Emery and Emery, *The Press and America*, 515; Mick Mulcrone, "'Those Miserable Little Hounds:' World War I Postal Censorship of the Irish World," *Journalism History* 20 (Spring 1994): 15-16.

18. Carroll and Noble, *The Restless Centuries*, 405; Linda Cobb-Reiley, "Aliens and Alien Ideas: The Suppression of Anarchists and the Anarchist Press in America, 1901-1914," *Journalism History* 15 (Summer-Autumn 1988): 57; Morris, En*cyclopedia*, 374; Bailyn et al., *The Great Republic*, 1043-1044.

19. Michael Emery and Edwin Emery, *The Press and America: An Interpretative History of the Mass Media*, 7th ed. (Englewood Cliffs, NJ: Prentice-Hall, 1992), 260-262; Paul L. Murphy, *The Constitution in Crisis Times, 1918-1969* (New York: Harper Torchbooks, 1972), 28.

20. Bailyn et al., *The Great Republic*, 1058-1060.

21. Robert H. Wiebe, *The Search for Order, 1877-1920* (New York: Hill & Wang, 1967), 245, 290; James D. Startt, "The Media and National Crises, 1917-1945," in *The Media in America: A History*, ed. William David Sloan, James G. Stovall, and James D. Startt (Worthington, OH: Publishing Horions, 1989), 292.

22. Roberts, *The Washington Post*, 157.

23. Washington *Post*, 2 February 1919, quoted in ibid., 156-157.

24. Nerone, *Violence Against the Press*, 176; Joy D. Humes, *Oswald Garrison Villard: Liberal of the 1920's* (Syracuse, NY: Syracuse University Press, 1960), 46-47.

25. Zechariah Chafee, Jr. *The Blessings of Liberty* (Philadelphia: J. B. Lippincott Co., 1956), 67.

26. New York *Times*, 17 October 1919, quoted in Stanley Coben, *A. Mitchell Palmer: Politician* (New York: Columbia University Press, 1963), 214.

27. Coben, *A. Mitchell Palme*r, 196, quoted in Justin Kaplan, *Lincoln Steffens: A Biography* (New York: Simon and Schuster, 1974), 256.

28. Bailyn et al., *The Great Republic*, 1046; Murray, *Red Scare*, 71; Preston, *Aliens and Dissenters*, 216; Carroll and Noble, *The Restless Centuries*, 406; Emery and Emery, *The Press and America*, 260; Humes, *Oswald Garrison Villard*, 52.

29. Murray, *Red Scare*, 83; Los Angeles *Times*, 8 February 1919, Rocky Mountain *News*, 8 February 1919, Washington *Post*, 10 February 1919, Cleveland *Plain Dealer*, 8 February 1919, Chicago *Tribune*, 7 February 1919, all quoted in Murray, *Red Scare*, 65; New York *Times*, 11 March 1919, Boston *Evening Transcript*, 11 March 1919, Atlanta *Constitution*, 11 March 1919, all quoted in Murray, *Red Scare*, 98.

30. Lofton, *Justice and the Press*; Chicago *Tribune*, 6 March 1919, quoted in Murray, *Red Scare*, 69; idem, 72.

31. Washington *Post*, 3 June 1919, quoted in Roberts, *The Washington Post*, 157.

32. Washington *Post*, 3 May 1919, and Salt Lake *Tribune*, 3 May 1919, p. 6, quoted in Murray, *Red Scare*, 77.

33. New York *Call*, 2 May 1919, quoted in Murray, *Red Scare*, 75; Murphy, *The Constitution in Crisis Times*, p. 93; New York *Times*, 28 July 1919, and Cincinnati *Enquirer*, 6 October 1919, quoted in Murray, *Red Scare*, 178-179.

34. San Francisco *Examiner*, 10 September 1919, Rocky Mountain *News*, 11 September 1919, and Salt Lake *Tribune*, 10 September 1919, quoted in Murray, *Red Scare*, 129.

35. Boston *Herald*, 10 September 1919, Boston *Globe*, 10 September 1919, and

Boston *Evening Transcript*, 28 October 1919, quoted in Murray, *Red Scare*, 127 and 148.

36. Kaplan, *Lincoln Steffens*, 256; Portland *Oregonian*, 1 October 1919, and Toledo *Blade*, 14 November 1919, quoted in Murray, *Red Scare*, 172.

37. Emery and Emery, *The Press and America*, 520; *The Nation*, 15 November 1919, quoted in Villard, *Fighting Years*, 463.

38. Zechariah Chafee Jr., *Free Speech in the United States* (Cambridge: Harvard University Press, 1941; Atheneum Books, 1969), 217; Villard, *Fighting Years*, 464.

39. Chafee, *Free Speech in the United States*, 206-207, 211-212; Carroll and Noble, *The Restless Centuries*, 407.

40. Chafee, *Free Speech in the United States*, 206-224.

41. New York *Times*, 5 January 1920, quoted in Lofton, *The Press as Guardian*, 201; Emery and Emery, *The Press and America*, 261-262.

42. Washington *Evening Star*, 3 January 1920, and Washington *Post*, 4 January 1920, quoted in Murray, *Red Scare*, 217; Denver *Times*, 3 January 1920, St. Louis *Globe-Democrat*, 4 January 1920, and Rocky Mountain *News*, 5 January 1920, quoted in Lofton, *The Press as Guardian*, 201-203; Bowles, "Newspaper Support for Free Expression," 278.

43. Murphy, *The Constitution in Crisis Times*, 28-29; Bowles, "Newspaper Support for Free Expression," 278-279; Ronald Steel, *Walter Lippmann and the American Century* (Boston: Little, Brown, 1980), 167; Humes, *Oswald Garrison Villard*, 52-53; Murray, *Red Scare*, 218-219; Lofton, *The Press as Guardian*, 202.

44. Murray, *Red Scare*, 251; New York *Times*, 2 May 1920, quoted in Murray, *Red Scare*, 253; Chicago *Tribune*, 4 May 1920, reprinted in Coben, *A. Mitchell Palmer*, 236; Indianapolis *News*, 2 June 1920, quoted in Coben, *A. Mitchell Palmer*, 241.

45. Murray, *Red Scare*, 240-241; Bailyn et al., *The Great Republic*, 1067.

46. Bailyn et al., *The Great Republic*, 1058-1059, 1067-1068; Murray, *Red Scare*, 269-271; Nerone, *Violence Against the Press*, 183-185.

9 ⁓

THE JAPANESE-AMERICAN
ENIGMA

Lloyd Chiasson Jr.

Togo Tanaka had the look of success. In 1936 he graduated from UCLA and within a year began working as an editor for *Rafu Shimpo*, the largest Japanese daily newspaper in southern California. For the next five and a half years he edited the English section of that journal.

In 1941 Tanaka was 25 years old, married a year, and about to become a father. In October of that year, he visited Washington, D.C., to ask U.S. Attorney General Francis Biddle for permission to continue publishing *Rafu Shimpo* if war came. During that trip to the Capitol, Tanaka visited the White House and met first lady Eleanor Roosevelt.

Two months later on December 8, the day after the Japanese air strike at Pearl Harbor, Tanaka was arrested by the FBI and imprisoned. He was held without being charged and freed 11 days later with no explanation of his imprisonment or release.

Tanaka's freedom was short-lived. Soon he was taken into custody again. Next stop, Manzanar, a barbed-wire home for thousands of people like Togo Tanaka: the Japanese Americans.[1]

During those tumultuous weeks after Pearl Harbor, people of Japanese heritage witnessed firsthand what many believed could never happen in the United States. They saw themselves tried not by jury but by implication, and, suddenly, reputable citizens somehow had become potential saboteurs. In the blink of an eye, an entire population witnessed the repudiation by the United States government of the Japanese-American Citizens League creed, a beautiful, albeit naive, statement:

Although some people may discriminate against me, I shall never become bitter or lose faith. . . . I am firm in my belief that American sportsmanship and the attitude of fair play will judge citizenship and patriotism on the basis of action and achievement, and not on the basis of physical characteristics.[2]

The spring of 1942 was not a time for simple creeds, nor for fundamental beliefs in American fair play. Long-standing emotions were unleashed, and hysteria and racism gripped the West Coast of the United States.[3] People did discriminate. Citizenship did become secondary to physical characteristics. And Japanese Americans discovered that security lay not in constitutional guarantees.

In the spring of 1942, naive beliefs in legal rights were inconsequential compared to the attitudes of neighbors, to the harping of the press, to the cold, hard reality of mass evacuation and internment. In the flourish of a pen a presidential executive order turned Japanese Americans into second-class citizens, confused and disheartened by events not of their making.

After the surprise attack at Pearl Harbor in December 1941, fear of a Japanese air strike on the West Coast of the United States was widespread,[4] and concern over the possibility of sabotage gripped the region. Following recommendations by top officials from Washington, Oregon, and California, along with recommendations by the War Department,[5] President Franklin Delano Roosevelt issued Executive Order 9066. This gave the War Department the authority to designate "military areas" in the far western states and exclude from those zones anyone considered a potential threat to the country's safety.

This resulted in the evacuation of more than 110,000 people of Japanese ancestry from the West Coast, approximately 75,000 of whom were United States citizens, into temporary, then permanent (for the duration of the war) military camps. Designated as enemy aliens, these Issei (first-generation Japanese immigrants) and Nisei (second-generation) remained in ten camps established throughout the West, Southwest, and Middle America until 1945 when the war with Japan ended. Japanese Americans living in Hawaii and other areas outside of the designated military zone did not face internment and were not placed in military camps.

The citizens placed in internment centers were never charged with any crimes. In fact, there were no reported cases of any Japanese Americans being convicted of disloyalty or espionage.[6] Although many opponents of mass evacuation argued before local and federal authorities for individual, case-by-case evaluation of Japanese-American residents, persons with as little as one-sixteenth Japanese ancestry were included in the mass evacuation that began in March 1942.[7]

Much of the history of the Japanese in the United States has been controversial. In 1869 the first Japanese immigrants settled at Gold Hill near Sacramento. One year later Congress granted naturalization rights to free whites and blacks, explicitly omitting Oriental races from the law. In 1906, the San Francisco School Law called for segregation of Oriental students. By 1911, the Bureau of Immigration and Naturalization ordered that declarations of intent to file for citizenship include whites and blacks. This gave the courts room to refuse naturalization to the Japanese.[8]

With the passage of the Alien Land Bill in 1913, Japanese aliens were prevented from owning land in California. As recently as 1924, Congress passed the Asiatic Exclusion Law, which held that aliens ineligible for citizenship would not be admitted to the United States.[9] Immigration from Japan was effectively discontinued. Following Pearl Harbor came Executive Order 9066, which essentially gave the War Department the power to evict from the West Coast all Japanese residents, including U.S. citizens.[10]

Reasons for abundant anti-Oriental legislation appear varied, but hostility to the Japanese immigrants was rooted mainly in racial and economic factors.[11] Viewed as cheap farm labor, the first Japanese immigrants had been welcomed to the West Coast in the last decade of the 1800s. By 1900, however, economic and social antagonisms had emerged, as can be seen in the San Francisco School Law, the California Alien Land Law, and similar land laws in Oregon and Washington. In addition, these three coastal states were instrumental in organizing congressional legislation terminating all Japanese immigration.[12]

Racism toward Japanese in California was fed by a legacy of anti-Chinese sentiment, and Californians persecuted Asians because they feared cheap labor would steal jobs from the white working people. The annexation of Hawaii in 1900 caused an influx of Japanese laborers to the United States, and nativist groups warned that "the West would be 'Japanized' as the South had become 'Negroized.' "[13] The possibility of racial mixing through marriage was another concern of those opposing Japanese immigrants.[14]

Anti-Japanese policy in California become so intense during this period that officials in Japan considered dealing directly with California as they would with an independent nation.[15] In 1910 there were fewer than 75,000 Japanese immigrants in the United States. None could become naturalized citizens. None could buy property because of antialien laws forbidding such transactions. Those affected were almost exclusively Issei.

Following World War I, propaganda about the Japanese "yellow peril" grew, principally in California and led by the Joint Immigration Committee composed of the American Legion, State Federation of Labor, Native Sons of the Golden West, and the California State Grange. Editorials, pamphlets, broadsides, and novels, such as *Seed of the Son* and *Pride of Palomar*, were prejudicial, no doubt for many West Coast residents. In addition, some seeds of racial hatred may have been planted by newspapers, specifically the Hearst newspaper chain.[16]

As early as 1920, high government officials such as California Governor William D. Stephens urged social exclusion of the Japanese for "self-preservation and the ethnological impossibility of successfully assimilating this . . . flow of Oriental blood."[17] Although the 1924 exclusionary law prohibited further immigration from Japan, the Nisei benefited since they now qualified to become American citizens by birth.[18] The same year, however, a law was passed that called for the deletion of all positive comments about Japanese in textbooks used in California schools.[19]

Interwoven with propaganda and the labor situation was the immigrants' tightly knit social structure, which stood out from the more loosely knit social structure on the West Coast.[20] Over time the Nisei did begin to integrate into the American socioeconomic fabric, but there was a continuation, if not a growth, of racial hatred.[21]

As the Nisei matured, they moved from the traditional work patterns of the Issei and became more integrated into the white society. The Nisei increasingly pursued traditionally Caucasian work as salesmen, as clerks. To varying degrees, they began to leave their rural roots and the traditional Japanese enterprises tied to farming. A shift to urban areas resulted. In 1927 the Japanese were the least urbanized immigrants in the United States. By 1941, half of the Pacific Coast Japanese lived in urban areas.[22] However, neither the Issei nor the Nisei were assimilated into American society when the war began. Only when the Nisei branched out into businesses outside the wholesale-retail cycle did assimilation noticeably begin. And this assimilation appears to have been minimal. The Japanese Americans were socially isolated, left to themselves and their "old country" customs and lifestyles.

For those of Japanese ancestry, a parallel society was established and became a community within a community. This separatism emphasized the gulf and the resulting occupational specialization, the concentration in residential districts, aggravated the situation, and created barriers to communication between groups. The result: prejudice.[23]

Urbanization did not mean that the Issei and Nisei had rejected their agricultural ties. By 1940 more than 5000 California farms valued at over $65 million were operated by the Issei and Nisei. By 1941 Japanese Americans controlled 42 percent of the state's commercial truck crops valued at $35 million, significant numbers that may partially explain why California labor and farm lobbies strongly supported mass evacuation after Pearl Harbor.

By February 1942, persons of Japanese heritage came under attack from organized pressure groups, politicians, and the mass media of the region,[24] and at times it seemed as though there were as many rationales for mass evacuation as there were people who favored it. One of the more popular arguments for internment centered on the importance of lifting the public's morale. Others believed that the Japanese had migrated to the United States for disloyal ends. Of course, the charges were as difficult to prove as they were to disprove. And still another justification for mass evacuation: Fear of the Japanese Americans and anxiety about what they might do could result in race riots. In fact, this concern was not without basis. In the months preceding the mass evacuation, seven Japanese-Americans were murdered.[25]

One appeal for mass removal that appears to have convinced many Issei and Nisei was based upon patriotism. The argument followed the lines that if the Japanese Americans were guiltless, they should accept evacuation to prove their loyalty. What irreparably weakens this stance is there were more German-Americans in New York State alone than Japanese on the entire West Coast.[26] Persons of Japanese ancestry represented approximately .01 percent of the U.S. population and less than 2 percent of California's population.[27] Unlike German and Italian Americans, however, Japanese Americans had virtually no political power.[28]

In addition, German aggression and German enemies were often portrayed in the person of Adolf Hitler, while Japanese were depicted in caricatures that could be interpreted as any person of Japanese heritage. Viewed in terms of nationality, the German enemy was Hitler; the Japanese enemy was the Japanese people.[29]

By the beginning of February 1942, it was more a matter of when rather than if a mass evacuation would take place. Groups such as the California Joint Immigration Committee, the American Legion, The Native Sons and Daughters of the Golden West, chambers of commerce, and agricultural and business groups headed a strong and broad-based proevacuation movement in the Pacific states.[30] In addition, the mayors of Seattle, Portland, San Francisco, and Los Angeles supported mass evacuation in testimony before the Tolan Committee (whose purpose it was to determine whether evacuation demands were based on fact or fiction).[31] The same was true for several city councils, boards of supervision and law enforcement officials.

Groups that opposed mass evacuation, such as the Northern California Committee on Fair Play for Citizens and Aliens of Japanese Ancestry, and the President's Committee on Fair Employment Practices, faced a single, albeit massive, obstacle: national and local politicians who disagreed with the antievacuation groups and made their feelings known, at first quietly and later publicly, on Capitol Hill.[32]

Washington, specifically the Justice and War departments, increasingly felt pressured from West Coast officials who supported mass evacuation.[33] It was the old story of the determined and raucous minority united against indifferent federal officials who were unsure, irresolute, and uncommitted against racism.[34] Finally, on February 19, President Franklin Delano Roosevelt signed Executive Order 9066.

By August 7, 1942, Japanese Americans were taken to assembly centers in Washington, Oregon, California, and Arizona, although some evacuees had already been taken in March of that year to Manzanar, the first camp to open. Within a week, the successful evacuation of 110,000 persons of Japanese descent into ten permanent camps had been accomplished.

Not until 1944 when the Supreme Court heard two cases concerning the rights of two Japanese-American internees did the question of internment get a full public airing. The decisions in *Ex parte* Endo and *Korematsu v. United States* were moot in one respect. The day after the Court ruled on both cases, the army announced that the relocation centers were being closed.

How did it happen? How could thousands of innocent American citizens end up in what were, at best, relocation centers and, at worst, concentration camps? American citizens were incarcerated without benefit of trial, and the government never provided the public with a factual reason for its actions. What newspapers wrote about a mass evacuation of American citizens should speak volumes about how the press perceived its watchdog role, particularly in a pretelevision era in which newspapers served as a primary source for both news and opinion.

California newspapers overwhelmingly favored mass evacuation. Although the majority of editorials during December 1941 urged tolerance toward Japanese Americans, a dramatic shift occurred in the middle of January and continued well past the mass evacuation order in February. An editorial evaluation of 112 newspapers revealed that from mid-January to mid-March 77 percent of the editorials supported mass evacuation or other restrictive measures. If letters to the editor are an accurate gauge, then public opinion ran about the same.[35]

Across the West Coast, newspapers were fairly consistent in their support of the mass evacuation program and generally differed only in whether they favored it before or after the government said it was necessary.

After the mass evacuation decision was made, few newspapers questioned its legality or its necessity, and some, like the Los Angeles *Times*, felt it was an issue of loyalty: "Those [Japanese Americans] truly loyal will understand and make no objection."[36]

In areas with large Japanese-American populations, newspapers played a particularly important role in the unfolding drama. Newspaper commentary in those cities was active, and prominent journals like the San Francisco *Chronicle*, the San Diego *Union*, the Los Angeles *Times*, and the Sacramento *Bee* commented extensively on the issues involving the Japanese Americans.

The San Francisco *Chronicle* demonstrated a wide range of editorial opinion, as well as a dramatic shift in stance. Prior to the mass evacuation order, the journal opposed restrictions that might be placed upon Japanese Americans up to and including mass evacuation. Following the order, however, it reversed its stance and supported government policy.

Prior to the mass evacuation decree, the *Chronicle* consistently called for public calm and fair treatment of all loyal persons of Japanese descent. The newspaper was also concerned that both Japanese Americans and Japanese aliens would be persecuted because of race. "Of the three groups with the countries whose origin were at war, the Japanese are the hardest case merely because they are the most easily recognizable."[37] In addition, the *Chronicle* opposed what it termed "the mass injustice of an emergency"[38] and wrote that grass-roots reports indicated the government was responsible for reflecting a popular hysteria that simply did not exist.[39] "We deny the very principles we are fighting for when we begin convicting and punishing people on suspicion or by guess."[40]

A month and a half later, however, the journal informed its readers that "we have to be tough even if civil rights do take a beating."[41] The *Chronicle* wrote that its reversal in stance was patriotic in nature. "They [the Japanese Americans] will, like the rest of us, take military orders as orders, and obey them without questions, as befits good citizens in times of war."[42]

The *Chronicle* also wrote that loyalty should be determined by the conduct and attitude of the Japanese-Americans, "not by the attitude of Japan."[43] That appeared before the mass evacuation order. After the order, the *Chronicle*'s position was that persons of Japanese ancestry "who are loyal to the United States and its ideals can show that loyalty by recognizing necessity."[44]

The San Diego *Union* provided its readers with a much clearer message: The necessity for mass evacuation superseded Japanese Americans' civil liberties. According to the *Union*, sabotage was an imminent threat because the majority of persons of Japanese ancestry could not be trusted. Over time this belief hardened as the newspaper asked first for controls on Japanese aliens,[45] then controls on persons with dual citizenship,[46] and finally controls on all "Japs."[47] (Since all Nisei were considered Japanese citizens under Japanese law, no categories other than the first two could exist.) In more than one editorial, the *Union* also used the derogatory term "Japs" when referring to Japanese Americans.[48]

The *Union* supported the mass evacuation and incarceration before and after the executive order and strongly criticized the government for not having enacted the mass evacuation program sooner.[49] The newspaper consistently printed rumors of unsubstantiated fifth-column activity at Pearl Harbor, as well as undocumented information of spy activity on the Pacific Coast.[50]

Over time the *Union* also became more virulent in its racial criticism.[51] For example: "[I]t is doubtful if there exists in any racial or national group potential treason to the degree that it is found in the ranks of the Japanese. They have contributed nothing to the cultural, political or economic life of this nation."[52]

The *Union* also painted a somewhat tainted view of the evacuation when it wrote the evacuees were "merely a large group of tourists journeying from one part of the country to another"[53] and that the camps were "admirably suited to health and they will give their new residents an opportunity to develop their talents. Comfortable living quarters, plenty of food until they are able to grow their own, quiet scenic surroundings, place many of them in a far better location, from an economic standpoint, than the ones which they are leaving."[54]

Although much of the *Union*'s editorial commentary was founded upon distrust of Japanese-Americans, the newspaper never provided its readers with evidence to substantiate its claims. The majority of the editorials read as vague, frightening forecasts. For example: "A well paid plan for sabotaging California's oil resources" is known by an oil industry spokesman (no attribution given) and "it has been established that we have been marked for attack for many years."[55] Also: "[E]very kind of potential fifth column activity has been revealed in hundreds of raids,"[56] and the movement of Japanese Americans during a blackout represented "a foretaste of what we might expect in the event of a large scale attack."[57] According to the *Union*, the solution to the threat of sabotage and fifth-column activity was simple: a mass relocation into government camps.

The Los Angeles *Times* exhibited neither an abrupt shift in editorial position nor a racial distrust for Japanese-Americans. Instead, its straightforward stance appeared to evolve at the same pace as did its concern about sabotage. Before the evacuation order, the newspaper regularly wrote about the possibility of fifth-column activity and approved of mass evacuation as a preventive action.[58] However, the *Times* was willing to accept less restrictive measures that would achieve the same results as a mass relocation.[59]

Although the *Times* felt many aliens and Japanese-Americans were "fully loyal and deserved sympathy rather than suspicion,"[60] by the end of January the newspaper wrote that demands by the federal government to "remove Japanese from vital military areas represents no sudden burst of hysteria" but "calm common sense conclusions of patriotic citizens who are determined there shall be no Pearl Harbor here."[61] Shortly thereafter, the newspaper supported mass relocation[62] but later wrote it hoped a plan to license all Pacific Coast residents would alleviate the threat of sabotage. According to the *Times*, the plan would meet "objections raised to the wholesale removal of alien and second generation Japanese from vital defense areas in this region" while possibly gaining support from officials "concerned with civil rights."[63]

Once President Roosevelt approved the mass relocation, however, the *Times* supported it and continuously wrote about its necessity due to the threat of sabotage.[64] Like the San Diego *Union*, it sometimes relied upon unsubstantiated information. For example, the *Times* wrote it was probable that Japanese submarines were manned "by crews trained in the Los Angeles fishing fleet" since Japanese naval forces had shown an intimate acquaintance with California's coastal waters.[65]

At times, the editorial stance of the Sacramento *Bee* seemed to be a composite of the other three newspapers. The *Bee* was similar to the *Union* in that it supported the decision for mass evacuation in 1942 and opposed the return of the evacuees in 1944.[66] Like the *Times*, the *Bee* was concerned with fifth-column activity and felt that threat was real and therefore justified Executive Order 9066.[67] Like the *Chronicle*, the *Bee* also expressed concern about the threat of vigilantism against persons of Japanese ancestry.[68]

Just one day after the Pearl Harbor attack the *Bee* was prophetic when it wrote that "these second generation Japanese . . . now find themselves caught in a situation not of their making, but which at best is going to cause them trouble and grief aplenty."[69] The *Bee* clearly believed that although many Japanese Americans were loyal to the United States, others were not. From the outset, the *Bee* seemed to know that strong action would be taken, and that sooner or later it would support that action.

By early February the newspaper wrote that it hated the idea of internment but that it opposed the American Civil Liberties Union for "standing flatfooted on the Bill of Rights as if there were no war. . . . This is war, and in war people get hurt, oftentimes the innocent."[70] Less than a week after Executive Order 9066 was issued, the *Bee* informed its readers that it supported the action, adding that "if such persons [Japanese Americans] are truly loyal, they will accept such hardships as part of their obligation to their adopted country."[71]

California newspapers were not unique in their opinions nor in their solutions to the problems facing the region. Although the following does not cover every editorial stance of every newspaper in the affected areas, it is representative of commentary published by the majority of newspapers on the Pacific Coast.

Prior to the mass evacuation order, the Ashland (Oregon) *Daily Tidings* wrote that a "citizen is a citizen, and all are equal under the law. That is a basic American principle." The Constitution is for all Americans "equally in war and peace . . . under all circumstances."[72] After the order, however, a dramatic shift occurred.

Certainly Americans of Japanese ancestry removed from those zones [the entire Pacific Coast] suffer loss of liberty. But isn't it preferable that they lose a few freedoms than for the traitors among them to blast war plants, air fields or guide invading forces? . . . [W]e are fighting to save the Bill of Rights and the way of life with which it blesses us. Let's don't let anyone crawl safely behind that Bill of Rights in an effort to tear it down from us permanently.[73]

One of the staunchest supporters of mass evacuation was the Corvallis

Gazette Times in Oregon. From the opening days of the war to the closure of the camps in 1944, the newspaper favored mass evacuation, opposed the return of the evacuees, and was often racist in terminology. Prior to mass evacuation the *Gazette Times* wrote: "Sixty per cent of 594 draftees in Honolulu recently inducted into the army are Americans of Japanese parentage. If we were their commanding officer, we would remember the fate of Pearl Harbor."[74] After the order: "[I]f Hitler can get away with several million aliens by keeping them in concentration camps, we ought to be able to have comparatively few Japanese here the same way."[75] Just days after announcement of the closure of the camps, the *Gazette Times* wrote: "If they are smart, they will not return."[76]

Another Oregon newspaper, the Albany *Democrat Herald*, also had strong anti-Oriental feelings. In early January the paper wrote that "anyone familiar with facts of Asia knows the Japs are a cruel, fanatical people, few of whom ever are altered by occidental environments."[77] Following the mass evacuation order, the journal wrote that "over here it [mass relocation] isn't a grimly ironical phrase that calls up tragic stories of concentration camps and seizure and slaughter. It actually denotes protection and guardianship."[78] Time altered little for the *Democrat Herald*. With the closure of the camps, the newspaper wrote that "most Japs came to this country with expectations of . . . ultimately conquering the United States ... the Tulelake [*sic*] relocation center is full of such Japs."[79]

In Washington, the *Olympian* immediately announced its support of civil liberties. "Freedom must be the inalienable right of all people—no matter where they live."[80] Two months later, however, the newspaper wrote: "Would a young Jap who really is trying to be a good American attend a Shinto school?"[81]

Concerning the closure of the camps, the *Olympian* authored perhaps the most original commentary of the war:

[T]housands of Americans were victims of the sneak attack on Honolulu. 119,000 persons of Japanese ancestry were evacuated to inland areas and placed in camps equipped with all modern conveniences, and warehouses were crammed with food. This despite the fact that white folks were unable to replace broken or wornout household and farm appliances, and were disturbed by the discovery that the grocer's shelves were getting barer by the day. Reports were heard that the Japs were being coddled—were, in brief, enjoying the life of Riley![82]

In Seattle, the *Post-Intelligencer* prior to the mass evacuation order wrote that the "saddest figures in the Seattle picture today are the nisei—the second generation Japanese American by birth, with full claim to all rights of American citizenship, yet inevitably marked by nature as of Japanese race. . . . [L]oyalty is not to be determined by the slant of an eyelid or the color of the skin."[83] A few days later the newspaper added a postscript to its earlier comments when it wrote that a "government which prescribes duties for citizens but no rights or sharply restricted ones, is a tyranny."[84]

After it was announced that the camps would be closed, the newspaper distanced itself from its early and strong pro–civil rights stance. "The impossibility of making any accurate classification [as to loyalty] is generally acknowledged."[85]

The Aberdeen *Daily World* in Washington also supported civil liberties immediately after the attack at Pearl Harbor: "[W]ar or no war . . . the American resolve should be that the bill of rights, under any circumstances, will not be surrounded or abandoned."[86] By March, however, it seemed ready to alter its editorial position: "[A]sk yourself whether an American-born Japanese is an American or Japanese. There need be no ill-will in your answer, no injustice, no hatred, but it will be hard to reach any conclusion but that the Japanese is a Japanese. Whether he would aid Japan . . . is another question, and depends on the individual."[87]

Two other Washington journals, the Everett *Daily Herald* and the Longview *Daily News*, viewed the internment in positive terms. According to the *Daily Herald*, "Only America would do for an alien race what we have and are doing for our Japanese aliens and citizens alike."[88] The *Daily News* was even more upbeat when it wrote that the Japanese Americans were "the luckiest racial group ever to be forcibly moved—lucky that it happened in a country like America."[89]

When the military announced the camps would be closed in December 1944, opposition to a mass return took various forms. Some newspapers wrote that the Japanese Americans could not be assimilated. Others wrote that loyalty of the internees could not be proven. Some newspapers felt aliens remained a fifth column danger. To others, vigilantism was a threat to anyone of Japanese descent.

On assimilation: "The idea of Americans assimilating the Japs is abhorrent. They are a tribe apart."[90]

On loyalty: "[I]t is known that some nisei Japanese have given their very lives on the field of battle for the country of their birth. Yet on the other hand it is true that both nisei and immigrant Japs have committed acts of sabotage and espionage and that the majority are at heart Japs, and will always be so."[91]

On fifth-column activity: "We have had enough experiences with Japs in times of peace to emphasize the opinion that they are not to be trusted."[92]

On vigilantism: "The loyal Jap American citizens have the law on their side, but that may not protect them. Besides, what is law and what is the Constitution to a dead Jap?"[93]

Once the conflict in 1944 appeared to be nearing a favorable conclusion, support for internment dropped dramatically and sometimes displayed a complete reversal editorial stance at the time of the mass evacuation decision. Commentary from the San Francisco *Chronicle* on December 19 is representative: "Loyalty is a thing of heart and mind, not of race, creed or color. This, a universal truth, is the American denial of Hitlerism."[94]

Three years before, most newspapers had benignly accepted the president's order without question. When the government said evacuation was a military necessity, editorial discussion of the constitutionality of the incarceration was minimal. The press issued few challenges to government's right to suspend the writ of habeas corpus. However, when the war was winding down in 1944 and an Allied victory was no longer in jeopardy, many newspapers that supported the government without question in 1942 questioned the constitutionality of a mass evacuation.

The majority of West Coast newspapers seem not to have evaluated governmental policy but blindly supported it. Editorial stances often appear based upon acquiescence to presidential fiat rather than upon fact. This resulted in support for strong authoritarian measures rather than individual freedom.[95] By omission the press may have relinquished its watchdog role and, to varying degrees, served as governmental publicist. For many newspapers, the government functioned as the gatekeeper, and the journals appear to have served as opinion leaders interpreting, then relaying, a message based upon rumor and not fact.

Although the constitutional guarantees to the Japanese Americans did not change over time, perhaps the fear of recognizing, and supporting, those guarantees did. Little information concerning the social, cultural, or historical contributions of the Japanese Americans found its way onto the editorial pages. In regards to editorial guidance, the result was twofold: the message readers received was that restrictions were necessary because of the existence in the community of a certain group; and the readers learned nothing about that group. To varying degrees, news articles and features may have helped fill this void, but more depthful commentary regarding assimilation, religion, education, and Japanese traditions may have reduced the anxiety levels of the government, the military, the public, and the press.

Although military necessity was by far the most-used reason given for the need of mass evacuation, not a single instance of sabotage was ever proven and the newspapers often chose to print rumors of unlawful activity rather than substantiated fact.[96]

It would be misleading to suggest that the editorial stance of every journal can be pigeonholed into one or two categories or that the journals supporting mass evacuation did so without concern for the plight of the evacuees. The San Luis Obispo *Telegram-Tribune*, for example, supported moving all aliens inland,[97] but believed that any proposal curtailing civil liberties should be carefully studied.[98] However, the one issue that stretched across time and emerged in almost every journal was the question of military necessity.

One point appears clear. A multiplicity of factors were at work prior to and during the internment of the Japanese-Americans. Military concerns became interwoven with racial and economic issues, and laid the groundwork for large scale acceptance of the government's claim of military necessity. At some point in the crisis, either at its beginning or by its end, some newspapers supported those unsubstantiated claims, and, in so doing, almost certainly fueled racial discord.

Although the press has at times been termed the loyal opponent to the government, this may not be the case in periods of crisis. In addition, concern about press controls in wartime may be misplaced. The issue might not be the First Amendment conflict over what information the media is allowed to gather in regards to national security but rather the interpretation of the information it does collect and disseminate.

In unstable times, and to varying degrees, the press may subordinate its duties to those of the government. However dangerous to First Amendment guarantees, this is understandable given the proper circumstances. When the government provides no factual justification for its actions, the erosion of freedom begins.

On August 10, 1988, President Ronald Reagan signed Public Law 100-383, providing $20,000 reparations to every Japanese-American interned during World War II. According to the President, no payment could make up for those lost years, and Congress officially declared that the evacuation, relocation, and internment were carried out without adequate security reasons and without proof of espionage or sabotage by even a single Japanese-American. On September 29, 1989, the Senate voted to waive budget restrictions and grant an estimated 60,000 Japanese-Americans compensation for their forced internment. The cost is estimated at more than $1 billion.

NOTES

1. Hansen, Arthur A., and Betty E. Mitson, eds., *Voices Long Silent, An Oral Inquiry Into the Japanese American Evacuation* (Fullerton: California State University, 1974), 88-96.

2. Maisie and Richard Conrat, *Executive Order 9066, The Internment of 110,000 Japanese Americans* (Cambridge, MA: The MIT Press, 1972), 33.

3. Idid., 11.

4. Morton Grodzins, *Americans Betrayed* (Chicago: The University of Chicago Press, 1949), 2-3.

5. Carey McWilliams, *Prejudice: Japanese-Americans, Symbol of Racial Intolerance* (Boston: Little, Brown and Company, 1945), 117-120.

6. Grodzins, *Americans Betrayed*, 2.

7. Ibid., 3.

8. James Houston and Jean Wakatsuki Houston, *Farewell to Manzanar* (Boston: Houghton Mifflin Company, 1973), xi.

9. 86 Stat 161 (1924).

10. Executive Order No. 9066, 3 CFR 1092 (1938-43).

11. Grodzins, *Americans Betrayed*, 3.

12. Syngman Rhee, *Japan Inside Out* (London: F.H. Revell Co., 1941), 172.

13. William E. Hunticker and James Mackey, "Racism and Relocation: Telling the Japanese-American Experience," *Social Education* 55(7) (Nov./Dec. 1991): 415.

14. Patricia Nelson Limerick, *The Legacy of Conquest* (New York: W.W. Norton, 1987), 270-73.

15. Grodzins, *Americans Betrayed*, 6.

16. Anne Reeploeg Fisher, *Exile of a Race* (Seattle, WA: F and T Publishers, 1965), 43. For more information about newspaper coverage, see Oliver Carlson and Ernest Sutherland Bates's *Hearst, Lord of San Simeon;* Grodins's *Americans Betrayed;* and two articles by the author, Lloyd Chiasson Jr., "The Japanese-American Encampment: An Editorial Analysis of Twenty-seven Newspapers," *Newspaper Research Journal* 12, no. 2, (Spring 1991); and idem, "An Editorial Analysis of the Japanese-American Evacuation and Encampment, 1941-1942," *Journalism Quarterly,* 68, nos. 1-2, (Spring-Summer 1991).

17. Governor Williams D. Stephens, *California and the Oriental* (Sacramento: California State Printing Office, 1920), as cited by Grodzins in *Americans Betrayed,* 7.

18. Bill Hosokawa, *Thirty-five Years in the Frying Pan* (San Francisco, CA: McGraw-Hill, 1978), xiv.

19. Grodzins, *Americans Betrayed*, 10-11.

20. McWilliams, *Prejudice: Japanese-Americans*, 89.

21. Ibid.

22. Ibid.

23. Gordon W. Allport, *The Nature of Prejudice* (London: Addison-Wesley Publishing Company, 1954), 228-229.

24. Ives Neely, "The Press Was an Accessory," *The Quill* 64 (April 1976): 19-20.

25. Grodzins, *Americans Betrayed*, 138-139.

26. Harrop A. Freeman, "Genesis, Exodus and Leviticus–Genealogy, Evacuation and Law," *Cornell Law Quarterly* 28 (June 1943): 414-458.

27. Hunticker and Mackey, "Racism and Relocation: Telling the Japanese-American Experience," 416.

28. Grodzins, *Americans Betrayed*, 21.

29. Donna Nagata, "The Japanese-American Internment: Perceptions of Moral Community, Fairness, and Redress," *Journal of Social Issues* 46 (Spring 1990), 135; and Hunticker and Mackey, "Racism and Relocation: Telling the Japanese-American Experience," 416.

30. Grodzins, *Americans Betrayed*, 81.

31. *Second Interim Report of the Select Committee Investigation National-Defense Migration*, by John H. Tolan, chairman (Washington, DC: Government Printing Office, 1942), 139-156.

32. Grodzins, *Americans Betrayed*, 180.

33. James MacGregor Burns, *Roosevelt–The Solider of Freedom* (New York: Harvest/Harcourt Brace Jovanovich, 1970), 215.

34. Ibid.

35. Grodzins, *Americans Betrayed*, 377-384. For a good starting point into an evaluation of the role of the press in periods of crisis–prior to television–see D. W. Harding, "General Conceptions in the Study of the Press and Public Opinion," *Sociological Review* 29 (October 1937): 390; Neely, "The Press Was an Accessory," The *Quill*, (April 1976), 19-20; Raymond Y. Okamura, "The American Concentration Camps: A Cover-Up Through Euphemistic Terminology," *Journal of Ethnic Studies* 10 (Fall 1982): 102; Richard Polenberg, *War and Society: The United States, 1941-1945* (New York: J. B. Lippincott Company, 1972), 37-72; Robert K. Murray, *Red Scare: A Study of National Hysteria, 1919-1920* (New York: McGraw-Hill, 1955), 35-36; Marcus W. Wilkerson, *Public Opinion and the Spanish-American War* (Baton Rouge: Louisiana State University Press, 1932). Perhaps the most exhaustive study of the encampment can be found in Grodins's excellent historical analysis, *Americans Betrayed*. Grodzins relates events leading up to the evacuation and encampment and, as cited above, his Appendix I contains an evaluation of news articles, columns, letters to the editor and editorials that appeared in 112 California newspapers.

36. Los Angeles *Times*, 28 February 1942.

37. San Francisco *Chronicle*, 16 December 1942.

38. San Francisco *Chronicle*, 9 February 1942.

39. San Francisco *Chronicle*, 6 February 1942.

40. San Francisco *Chronicle*, 3 January 1942.

41. San Francisco *Chronicle*, 21 February 1942.

42. San Francisco *Chronicle*, 4 March 1952.

43. San Francisco *Chronicle*, 20 January 1942.

44. San Francisco *Chronicle*, 21 February 1942.

45. San Diego *Union*, 3 February 1942.

46. San Diego *Union*, 7 February 1942.

47. San Diego *Union*, 27 February 1942.

48. San Diego *Union*, 27 February, 1942, 24 March 1942.

49. San Diego *Union*, 17 February 1942, 4 March 1942.

50. San Diego *Union*, 7 February 1942, 17 February 1942, 27 February 1942, 6 March 1942.

51. San Diego *Union*, 7 February 1942, 23 February 1942, 25 February 1942, 6 March 1942.

52. San Diego *Union*, 16 March 1942.

53. San Diego *Union*, 16 March 1942.

54. San Diego *Union*, 4 April 1942.

55. San Diego *Union*, 7 February 1942.

56. San Diego *Union*, 6 March 1942.

57. San Diego *Union*, 25 February 1942.

58. Los Angeles *Times*, 28 January 1942, 30 January 1942, 3 February 1942, 6 February 1942, 7 February 1942.

59. Los Angeles *Times*, 12 February 1942.

60. Los Angeles *Times*, 23 January 1942.

61. Los Angeles *Times*, 28 January 1942.

62. Los Angeles *Times*, 28 January 1942.

63. Los Angeles *Times*, 7 February 1942..

64. Los Angeles *Times*, 21 February 1942, 25 February 1942, 29 February 1942, 7

March 1942, 7 March 1942, sec 2, 13 March 1942.

65. Los Angeles *Times*, 28 February 1942.

66. Sacramento *Bee*, 23 February 1942, 19 December 1944.

67. Sacramento *Bee*, 23 February 1942, 19 December 1944.

68. Sacramento *Bee*, 8 December 1941, 10 December 1941, 31 January 1942.

69. Sacramento *Bee*, 8 December 1941.

70. Sacramento *Bee*, 6 February 1942.

71. Sacramento *Bee*, 23 February 1942.

72. Ashland *Daily Tidings*, 13 February 1942.

73. Ashland *Daily Tidings*, 28 March 1942.

74. Corvallis *Gazette Times*, 16 December 1941.

75. Corvallis *Gazette Times*, 28 March 1942.

76. Corvallis *Gazette Times*, 20 December 1944.

77. Albany *Democrat Herald*, 5 January 1944.

78. Albany *Democrat Herald*, 19 March 1942.

79. Albany *Democrat* Herald, 20 December 1944.

80. *Olympian*, 14 December 1941.

81. *Olympian*, 24 February 1942.

82. *Olympian*, 19 December 1944.

83. Seattle *Post-Intelligencer*, 11 December 1941.

84. Seattle *Post-Intelligencer*, 16 December 1941.

85. Seattle *Post-Intelligencer*, 24 March 1942.

86. Aberdeen *Daily World*, 15 December 1941.

87. Aberdeen *Daily World*, 2 March 1942.

88. Everett Daily *Herald*, 3 April 1942.

89. Longview Daily *News*, 2 April 1942.

90. *Olympian*, 19 December 1944.

91. Albany *Democrat Herald*, 20 December 1944.

92. Bakersfield *Californian*, 15 December 1944.

93. Corvallis *Gazette Times*, 20 December 1944.

94. San Francisco *Chronicle*, 19 December 1944.

95. The findings of Grodins's editorial analysis, *Americans Betrayed*, appendix I, 377-399), were almost identical to those of this chapter. Although a shorter time frame was analyzed (8 December 1941 to 8 March 1942), Grodzins found that favorable comments regarding civil liberties were lost in an avalanche of rumors about disloyalty by the end of January. According to Grodzins, after this period almost every newspaper had a "shift in sentiment." He found that the San Francisco *Chronicle*'s editorial pattern was representative of several newspapers that supported civil liberties, then reversed position. Grodzins also found both the *Chronicle* and the *Times* to be representative of many of the journals evaluated, and his specific findings regarding those two newspapers parallel those of this chapter. In regard to the San Diego *Union*, Grodzins found every editorial the newspaper printed to be a demand for mass evacuation.

96. *Report of the Select Committee Investigation on National Defense Migration*, by John H. Tolan, chairman (Washington, DC: Government Printing Office, 1942), 40-48.

97. San Luis Obispo *Telegram-Tribune*, 28 January 1942, 20 February 1942, 3 March 1942.

98. San Luis Obispo *Telegram-Tribune*, 10 February 1942.

10 ⌒

MCCARTHY'S
JOURNALISM

Lloyd Chiasson Jr.

On a cold January day in 1950 the basic outline for one of the most outrageous and spectacular careers in the history of American politics was born. The setting was innocent enough: the Colony Restaurant in Washington, D.C.

Engaged in after-dinner conversation were attorney William Roberts, Georgetown University professor Charles Kraus, Father Edmund Walsh, and Senator Joseph McCarthy. The subject was a campaign issue, something McCarthy could use in his next senatorial campaign.

Father Walsh: "How about Communism as an issue?"

McCarthy: "The government is full of Communists." Here was an issue the senator could use, one he liked. "The thing to do is hammer at them."[1]

And for the next four years, that is what the senator from Wisconsin did. He hammered at the Communists, be they real or imagined; he hammered at his opponents; he hammered at the public's doubt; and he hammered at the press, which was always anxious for a story but was often mystified that McCarthy's facts rarely matched McCarthy's promises.

The senator's crusade began in the quiet hills of West Virginia. Just one month after his legendary supper meeting at the Colony Restaurant, McCarthy made one of the most, and certainly not the last, electrifying statements of his career. Speaking before the Ohio County Women's Republican Club on February 9, the senator claimed he had the names of 205 Communists who worked in the State Department (different accounts have put the number at 81 and 57).[2]

McCarthy would later deny he had said 205 Communists, and a day later in Denver, he told reporters what he had actually said in Wheeling

was that 207 "bad risks" worked in the State Department.[3] His next scheduled stops were Salt Lake City, Utah, and Reno, Nevada, where the number dropped from 207 to 57.

Regardless of the number cited, McCarthy's speeches and impromptu
press conferences the next two days attracted the attention of the local
newspapers, as well as the Associated Press (AP), and a smattering of
newspapers across the country reported his comments.[4] Coverage of
McCarthy's charges increased markedly the following week, although
specifics of what the senator had to say were essentially nonexistent. The
reason was simple: McCarthy offered no specifics. As AP correspondent
Edward Olsen put it: "The man just talked circles. Everything was by
inference, allusion, never a concrete statement of fact. Most of it didn't
make sense. I tried to get into my lead that he had named names but he
didn't call them anything."[5]

What he talked about was the number of unnamed cases, which in
three days changed three times. Ten days and no names later, McCarthy
appeared before the Senate, ostensibly to explain himself and provide evidence of his charges. What he provided was the first episode of a show
that would run for four years. In what one biographer termed "one of the
maddest spectacles in the history of representative government,"
McCarthy rambled for six long hours, often incoherently, about unnamed,
yet numbered cases of Communists in the State Department, about loyal
Americans in the State Department, about someone who was on his list
but was still, somehow, inexplicably, a "Democratic American."[6] And once
again, the number changed. Now there were 81 Communists working for
or influencing the State Department.

Even this type of disarray worked for him. McCarthy changed his
story so often that, for most reporters, covering the senator was like trying
to solve a Rumplestilskin riddle. For what reporter could make sense of
his six-hour Senate presentation? Of rambling press conferences, incon-
gruous statements, unverifiable facts? Who could write the truth when
the truth was not yet known? In the meantime, McCarthy's comments
were picked up by the wire services, and people across the country read
reports of a United States senator who claimed Communists helped shape
the country's foreign policy. The public could discern that he had changed
figures, that he had met with criticism, that he failed to convince his colleagues in the Senate. But his charges were national news, and he was
either a man shouting fire where none existed or someone telling the truth.

It is with the last possibility that McCarthy's newsworthiness can be
explained. If what he said was true, even just a little, then there was cause
for concern. If his figures were inflated, just one Communist in the State
Department was too many. In any case, the charges were news, and as
long as they couldn't be proven false, the wire services and many newspapers believed they had an obligation to cover the story.

According to McCarthy biographer Richard Rovere, readers had only to ask themselves a series of questions in evaluating McCarthy's claims. Would a United States senator appear before Congress and make false claims? What were the chances of a senator making charges of this magnitude without some sort of substantiation? How could anyone expect the senator to have exact numbers since the Communists certainly would not provide him with a directory of agents working in or around the State Department? Finally, how could charges so vast not contain, at the very minimum, a kernel of truth?[7]

Now to the secret to McCarthy's notoriety. If the untruth is bold enough and multifaceted enough, the Big Lie (also referred to as "The Multiple Untruth" by Rovere and "The Great Conspiracy" by historian Dale Leathers) becomes believable simply because it is not small, simple, or easily understood.[8] Because what McCarthy said sounded plausible, two things happened almost simultaneously: [T]he media reported what he said, and what he said attracted the public's attention. What emerged was an audience, and from the audience came a following.[9] McCarthy became important because people believed it to be so. He was a senator. He was a senator with important information. He was a senator on a righteous crusade. He was news.

Joe McCarthy blazed across the American political landscape in the early 1950s. In a span of weeks, he was transformed from a Washington Lilliputian into one of the most visible figures in the nation. In just months, he became one of the most feared men in the United States. McCarthy was the master of the pseudoevent; his was the art of accusation without documentation.

McCarthy's mercurial rise was not without casualties, however. Amidst the unfounded accusations, the concept of fair play was lost. Reputations were destroyed, lives ruined. Thirty years after it faced the first Red Scare, America once again was gripped by a fear of an unseen, monolithic Communist conspiracy. The country's domestic and foreign agendas were altered.[10] And the press faced the dilemma of covering news that was not quite news, press conferences that were ambiguous but somehow important, allegations by important people against persons of lesser notoriety, and therefore lesser news value. Holding high the standard of objectivity, the press transmitted the news as an unbiased observer. Interpretation was often infrequent and after the fact. Truth became an elusive shadow on the wall, and the press became a casualty of McCarthyism.

Several incidents prior to McCarthy's first claims of Communists in the State Department helped pave the way to much of the publicity McCarthy received. The country was deeply concerned about the threat of communism, due in part because of the Canadian government's announcement in 1946 that a spy ring existed within its political superstructure. In 1947 President Harry Truman began a stern loyalty program, and in July of the following year, several Communists were indicted under the Smith Act for plotting the overthrow of the government. A month later Whittaker Chambers accused Alger Hiss of being a Communist spy, and in 1950, Hiss became national news when he was found guilty of espionage, while Chambers made headlines by committing suicide.[11]

Coincidentally, the day after McCarthy made his first Communists-in-the-government speech, Klaus Fuchs was arrested for atomic espionage. Less than two weeks later Senate Democratic leader Scott Lucas offered a resolution to the Senate that would direct the Foreign Relations Committee (also known as the Tydings Committee) to probe earlier charges by Senator McCarthy that Communists worked in the State Department.[12] Although President Truman immediately called McCarthy's charges false, a subcommittee was appointed to study the allegations. Suddenly, the story was larger than McCarthy, and for as long as the issue had life in Washington, McCarthy stayed near or at the top of the news agenda.

In early March the subcommittee hearings opened with McCarthy as its first witness. Almost immediately the senator accused American Ambassador-at-Large Philip Jessup of having an "affinity for Communist causes."[13] Although Jessup denied the charges, McCarthy was successful in focusing national attention on the hearings. He continued his attacks later that month when he alleged that the State Department was a haven for Communists and that the Alger Hiss ring was still there. (Hiss had been a State Department employee when convicted of subversion in 1948.)

McCarthy probably garnered support in Washington as much for his ability to put the Democrats on the defensive as for his anti-Communist stance. His aggressiveness also created rifts within the Republican Party, and the Senate Republican Policy Committee announced the senator's accusations were not a matter of party policy.[14] On the Democratic side, both liberals and conservatives were poised to see how the president and Secretary of State Dean Acheson would emerge from the State Department tempest.[15]

From March through July, the Tydings Committee had no more success in extricating information from McCarthy than did the press. McCarthy provided the committee with names—but no evidence. When asked by committee members to provide evidence, McCarthy said that information was in the State Department files. Without evidence, there could be no formal charges. Without charges, the committee wasn't empowered to subpoena the records. Finally, when the president agreed to open the files to the committee, McCarthy called the president's action "a phony offer of phony files."[16]

By March, McCarthy named a professor from Johns Hopkins University, Owen Lattimore, as "the top Russian agent" in America. Although Lattimore had never worked for the State Department, he had traveled in the Far East in the 1930s and 1940s. If not a household name, Lattimore was anything but an unknown commodity. He had been criticized by right-wing politicians for his opposition to Nationalist Chinese leader Chiang Kai-shek, and in 1949 Lattimore had advocated U.S. withdrawal from South Korea.[17] According to United Press correspondent George Reedy, "Lattimore was a kind of fuzzy professor who never had any influence in the State Department. The Communist spy business was ridiculous nonsense, and we all knew it."[18]

Where McCarthy was involved, however, knowing something and writing about it was akin to holding water in your hands. Time pressures that the wire services faced sometimes led to stories that, under more normal circumstances, would never have been published. But dealing with the senator was anything but normal. His methods, although appearing simple and straightforward, somehow confused the most astute reporters, leaving more than one in a convoluted state of mind. In the morning, McCarthy would call a press conference to call a press conference at midday, which would afford the senator the opportunity to announce a press conference for the evening. If there was hard news to be found in between, it was often an accident. It also became abundantly clear that McCarthy's "electrifying" morning statements were somewhat less than electric and almost always timed to squeak in under the early deadlines of newspapers in the eastern time zone. Any confusion or lack of balance to the early stories would be clarified, somewhat, by noon. Of course, McCarthy still had reached the public with a double "news" whammy by noon. In addition, McCarthy rarely looked bad. He simply grabbed more headlines. AP filing editor Allen Alexander explained how the early story was often "corrected" by the second wire story, and how competition sometimes led to poor news judgment:

[I]nstead of the original unvarnished "Senator Joe McCarthy declared today that John Doe is a lousy, no-good Communist," it would state "John Doe denied today that he is or whether was a lousy, no-good Communist." (This new lead was great for noon newscasters with their in-depth coverage.) By 2 P.M., in time for final afternoon editions, the semblance of a balanced, fair story on the Senator's charges and allegations might be available. All too often, however, this did not take place during the same news cycle.

If this first bulletined story was too blatantly irresponsible, I would on occasion try to delay filing it, knowing that a new, better balanced lead was expectable. . . . I had trouble with an overwhelming tide. AP member newspapers subscribing to competing UP And INS service would message frantically: "Opposition reports that McCarthy said xxx. Where's ours?" What do you tell your superiors when they see a message like that? And when a boss states, "We report the news. Local editors make the judgment as to whether to use it." Filing editors are not in a position to discuss philosophy, ethics, or the definition of news. At least they weren't back then.[19]

During the next three months the subcommittee hearings surfaced as a major news event for many Americans, and McCarthy's famous quote: "I believe you can ask any school child who the architect of our Far Eastern policy is, and he will say 'Owen Lattimore'" was true for many children.[20]

Lattimore was not the only witness to appear before the Tydings Committee. Throughout the summer, witness after witness was paraded before the committee. Then in June, North Korea invaded South Korea, and McCarthy had additional fodder with which to fuel his anti-Communist campaign. After Red China joined in that conflict, McCarthy quickly blamed the entire Korean situation on the State Department.[21] In July, however, the Tydings Committee handed McCarthy a setback when it issued an interim report that referred to McCarthy's Communist hunting as a "fraud and a hoax."

After the Tydings report, McCarthy dropped down, but not off, the news agenda. The Korean Conflict had turned into a shooting war, and both public and media interest turned from domestic to foreign affairs. With concern about Communists now relegated to a more distant front, the Tydings Committee report was less harmful to McCarthy than it might have been in other circumstances.

The timing of the upcoming senatorial election in Maryland was tailor-made for McCarthy to demonstrate that his popularity had not taken a significant downturn. Maryland was Senator Millard Tydings's home state, and McCarthy made several speeches on behalf of Senator Tydings's opponent, John Butler. If anyone doubted the political power of the Communist issue, those doubts were quelled with Tydings's defeat.

By 1951 McCarthy shifted his investigation temporally from the State Department to the secretary of defense. On June 14, McCarthy gave perhaps his best-known speech in which he assailed General George Marshall, who was considered by many Americans, not the least of them President Truman, as the "greatest living American."[22] (Claiming that he did not want "his colleagues to miss the ball game this evening," McCarthy gave only the opening of the speech and simply had the entire speech entered into the *Congressional Record*. Later it was printed as a book, *America's Retreat from Victory: The Story of George Catlett Marshall*.)

Essentially, McCarthy attempted to link Marshall to a foreign policy that the Wisconsin senator claimed encouraged both foreign and domestic communism. This was a conspiracy, McCarthy said, "so immense as to dwarf any previous such venture in the history of man."[23] According to Richard Rovere, the speech was also a classic example of the Multiple Untruth, "composed, for the most part, of a mass of historical truths— tendentiously chosen, to be sure, and meanly organized."[24]

After the Marshall speech, McCarthy popularity with Republican organizations increased, and his investigations, no matter how flimsy in evidence, consistently garnered media attention.

In 1952 McCarthy was reelected, and McCarthy was soon named chairman of the Committee of Governmental Operations. The senator, however, used an arm of this committee, the Permanent Subcommittee on Investigations, to continue his investigations. By naming himself chairman of the subcommittee, which was not limited in the scope of its activities, McCarthy had a mechanism by which he could not only make charges but call witnesses. By ignoring the responsibilities of the parent committee and concentrating his efforts on the subcommittee, McCarthy at once created a podium for himself and a clearinghouse for information for the news media.

In organizing a staff, McCarthy hired Roy Cohn as chief counsel to the subcommittee and David Schine as chief consultant. Although the reasons behind the selection of Schine are unclear, Cohn seemed ideally suited to assist McCarthy. He had helped prosecute Julius and Ethel Rosenberg for stealing atomic secrets, in 1948 he had prosecuted 13 Communists for conspiring to overthrow the government, and he took part in the indictment of Owen Lattimore for perjury.

Cohn and Schine ran the subcommittee in 1953,[25] and although the investigations and hearings offered little in the way of Communist activities, they produced an enormous amount of publicity.[26] About this time, however, McCarthy's support in the Republican Party appears to have diminished, in part because he was increasingly at odds with President Dwight D. Eisenhower, who was intent on disassociating himself from McCarthy.[27]

In the fall of 1953, McCarthy embarked upon his final investigation. What resulted was the Army-McCarthy hearings, a political spectacle unique in American political history.[28] What began as an investigation into alleged subversion in the army turned into a dramatic television event—187 hours of televised coverage sometimes viewed by 20 million Americans at a time. At first glimpse, McCarthy's investigation into civilian scientists employed by the Army Signal Corps Engineering Laboratories at Fort Monmouth, New Jersey, seemed no different than previous investigations. But McCarthy soon enlarged the battleground to the Army and the Department of Defense and pressed hard for access to the Army's confidential loyalty files. Since President Eisenhower opposed public disclosure, the result was a highly publicized conflict between the right of Congress to access information and the right of a president to withhold it.

Oddly enough, the real clash between the army and McCarthy developed over an Army dentist named Irving Peress, who, despite having invoked the Fifth Amendment about questions pertaining to his political beliefs, was commissioned as a major.[29] Three days after being questioned by McCarthy, and following McCarthy's demand that the dentist be court-martialed, the Army granted Peress his request for an honorable discharge.

Three weeks later, General Ralph Zwicker, Peress's commanding officer, refused to kowtow to McCarthy's demand that Zwicker reveal the names of those involved in the Peress case. McCarthy hammered at the general mercilessly and unsuccessfully, eventually saying that Zwicker was "not fit to wear that uniform."[30]

In the midst of this national drama, a melodrama blossomed when the Army reported that David Schine, the chief counsel for McCarthy's subcommittee, had been drafted despite what the army termed attempts by McCarthy and Roy Cohn to have Schine commissioned.[31] Schine's history as an army recruit was certainly not ordinary. Army records show he received an inordinate number of passes, was excused from drills, and gave the general appearance of being an officer rather than a private.[32] Eager for a full hearing, Senate Democrats demanded an immediate report from the Army and an investigation of charges by both McCarthy—who claimed the army was holding Schine "hostage,"—and the Army—which claimed McCarthy had attempted to exert unfair influence in the case of private G. David Schine.[33]

Seeming to sense a public clash of great magnitude, Congress appointed the Permanent Subcommittee on Investigations—McCarthy's subcommittee—to conduct hearing to air all the facts. Led by Senator Lyndon Johnson, the Democrats pushed for televised coverage of the hearings. Congress agreed. For the next two months a bitter drama, laced with healthy doses of confusion and confrontation, unfolded.

McCarthy dominated the hearings from the outset. The senator questioned witnesses relentlessly, much to the chagrin of Republican committee members anxious for the hearings to end as quickly and quietly as possible.[34] Perhaps because of the constant bickering among the committee members, the hearings never developed a logical pattern. Before what must have been an enthralled audience, millions watched as McCarthy doggedly questioned witnesses for 36 days. In one way, the hearings were inconclusive. Yet they may have had more of an emotional than substantive impact,[35] for they established McCarthy as a destructive personality who placed himself above any standard of fair play.[36]

After the hearings, it was clear that support for McCarthy had eroded with the public as well as with Congress. Republican Senator Ralph Flanders of Vermont introduced a bill to censure McCarthy,[37] and on December 2, 1954, the Senate voted 687 to 22 to condemn McCarthy for actions "contrary to senatorial ethics" and tending "to bring the Senate into dishonor and disrepute."[38] Although the condemnation meant no loss of senatorial privileges for McCarthy, it marked both the end of the senator's prominence and the beginning of an abrupt political decline. After enduring various physical ailments, McCarthy died just three years after his condemnation by the Senate.

Since he never provided substantive evidence to either the government or the media, and since no Communists were ever uncovered by his investigations, it would seem McCarthy's news value would have quickly diminished after the Wheeling speech. That did not happen, however, as McCarthy proved he could become a human pseudo event, a person known for his well-knownness.[39]

Reporters were astonished that McCarthy could produce so much news from such flimsy material.[40] The truth is, McCarthy developed techniques with the press that, although ridiculously simple, worked. He would call a press conference to announce another press conference. Even if the afternoon news conference had no worth, the announcement of an "important" McCarthy conference would make the afternoon editions. Editors who saw McCarthy's press conferences for what they were often were powerless in criticizing him. For every editorial that attacked McCarthy, the same editors were "building him up in front-page headlines."[41]

Technological advancements in communications prior to that period may have hindered complete and accurate news coverage of events surrounding McCarthy. Primarily because of "round-the-clock" news gathering, the news gap became so narrow that it became necessary "to plan in advance the stages by which any available news would be unveiled."[42]

Since world developments had become increasingly complex and deadlines more demanding, it may have been tempting for editors to report insignificant staged events such as newsless news conferences constructed on a foundation of hype. In addition, staged events like McCarthy's are often easier to report than spontaneous ones[43] and although they have the appearance of importance and can be reported in objective terms, the "news" remains ambiguous at best. In short, news gathering turns into news making.[44]

Daniel Boorstin also asserts that newsmen were McCarthy's most potent allies since they served as comanufacturer of pseudoevents because they were victims of what one termed their "indiscriminate objectivity."[45] According to Jack Anderson, McCarthy simply knew how to use the press because he understood the mechanics of the profession.[46] McCarthy recognized the importance of deadlines to reporters who were being manipulated "like Pavlov's dogs" and knew when "they were hungriest and needed to be fed, and when there was no time for substantiation."[47]

In addition, reporters seldom made McCarthy produce the goods. In 1950 when he first made his charges, rarely did they challenge him. Later, when he was firmly ensconced on the news agenda, it made little difference.[48] According to Jack Anderson, "[T]he real scandal in all this was the behavior of the member of the Washington press corps who, more often than not, knew better." Anderson adds that reporters "were delighted to be a part of his traveling road show, chronicling each charge and then moving on to the next town, instead of bothering to stay behind to follow up. They had little interest in reporting how careless he was or how little it all meant to him. It was news and he was news; that was all that mattered."[49]

A part of this attitude may be explained by what Douglass Cater refers to as "frozen patterns" of reporting, which primarily referred to a passive type of straight news reporting that relied on acceptance of the facts rather than a more aggressive approach including depthful backgrounding and explanation of the "hows" and "whys" of a story. As Cater points out, most reporters wrote straight news; only a select few did in-depth coverage. The result was twofold: The straight news stories with little insight into McCarthy's motives and claims tended to be the stories that were picked up by the wire services because they were viewed as hard news and not subjective interpretation;[50] and the readers ended up being acquainted with McCarthy's claims rather than knowledgeable about them. The bottom line was simple: McCarthy made unfounded claims, he told lies, and he got away with it. For the most part, reporters relied on convention, wrote what the senator said, and rarely commented on whether or not what he said was true.

Not all observers believed this was a mistake. Rovere wrote that the press was right to report on McCarthy in the traditional, objective fashion.

I suspect there is no surer way to a corrupt and worthless press than to authorize reporters to tell the readers which "facts" are really "facts" and which are not. Certainly in those countries where this is the press, the press serves the public less well than ours does.[51]

There is little doubt that journalistic objectivity was at the heart of McCarthy's success. Bayley writes that if the press was responsible for creating McCarthy, it did so in the first month after the Wheeling speech.[52] Indeed, several things could have occurred at this point. First, if the senator's comments generated interest in the press, then he would be placed on the agenda. If they failed to spark interest, it was a dead issue. The answer to this goes directly to the definition of news, and there exists little basis for debate that the senator's charges were not news.

Second, once McCarthy was placed on the agenda, how long could he, or should he, stay there? This second point is more difficult to analyze. McCarthy's charges against the State Department deserved coverage. But how much, and for how long? When substantiation for his claims were not forthcoming, newspapers and the wire services had to decide whether or not McCarthy stayed on their agenda. The answer to this was muddy at best. Fear of some sort of infiltration by Communists had been an issue since the first Red Scare in 1919–1920 and had markedly increased since World War II.[53] In 1947 the Hiss/Chambers controversy boiled, and in 1949 the State Department opposed further aide to the Chiang Kai-shek

and the Nationalists in China. Republicans strongly opposed this policy
as either stupid or traitorous. For the political parties, communism as both
a domestic and a foreign affairs issue was real.[54] The time was ripe for
someone to make communism less abstract for the public. Enter Joe
McCarthy.

What helped McCarthy with both the public and the press were the
specifics of his charges. Republicans had been criticizing the State
Department's policies for years but in general terms. McCarthy offered
numbers, and even though the numbers changed, they were there for the
press to print. Once printed, the agenda as it applied to McCarthy was set
in motion. For some, the question of whether McCarthy should have remained on the agenda for any length of time is moot.

In addition, agreement that the press failed to investigate McCarthy
or the validity of his claims is far from universal. Disagreeing with both
Cater and Anderson, Bayley writes that the investigation by newspapers
of "McCarthy's affairs was no less thorough [than the Watergate investi-
gation], and no minor wrongdoing was left undisclosed. But no one cared.
McCarthy's character was not important; only his accusations were."[55]

It is clear, however, that the wire services had a real time disadvantge
when it came to investigative reporting. Deadlines based upon competition forced the services to cover the "what." The "why" and "how" to
McCarthy stories came across the wires well after many papers had gone
to print. Wire services were also handicapped because of financial considerations. They simply couldn't afford to offend clients. To a McCarthy
supporter, an in-depth investigative piece about the senator "looked like
anti-McCarthy prejudice."[56]

History tells us, of course, that McCarthy not only got on the agenda;
he dominated it for four years. It was at the beginning, in the first month
after the Wheeling speech, when the decision to alter the agenda might
have been made. About this, Bayley writes: "What the press did that
month was important because it created first impressions—impressions
that lasted years, perhaps still last, in some minds."[57]

Once he became a major news figure, a natural evolution of events
occurred. In the linear world of politics, news coverage confers status and
status often confers money. Hate groups and authoritarians favoring a
stronger policing of leftist ideologies supported McCarthy, and a trickle of
funds soon became a substantial outpouring of contributions to stem the
subversive arsenal in America.[58] With this, McCarthy almost immediately
gained support from elite power groups.[59]

Of course, not just elite groups supported McCarthy. A substantial
segment of the public may have seen his anticommunism as a crusade to
cleanse the American establishment of what many conservatives viewed
as a naive liberalism eating away at the country from the inside.[60] Indeed,
for McCarthy and some of his constituents, the problem with America was

domestic subversion that was specifically the handiwork of the Democratic Party.[61] In addition, many Americans thought the federal government too pro labor at the expense of free enterprise, and McCarthy as someone who would fight the growing power of the labor organizations. David Oshinsky writes that some of McCarthy's supporters looked to him because "as the major political figure of that era he had become a symbol of defiance—a politician who refused to kowtow to new and Fair Dealers and their 'abusive doctrines.' "[62]

McCarthy's attack on liberalism may have backfired in a way he never expected. Diana Trilling writes that the senator was "[t]he greatest gift our country could have made to the Soviet Union. He robbed anti-communism of its base in liberalism."[63]

Religion may have played a role in McCarthy's popularity. The senator was Catholic, and many people felt that as McCarthyism grew in popularity, Catholic McCarthyites would increase in number and provide him with an immense power base. In his book about McCarthy and Catholicism, however, Donald Crosby found this was probably more myth than fact.[64]

Although an argument can be made that McCarthy's appeal was more broad based than anticommunism, it was the possibility of a Communist conspiracy that kept the McCarthy train on track. The groundwork for this was finely constructed by the large number of un-American investigating committees during the period, the very existence of which lent support to the timeless "Where there's smoke, there must be fire." Concern therefore existed that America's institutions were under attack by an internal Communist conspiracy.[65] From 1950 to 1954, for example, hearings were held to investigate Communist infiltration and/or subversion in labor unions, in the Department of Defense, in the State Department, in The Voice of America, in the United States Army, in the Printing Office, in the telegraph industry, in the motion picture industry, in the radio-television industry, and in secondary, high school, and college education.[66]

In the end, someone had to step forward to consolidate the movement. The junior senator from Wisconsin, the man voted the worst senator in Congress, became that person. In part, it was by accident. It was Providence. But it was also McCarthy. For when the opportunity presented itself, he seized it. He mastered the art of distortion. He misread documents; he created facts to fit either the audience or the moment, or both; when caught in an inaccuracy, he altered the statements, always claiming it wasn't altered.[67]

Simply, McCarthy had a knack for publicity perhaps unmatched by any politician of his generation.[68] There was a P. T. Barnum quality about his politics and press maneuverings and is perhaps the reason he was, if not popular with reporters, often difficult to dislike.

At times McCarthy seemed like a man dancing without music. He had no plan, which was probably the best plan. First here, then there. Without a rational plan and acting on impulse, neither his actions nor his motives were easily deciphered. Reporters, as well as the public, could only discern what they could understand.

Meanwhile, McCarthy kept on dancing.

NOTES

1. Thomas C. Reeves, ed., *McCarthyism* (Hinsdale, IL: Dryden Press, 1973); Robert Griffith, "The Making of a Demagogue," in ibid.; and Richard Rovere, *Senator Joe McCarthy* (New York: Harper & Row, 1959), 123. The quote is mentioned in each book.

2. Speech by Senator Joseph McCarthy, 20 February 1950, "Communists in Government–Wheeling Speech," *Major Speeches and Debates of Senator McCarthy: 1950-1951* (Washington, DC: U.S. Government Printing Office, 1953).

3. Edwin Bayley, *Joe McCarthy and the Press* (New York: Pantheon Books, 1981), 20.

4. Ibid., 20-21.

5. Ibid., 29.

6. Rovere, *Senator Joe McCarthy*, 132.

7. Ibid., 138-139.

8. Ibid., 139.

9. Ibid., 140.

10. Jack Anderson and Ronald W. May, *McCarthy: The Man, The Senator, the "Ism"* (Boston: Beacon Press, 1952), 249.

11. Richard M. Fried, *Nightmare in Red: The McCarthy Era in Perspective* (New York: Oxford University Press, 1990), 17-23.

12. New York *Times*, 22 February 1950.

13. New York *Times*, 9 March 1950.

14. New York *Times*, 23 March 1950.

15. Rovere, *Senator Joe McCarthy*, 151.

16. Ibid., 150.

17. Robert Griffith, *The Politics of Fear* (Lexington: University Press of Kentucky, 1970), 76.

18. Bayley, *Joe McCarthy and the Press*, 71.

19. Ibid., p. 70. (The author reports that the statement was in a letter by Alexander to Alfred Friendly, 28 February 1977.)

20. Rovere, *Senator Joe McCarthy*, 153.

21. Richard M. Fried, *Men Against McCarthy* (New York: Columbia University Press, 1976), 171.

22. *Cong. Record* 97 (14 June 1951): 6556-6603. For more information about General Marshall, see Anderson and May, *McCarthy*, 236-242, Rovere, *Senator Joe McCarthy*, 171-178, and Mark A. Stoler, *George C. Marshall: Soldier-Statesman of the American Century* (Boston: Twayne Publishers, 1989).

23. *Cong. Record* 97 (21 April 1951): 4259-70, (14 June 1951): 6556-6603.

24. Rovere, *Senator Joe McCarthy*, 177-178. See also Fried, *Nightmare in Red: The*

McCarthy Era in Perspective, 135-137.

25. Ibid., 136-137. See also Rovere, *Senator Joe McCarthy*, 195.

26. *Dictionary of American Biography*, Supplement Six, 1956-1960 (New York: Charles Scribner & Sons, 1980), 405.

27. Ibid.

28. Rovere, *Senator Joe McCarthy*, 207.

29. Fried, *Men Against McCarthy*, 279.

30. *Communist Infiltration in the Army*, 83rd Cong., 2nd sess., 1954, 107-108.

31. Griffith, "The Making of a Demagogue," 249.

32. Fried, *Men Against McCarthy*, 281.

33. Ibid.

34. Griffith, "The Making of a Demagogue," 261.

35. Fried, *Men Against McCarthy*, 282.

36. Rovere, *Senator Joe McCarthy*, 217-218.

37. Fried, *Men Against McCarthy*, 292-313.

38. Senate Resolution 301, 2 December 1954.

39. Daniel J. Boorstin, *The Image: A Guide to Pseudo-Events in America* (New York: Atheneum, 1980), 57.

40. Ibid., 22.

41. Ibid., 23.

42. Ibid., 14.

43. Ibid., 7-12.

44. Ibid., 14.

45. Ibid., 23.

46. David Halberstam, *The Fifties* (New York: Villard Press, 1993), 55.

47. Ibid.

48. Ibid.

49. Ibid.

50. Douglass Cater, "The Captive Press," *The Reporter* 2 (6 June 1950): 18.

51. Rovere, *Senator Joe McCarthy*, 166

52. Bayley, *Joe McCarthy and the Press*, 16.

53. Fried, *Men Against McCarthy*, 3-5. See also Bayley, *Joe McCarthy and the Press*, 17.

54. Fried, *Men Against McCarthy*, 4.

55. Bayley, *Joe McCarthy and the Press*, 216.

56. Ibid., 215.

57. Ibid., 16.

58. Rovere, *Senator Joe McCarthy*, 142.

59. Michael Paul Rogin, "Pluralists and Agrarian Radicalism," in Reeves, *McCarthyism*.

60. Symour Martin Lipset, "An Instrument Rather Than Creator," In Reeves, *McCarthyism*. See also Fried, *Nightmare in Red*, 17.

61. Halberstam, *The Fifties*, 53.

62. David M. Oshinsky, *Senator Joseph McCarthy and the American Labor Movement* (Columbia: University of Missouri Press, 1976), 183.

63. Diana Trilling, "How McCarthy Gave Anti-Communism a Bad Name," *Newsweek*, 11 January 1993, 32.

64. Donald F. Crosby, *God, Church and Flag: Senator Joseph R. McCarthy and the*

Catholic Church, 1950-1957 (Chapel Hill: The University of North Carolina Press, 1978), 69-70.

65. Dewitte Holland, *America in Controversy: History of American Public Address* (Dubuque, IA: William C. Brown, 1973), 352.

66. See Congressional Record during 1950-1954.

67. Nathan Glazer, "The Methods of Senator McCarthy," in Reeves, *McCarthyism.*

68. Rovere, *Senator Joe McCarthy*, 162.

11 ⇀

THE UNRAVELING
OF AMERICA

Arthur Kaul

*The Negroes of this country . . . are very well placed indeed to precipitate
chaos and bring down the curtain on the American dream.*
James Baldwin, *The Fire Next Time*[1]

Vietnam was where the Trail of Tears was headed all along
Michael Herr, *Dispatches*[2]

It was a time for our viciousness.
Bob Greene, *"Blaming LBJ"*[3]

America unraveled in the Sixties.

An assassin's bullets fired from a book depository building in Dallas
in November 1963 ended President John F. Kennedy's "New Frontier."
Five years later, Nobel Peace Prize winner Martin Luther King Jr. and U.S.
Senator Robert F. Kennedy were gunned down. Scores of American cities
exploded into "race riots," sending President Lyndon B. Johnson's "Great
Society" up in smoke. The war in Vietnam rapidly escalated into a "credibility gap" that entered the national political vocabulary with all the fe-
rocity of the Tet offensive. The 1968 Democratic National Convention in
Chicago set the stage for a "police riot"—and the whole world watched
the chaotic spectacle. Television entered millions of American homes in
the 1960s when Mayberry was an idyll of national life, its city limits sym-
bolically stretching to the Mekong Delta.

Urban violence and the Vietnam War sent shock waves through mass-mediated American culture between 1964 and 1968. Media coverage of urban violence prompted a devastating critique of its failure to communicate the alienation and estrangement of inner-city American minorities and the impact of racism in American society. The Vietnam War showed the nation the limits of its cold war military and political power and fundamentally altered America's role in the world. American news media were deeply implicated in the cultural crisis that beset a nation fighting a war in Southeast Asia and in the streets of its own cities. America unraveled—on the front page and on prime time—before our very eyes.

A decade after the U.S. Supreme Court in 1954 declared segregated public schools and the "separate but equal" doctrine unconstitutional, passage of the 1964 Civil Rights Act signaled modest success for the civil rights movement. President Lyndon B. Johnson's "Great Society" legislative agenda declared "war on poverty" with millions of dollars pumped into an array of education, health, housing, urban renewal, and welfare programs. Yet America's cities simmered. Harlem burned in 1964. The Watts area of Los Angeles exploded in six days of rioting in 1965, killing 35 and injuring 900. A year later, the Hough ghetto of Cleveland erupted in violence.[4]

Riots broke out in 70 American cities during the summer of 1967—40 in two weeks in July—with Newark and Detroit surpassing Watts to set new standards for urban violence. "When the ghetto finally exploded one muggy night last week," Newsweek said of Newark, "the riot was the worst since Watts for sheer destructive fury—and the only surprise in the aftermath was that the blowup has been so long in coming."[5] New Jersey Governor Richard Hughes declared Newark a "city in open rebellion . . . the line between the jungle and the law might as well be drawn here as any place in America," the governor said when he called up 2600 National Guard troops to quell the riot that resulted in 21 deaths, 1,600 arrests and property damage "into the millions."[6] By early August, Newsweek declared "Detroit's bloody arithmetic"—41 deaths, 2250 injuries, 4000 arrests, $250 million in property losses—"an American tragedy," "the new benchmark," and "a monument to the most devastating race riot in U.S. history—and a symbol of a domestic crisis grown graver than any since the Civil War."[7]

Images of war were interspersed with metaphors of epidemics, plagues, delerium and despair in national newsmagazines' assessments of the riots. Detroit was a "theater of war" with "combat zones," "paratroopers" fighting a "guerrilla war" with "looters" and "snipers."[8] "Busload after busload of POWs spilled out at jails," Newsweek wrote. [9] "It looks like Berlin in 1945," Time quoted Detroit Mayor Jerome Cavanagh.[10] Congressional reaction to Newark was straightforward: "[P]raise the Guard and pass the ammunition."[11] The nation needed "to extricate itself from a home-front war grown deeper, graver and more intractable than the distant battle for Vietnam," *Newsweek* wrote.[12] "An ugly mood of nihilism and despair" became a "mob delirium," according to *Time*.[13] *Newsweek*'s "1967 fever chart," a map showing the locations of "major" and "minor" outbreaks in "The U.S. Epidemic of Negro Riots," told readers: "No city seemed safe from the virus of racial violence."[14] "Yet, the message of this longest, hottest summer was plain: America could no longer run away from the endemic sickness of her cities," *Newsweek* wrote, the riots representing "the desperate, even suicidal revolt of the invisible man."[15]

President Lyndon Johnson spoke on national television July 27, 1967, about the week's riots. "We have endured a week such as no Nation should live through: a time of violence and tragedy."[16]

Two days later he issued Executive Order 11365 to establish an 11-member National Advisory Commission on Civil Disorders, telling the newly appointed Commission Chairman, Illinois Governor Otto Kerner, and the vice chairman, New York Mayor John Lindsay: "The American people are deeply disturbed. . . . No society can tolerate massive violence, any more than a body can tolerate massive disease. And we in America shall not tolerate it."[17]

The president charged the Advisory Commission with the task of avoiding "conventional wisdom" to answer three basic questions about the riots: What happened? Why did it happen? What can be done to prevent it from happening again and again?[18] Kerner told *Newsweek*: "We are being asked to probe into the soul of America."[19] In addition, President Johnson asked 14 other questions the Commission should address, including: "What effect do the mass media have on the riots?"[20]

The U.S. Justice Department's Office of Media Relations offered its own assessment of the news media and racial disorders in an October 12, 1967, paper distributed at a conference at Columbia University in New York City. The Justice Department found "ample evidence," based on "field reports" from Buffalo, Detroit, Houston and Newark, that "the media were the single most important factor helping to build tensions in some communities."[21] The "lack of understanding or plain indifference by most white persons" to the "socio economic ailments that plague our urban centers," the Justice Department stated, poses "the challenge to the news media."[22] News media were most vulnerable to criticism that their "perspective" in covering the disturbances amounted to "war correspondents attached to a conquering army"; Newark's coverage gave the impression of "a battle of 'good guys' in blues and fatigues against hordes of black snipers, bombers, and looters."[23] "If this nation is to veer from a course toward increasing racial polarization," the Justice Department stated, "the media will have to view racial disorders as much more than a Memorial Day casualty toll."

The phrase, "the white press," must cease to come so easily to the lips of Negroes. The challenge to the news media is whether they can do more than chronicle the fears and discomforts of whites caused by Negroes. The media should attempt to convey to both black and white the underlying causes of the dilemma and what must be done to resolve it.[24]

Phrasings in the Justice Department's final sentence—"underlying causes of the dilemma and what must be done to resolve it"—would reverberate through the Kerner Commission's report.

The Kerner Commission issued its massive report on March 1, 1968, devoting an entire chapter to "The News Media and the Disorders." The commission concluded that press coverage was "an exaggeration of both mood and event" and the media failed to report adequately on "the causes and consequences of civil disorders and the underlying problems of race relations."[25]

The disorders were "less destructive, less widespread, and less a black-white confrontation than most people believed," the commission observed, expressing concern that "millions of other Americans, who must rely on the mass media, likewise formed incorrect impressions and judgments."[26] For example, the Commission was critical of news reports of Detroit's property damage that put the figure in excess of $500 million when subsequent investigation showed damages between $40 and $45 million.[27] News media also were criticized for such "gross flaws" as " 'scare' headlines," "rumors that had no basis in fact," "staged riot events for the cameras" and "coverage of the disorders . . . [that] tended to define the events as black-white confrontations."[28]

A major thrust of the Kerner Commission's criticism focused less on the news media's coverage of the summer disorders than on reportorial omissions. The news media failed to "analyze and report adequately on racial problems" and to "meet the Negro's legitimate expectations in journalism" in large measure because they "report and write from the standpoint of a white man's world."[29] And in even stronger rhetoric, the Kerner Commission complained that American news media have "failed to communicate."

They have not communicated to the majority of their audience—which is white—a sense of the degradation, misery, and hopelessness of living in the ghetto. They have not communicated to whites a feeling for the difficulties and frustrations of being a Negro in the United States. They have not shown understanding or appreciation of—and thus have not communicated—a sense of Negro culture, thought, or history. . . . The world that television and newspapers offer to their black audience is almost totally white, in both appearance and attitude.[30]

The news media could make a contribution of "inestimable importance" to race relations, the Kerner Commission stated, simply by treating ordinary news about Negroes as other groups are treated. "By failing to portray the Negro as a matter of routine and in the context of the total society, the news media have," the commission charged, "contributed to the black-white schism in this country."[31] The Kerner Commission concluded its assessment of the news media and race relations with the comment that "the press has too long basked in a white world, looking out of it, if at all, with white men's eyes and a white perspective. That is no longer good enough."[32]

Paradoxically, the Kerner Commission's critical preoccupation with the "white press" created its own "failure to communicate." The Commission's report was strategically silent about the inadequacies of the "black press"—171 dailies, weeklies, and semiweeklies—and its news coverage during the summer racial disorders. Bernard Roshco's analysis of black newspapers, published several months before the Kerner Commission released its report, found that "the truly big racial stories have grown beyond their scope."[33] Caught in the "time-lag of the weekly press," financially strapped to "chase distant stories on their own or to buy top-flight coverage from news services," and "outgunned" by national magazines and television, Roshco wrote, "the Negro papers are usually out last with the least."[34] The black press provided exclusive and significant commentary in editorials, columns, and letters to the editor that "explained why Negroes thought the cities were exploding," providing "the essential element missing from the commentary printed in the daily press—an explicitly Negro interpretation of what the white politicians were saying and doing."[35] Roshco found "seemingly unanimous" black press editorial opposition to violence, riots, and extremist militancy. The Baltimore *Afro-American* in September 1967, for example, editorially responded to a letter from black power activist H. Rap Brown that castigated the black press for lack of militancy: "We see a very clear distinction between constructive militancy and destructive stupidity. In our view H. Rap Brown has set out on a perilous journey upon which we shall not embark, thank you."[36] Nevertheless, Roshco discovered in the black press "a specifically Negro side to the race-and-riot story, and it does not reach most white Americans."[37]

The Kerner Commission noted two "brilliant exceptions" to its relentless criticism of mainstream media, commending the Detroit *Free Press* for its August 20–22, 1967, "landmark survey of local Negro attitudes and grievances" and *Newsweek*'s November 20, 1967, special issue on "The Negro American—What Must Be Done." The *Free Press* embarked on a postriot project that combined "the precision of the scholar with the speed and efficiency of the journalist" to produce a three-part series based on quantitative social science survey research. According to Philip Meyer, who directed the *Free Press* project, the study turned up a few surprises:

Most Negroes generally agreed with the pre-riot image of Detroit as progressive in race relations. This progress, by raising hopes, was, ironically, a contributing cause to the riot.[38]

Newsweek's special issue acknowledged that "the black riots—the most sustained spasm of civil disorder in the violent history of a violent country—have already changed America's comfortable image of itself," prompting "the growing fear that the nation is drifting inexorably toward a showdown between its white majority and its black minority."[39] The newsmagazine devoted long articles to the "ABC's of Race," "Black Poverty," "Thinking Black," among others, concluding with a "twelve-point program for action now" in the areas of "presidential leadership," "top level direction," "inflation control," "state and local effort," "the private sector," "employment," "welfare," "housing," "education," "riot control," "enforcement powers," and "ghetto business." Unlike the Kerner Commission, *Newsweek* did not put the news media in its program of "what must be done" to counteract the "national atmosphere of drift and civil disorder" straining race relations in the nation.

One month and four days after the release of the *Report of the National Advisory Commission on Civil Disorders*, Nobel Peace Prize winner and civil rights activist Martin Luther King Jr. was assassinated in Memphis, Tennessee, the victim of a sniper's bullet. Four thousand National Guard troops were ordered into Memphis, where a curfew was imposed and sporadic shootings, fires, and looting broke out in the Negro districts and spread over the city.[40] The next day, President Johnson ordered 4000 regular army and National Guard troops into Washington, D.C., the New York *Times* reported, "to try to end riotous looting, burglarizing and burning by roving bands of Negro youths."[41] Washington looked like "the besieged capital of a banana republic with helmeted combat troops, bayoneted rifles at the ready, guarding the White House and a light-machine gun post defending the steps of the Capitol."[42] Vandalism, violence, and looting spread throughout more than two dozen American cities. *Newsweek* wrote:

It was Pandora's box flung open—an apocalyptic act that loosed the furies brooding in the shadows of America's sullen ghettos . . . a black rampage that subjected the U.S. to the most widespread spasm of racial disorder in its violent history.[43]

With the Kerner Commission criticism fresh in mind, according to Marvin Barrett, the news media made "a conscious attempt . . . to perform a constructive function which . . . did in many instances succeed in damping rather than inflaming the violence that followed the assassination."[44] Television and radio were "remarkably sensitive to their potential for stirring up trouble," Barrett wrote.

From coast to coast wherever violence flared the rules were: Don't put it on live, check all rumors before airing them, use unmarked cars, shoot only with available light, don't be obtrusive, tone down the emotion.[45]

Two months later, on June 5, 1968, yet another assassination—U.S. Sen. Robert F. Kennedy shortly after winning the California Democratic primary—brought the issue of violence once again into the mass-mediated public consciousness. The whole country had become "a vast hospital waiting room," waiting via television for the latest word on the condition of late President John F. Kennedy's younger brother. During the evening news, CBS News commentator Eric Sevareid wondered aloud if the media's preoccupation with violence contributed to Kennedy's death: "We ought . . . to think again about the cult of violence in our popular culture, the ideology of those who kill, in our television, films, literature and plays. The leaders of the first such industry to put a stop to all this will surely be honored men."[46] President Johnson's response to the killings of King and Kennedy was to form yet another blue-ribbon panel, the National Commission on the Causes and Prevention of Violence.

Nationally televised violence in Chicago during the Democratic National Convention in August 1968 brought the Vietnam War to the nation's second-largest city and into millions of American homes. Thousands of anti–Vietnam War demonstrators—some peaceful, some provocateurs—converged on the convention city to protest under the watchful eyes of more than 300 newsmen and photographers assigned to cover the convention. Demonstrators hurled epithets and obscenities, rocks, and sticks at police already on edge by widely published threats to disrupt the convention. Police retaliated, attacking demonstrators, bystanders, and media representatives. A study team under the direction of Chicago attorney Daniel Walker prepared an extensive report on the convention-week violence that was submitted to the National Commission on the Causes and Prevention of Violence in November 1968. Based on more than 3400 statements of eyewitnesses and participants, 20,000 pages of testimony, and 180 hours of local and network television film, the Walker Report found that "police violence against media representatives" was "plainly deliberate." "Newsmen and photographers were singled out for assault, and their equipment deliberately damaged."[47] Twenty percent of the press corps assigned to cover the convention were involved in incidents causing injury, damage to equipment, or arrest. For example, the Walker Report reproduced a partial transcript of an encounter between Chicago police and free-lance photographer Dan Morrill and NBC cameraman John Evans:

Unidentified Voice: *Give me that.*
Dan Morrill: *I'm sorry, I apologize, I apologize, please, I apologize.*
Unidentified Voice: *Give me the film.*

Dan Morrill: *I won't (?) give you the film.*
John Evans: *Why do you want the film, officer?*
Unidentified Voice: *None of your business.*
John Evans: *You don't have to surrender that film, sir.*
Dan Morrill: *No, I'll give it to him.*
Unidentified Voice: *Thank you.*
Unidentified Voice: *Mind your own business.*
Unidentified Voice: *Who are you?*
John Evans: *NBC News, who are you?*

Evans then was clubbed on the head, suffering a laceration that required six stitches.[48] *Newsweek* news editor Hal Bruno sent a telegram to
Chicago Mayor Richard Daley complaining that "our reporters and photographers were subject to unprovoked attacks by Chicago policemen."[49]
The Walker Report concluded that a dispassionate reading of the hundreds
of statements describing convention-week events provided convincing
evidence that law enforcement's "indiscriminate" and "unrestrained" attacks amounted to "a police riot."[50]

Media coverage of the Democratic National Convention set off a barrage of criticism. "Anyone who has read the letters column in his local
newspaper is not likely to challenge Mayor Richard J. Daley's contention
that his mail on the subject overwhelmingly praised the conduct of the
Chicago police," Jules Whitcover wrote in a postconvention analysis. "The
judgment carries with it a censure, specific or implied, that the press was
lying or distorting the facts when it reported that heads were being cracked
in Chicago without sufficient provocation."[51]

Whitcover wrote that public reaction to convention media coverage
disclosed "the American press has a credibility gap as wide as the one that
has afflicted President Johnson."[52] The unparalleled "crisis of credibility"
was an understandable result of "turbulent times," Whitcover stated. "In
a nation longing for peace at home and abroad, the messenger of conflict
inevitably is not going to be a welcome one."[53]

Whitcover's reference to foreign affairs proved no less accurate in its
application to the coverage of the Vietnam War, an oil and vinegar mix of
media and Administration credibility. From the beginning of the U.S. involvement, communication between the press and the administration, as
well as the press and the military, seemed either strained, garbled, or mis-
understood.

At the outset of a conversation with New York *Times* publisher
Arthur Ochs Sulzberger on October 22, 1963, President John F. Kennedy
asked: "What do you think of your young man in Saigon?" The young
man in Saigon was the *Times'* 29-year-old correspondent David
Halberstam whose Vietnam dispatches contradicted the Kennedy
administration's optimistic view of military and political affairs. Presi-

dent Kennedy suggested that Halberstam was too close to the story and should be reassigned. Sulzberger refused, canceling the correspondent's scheduled two-week holiday for fear of giving the impression that the publisher had acquiesced to pressure.[54]

The President's question came 11 days after *Time* magazine published a caustic critique of the Saigon press corps for its "we're-losing-the-war attitude." "Have they given their readers an unduly pessimistic view of the progress of the war and the quality of the Diem government?" *Time* asked. The New York *Herald Tribune's* Marguerite Higgins complained, "Reporters here would like to see us lose the war to prove they're right," and columnist Joseph Alsop characterized the Saigon correspondents as "young crusaders."[55] *Time*'s earlier assault on the correspondents' "view from Saigon" published in late September complained:

The newsmen have themselves become part of South Viet Nam's confusion; they have covered a complex situation from only one angle, as if their own conclusions offered all the necessary illumination. Such reporting is prone to distortions. The complicated greys of a complicated country fade into oversimplified blacks and whites. . . . [T]he correspondents have taken sides.[56]

Time's Southeast Asia bureau chief Charles Mohr was so incensed over the articles he resigned. In March 1964, shortly before winning the Pulitzer Prize for international reporting, Halberstam commented:

We maintained an independent position. While we were sympathetic to the aims of the U.S. government, we had to be critical of the representatives of our government who created a policy of optimism about the war that simply was not justified.[57]

The Halberstam/Mohr affairs, "the most violent argument over journalistic practice since the McCarthy era,"[58] signaled an initial breach in the emerging credibility gap between government and the media over American involvement in Vietnam.

On August 7, 1964, President Johnson was granted authority to "take all necessary measures" to prevent "further aggression" against American forces in Vietnam when Congress passed the Tonkin Gulf Resolution. The U.S. House of Representatives unanimously passed the resolution; the Senate approved with only two dissenting votes. Senator Wayne Morse of Oregon told his colleagues that "the place to settle the controversy is not on the battlefield but around the conference table," prophetically warning that they would "live to regret" their support of the resolution giving the president unbridled power to escalate American military involvement in Vietnam. The other dissenter, Ernest Gruening of Alaska, told the Senate that "all Vietnam is not worth the life of a single American boy."[59] More than 52,000 Americans died in the Vietnam conflict.

In the years leading up to the Tet offensive of January 1968, television coverage of the Vietnam conflict—Michael Arlen dubbed it America's first "living room war"[60]—presented flickering images of successful anti-Communist American intervention in Southeast Asia. ABC, CBS, and NBC ran nearly three minutes of Vietnam news daily, the coverage fluctuating in relation to America's combat role. Combat coverage was antiseptic, only minuscule amounts of it portraying graphic details of the dead, dying, and wounded.[61] The three networks' policies prohibited showing graphic film of wounded American soldiers and Vietnamese civilians, and nightly news editors routinely deleted detailed grisly footage believed to be inappropriate for dinnertime viewing; a CBS network policy prohibited showing identifiable American soldiers until their families had been notified.[62] Combat stories emphasized American "initiative"—bombings, patrols, and troop landings—and military technology.

Weekly casualty statistics began in September 1965, with daily combat summaries originating from government public relations offices, including the daily Saigon briefings that came to be known derisively as the "Five O'clock Follies."[63] Briefings came to sound like a "Naming of the Parts, and the language was used as a cosmetic, but one that diminished beauty," *Esquire* magazine correspondent Michael Herr later wrote. He added that "it would be as impossible to know what Vietnam looked like from reading most newspaper stories as it would be to know how it smelled."[64]

NBC correspondent Floyd Kalber told the audience of a network special on Vietnam: "To the degree that we in the media paid any attention at all to that small, dirty war in those years, we almost wholly reported the position of the Government."[65]

A legendary exception to the military-controlled number-driven Vietnam coverage was Morley Safer's CBS News story "The Burning of the Village of Cam Ne," aired on August 5, 1965. Film footage showed U.S. Marines with cigarette lighters setting fire to the huts of Cam Ne in retaliation for a Vietcong attack. With burning huts in the background, Safer told an *Evening News with Walter Cronkite* audience of 15 million: "This is what the war in Viet Nam is all about."

Today's operation is the frustration of Vietnam in miniature. There is little doubt that American firepower can win a military victory. But to a Vietnamese peasant whose home means a lifetime of back-breaking labor—it will take more than Presidential promises to convince him that we are on his side.[66]

Critics of the Cam Ne story, including Pentagon spokesman Arthur Sylvester, remembered for his glib quip that government has a "right to lie," complained that the vivid footage and narrative were "unpatriotic" in their one-sided and negative portrayal of American soldiers in Vietnam and the policies that put them there.[67]

More strident criticism greeted New York *Times* correspondent Harrison E. Salisbury's controversial "behind the lines" reports from North Vietnam's capital of Hanoi between December 25, 1966, and January 9, 1967. His dispatches directly contradicted the Johnson administration's position that the escalation of bombing North Vietnam was aimed only at military targets. The President was elected in November 1964 "by setting his face firmly against deeper involvement in Vietnam," Salisbury wrote. "He had rejected Barry Goldwater's call for bombing of the North."[68] In his first story, dated December 24 and published in the *Time*'s Christmas Day edition, Salisbury wrote:

Contrary to the impression given by United States communiqués, on the spot inspection indicates that American bombing has been inflicting considerable civilian casualties in Hanoi and its environs.[69]

A Defense Department statement issued the next day tersely acknowledged: "It is impossible to avoid all damage to civilian areas."[70] Salisbury's second story, published on December 27, described "block after block of utter desolation" in Nam Dinh: "United States planes are dropping an enormous weight of explosives on purely civilian targets...it is the civilians who have taken the punishment."[71] Three days later, "Pentagon sources" called Salisbury's civilian casualty figures "grossly exaggerated."[72] The Hanoi reports touched off domestic media criticism before Salisbury even arrived back in New York. William Randolph Hearst Jr.'s New Year's Day column compared him to World War II propagandist Tokyo Rose; the Washington *Post*'s Chalmers Roberts tagged Salisbury for being "Ho's chosen instrument"; and columnist Joseph Alsop complained that Salisbury had lent "the authority of his byline to enemy propaganda."[73]

Two other journalists visited Hanoi in January 1967—former Arkansas *Gazette* Editor Harry Ashmore and Miami *News* Editor William C. Baggs—both affirming Salisbury's assessments of civilian damages. Baggs's series of articles for the Associated Press confirmed that neighborhoods of Nam Dinh with no military value had been bombed. On January 21, an Associated Press story quoting "intelligence sources" said that "aerial photographs showed considerable damage to civilian structures as well as to military targets in some places in North Viet Nam."[74] The credibility gap widened.

Walter Lippmann's aggressively acerbic criticism of President Johnson in March 1967 enshrined "credibility gap" in a two-part column following a "farewell address" to the Federal City Club. "I would have carved on the portals of the National Press Club: 'Put Not Your Trust in Princes,' " he told an admiring audience.[75] Johnson's press relations style included calculated attempts to court columnists, publishers, and reporters like any other potent political interest group. Lippmann's immense influence among Washington's media and political elite prompted Johnson early on to make concerted efforts to win the columnist's support for the administration's Vietnam policy.[76] Lippmann believed the president had deliberately "misled" him during a 1965 conversation—"He was either lying to me or to the others," Lippmann later said—about Vietnam War policy.[77]

The two-part "Credibility Gap" columns Lippmann authored in late March 1967 culminated from that disenchantment. The credibility gap phrase was a "polite euphemism for deception" that put the nation in the "perilous position of not believing that it can trust its government," Lippmann wrote.

[T]here is no longer much pretense that the news is not being manipulated in order to make the Congress, the newspapers, the networks, and the public at large support the President.[78]

The credibility gap was the result of "a deliberate policy of artificial manipulation of official news," Lippmann wrote.

The purpose of this manipulation is to create a consensus for the President, to stifle debate about his aims and his policies, to thwart deep probing into what has already happened, what is actually happening, what is going to happen.[79]

Moreover, Lippmann charged President Johnson with being "a pathologically secretive man" who believed in his right to manipulate the news in his own political interest.[80]

The phrase "credibility gap," first used in a May 1965 New York *Herald Tribune* headline,[81] had become a well-established commonplace in the mounting critical vocabulary of the Vietnam War.

By July 1967, only weeks before the urban riots exploded, *Newsweek* described America as "A Nation at Odds" over the Vietnam war. "Cleft by doubts and tormented by frustration," *Newsweek* wrote, America was "haunted by its most corrosively ambiguous foreign adventure—"

a bloody, costly jungle war half a world away that has etched the tragedy of Vietnam into the American soul. . . . More than anything, Vietnam had made Americans question their fundamental assumptions about themselves and their country. . . . [T]he problem is distilled into a single, cryptic phrase: the credibility gap.[82]

The Vietnam "victory gap" had "punctured the myth of American innocence," *Newsweek* wrote, and "served as the nation's sobering introduction to the limits of America's seemingly unlimited power." The newsmagazine found "no romance in jet-strewn napalm, in raids by mammoth B-52s on remote jungle trails, in murderous battles for hills known

only as numbers or obscure villages abandoned as soon as they are captured."[83] Noting that "never in the history of warfare has so much information been inflicted upon so many," *Newsweek* found "room for improvement" in the media's Vietnam coverage, blaming both the press for "scant-
ing stories it finds difficult to tell" and the administration for "repeated
self-delusion, if not necessarily deliberate deceit."[84] "Nobody really believes the pipe dreams of the earlier days anymore," David Halberstam
told *Newsweek*.[85] A month later, President Johnson held his first televised
press conference since March, indignantly dismissing as "nothing more
than propaganda" press reports that the Vietnam War was in stalemate.[86]

A vocal New Left on many American college campuses led a growing
youth-driven antiwar movement that staged highly visible protest demonstrations in the spring and fall of 1967. Anti-Vietnam demonstrations in
New York City in April drew 100,000 protesters. Thousands arrived in
Washington, D.C., in October to stage "the biggest 'peace' demonstration
in the history of the nation's capital" at the Lincoln Memorial and the Pentagon.[87] Protesters included such high-profile figures as novelist Norman
Mailer and Dr. Benjamin Spock, many carrying placards saying "Babies
Are Not for Burning" and "Dump Johnson," waving red and blue Vietcong
flags, chanting, "Hell, No, We Won't Go," and burning their draft cards.[88]

Editorial support of the administration's Vietnam War policy showed
strains in fall 1967. "A gradual shift has taken place in the support that a
majority of U.S. newspapers had been giving President Johnson's policies
in Vietnam," *Time* reported in late October.[89] Three days later, *Newsweek*'s
"Press" column expressed "doubts about Vietnam": "More and more, U.S.
newspapers and magazines are becoming impatient with Administration
policy in Vietnam and inclined to nest with the doves."[90] Many newspapers' editorial pages worried over continuing escalation of U.S. bombing
in Vietnam where American troop strength had reached nearly 500,000.
Wall Street *Journal* editor Vermont Royster continued to back the
Administration's bombing policy. "We are skeptical of the view that if we
stopped the bombing, " he said, "those nice people would be so grateful
they would come to the bargaining table."[91] Denver *Post* editorial page
Editor James Idema told *Newsweek*: "The staff is divided, but the prevailing voice right now is in support of the American presence. As far as I can
tell, our policy will continue—at least for the next few weeks."[92] The Tet
offensive changed that fence-straddling.

Some 70,000-plus Communist North Vietnamese troops surged into
more than 100 cities and towns in South Vietnam, including Saigon, during a cease-fire on the eve of Tet, the lunar New Year, on January 30, 1968.
The U.S. Embassy in the heart of Saigon came under attack about 3 a.m. on
January 31, 19 commandos blasting a hole in the embassy wall, entering
the compound and killing five American soldiers before they were killed.
Nearly six and a half hours later, the embassy site was declared secure.

General William Westmoreland delivered a televised statement saying that "the enemy's well-laid plans went afoul"; President Johnson told the White House press corps that the attacks were a "complete failure."[93] Television coverage beamed into 50 million American homes showed dead bodies amid the embassy rubble, with soldiers and civilians caught in scenes of confused fighting in Saigon and other cities. The most shocking film image appeared on February 2 on NBC's *Huntley-Brinkley Report*: Vietnamese General Nguyen Ngoc Loan drew his revolver on a Saigon street, aimed it at the head of a Vietcong officer wearing a plaid shirt, and pulled the trigger—an execution on network television.[94]

"What the hell is going on," Walter Cronkite asked as he watched the Tet offensive film reports flooding into the CBS newsroom. "I thought we were winning the war!"[95] His dismay over government and military pronouncements of Communist failure during the Tet offensive and the startlingly contradictory reports arriving from the field prompted him to visit Vietnam to see for himself. Upon his return, Cronkite's nationally televised "*Report from Vietnam*" on February 27 summed up his findings about who won and who lost the Tet offensive. "The Vietcong did not win by a knockout," he concluded, "but neither did we."

To say we are mired in stalemate seems the only realistic, yet unsatisfactory, conclusion. . . . But it is increasingly clear to this reporter that the only rational way out then will be to negotiate, not as victors, but as an honorable people who lived up to their pledge to defend democracy, and did the best they could.[96]

The Cronkite broadcast "shocked and depressed" the president and "the shock waves rolled through the Government."[97] Three days before the broadcast, the pro–Johnson administration *Wall Street Journal* published an editorial, "The Logic of the Battlefield," that displayed a significant erosion of support for the Vietnam War.

We believe the Administration is duty-bound to recognize that no battle and no war is worth any price, no matter how ruinous, and that in the case of Vietnam it may be failing for the simple reason that the whole place and cause is collapsing from within.

The American people must be prepared for "the bitter taste of a defeat beyond America's power to prevent," the *Journal* warned.[98]

Meanwhile, the New York *Times* on March 10 reported that U.S. General William C. Westmoreland's request for an additional 206,000 American troops for Vietnam set off "a divisive internal debate" within the upper echelon of the Johnson administration.[99] Two days later, U.S. Senator Eugene McCarthy won 42 percent of the vote in the New Hampshire Democratic Primary, emerging as a major challenger to Lyndon Johnson. And four days after McCarthy's impressive primary showing,

U.S. Senator Robert F. Kennedy announced his anti–Vietnam War candidacy for the Democratic presidential nomination. Ironically, on that day, March 16, 1968, the troops of Charlie Company, 1st Battalion, 11th Infantry Brigade, under the command of Second Lieutenant William L. Calley Jr., entered the Vietnamese village of My Lai, killing between 300 and 400 people, most of them women, children, and old men. The My Lai Massacre was not made public for another 18 months.[100]

On March 31, 1968, President Johnson delivered a nationally televised address on Vietnam. He announced a unilateral halt in the U.S. air and naval bombardment of most of North Vietnam to de-escalate the conflict, asking Ho Chi Minh's Hanoi government to "respond positively, and favorably, to this new step toward peace." The United States is "ready to send its representatives to any forum, at any time," Johnson said, "to discuss the means of bringing this ugly war to an end." Acknowledging "division in the American house" and "divisiveness among us all," Johnson pledged to avoid "any personal partisan causes," then announced: "Accordingly, I shall not seek, and I will not accept, the nomination of my party for another term as your president."[101] A day after the Sunday night speech, The New York *Times* editorialized that the president's renunciation reflected "the profound malaise" Americans were experiencing over the Vietnam war and "embittered" domestic race relations.[102]

President Lyndon B. Johnson became a casualty of the credibility crisis. America learned the limits of its power after half a million American soldiers showed up with bombs and napalm and freedom and justice for all. Media coverage of the Vietnam War, with notably few exceptions, uncritically accepted government and military pronouncements. After political and power elites began withdrawing their support of the Vietnam War in the months leading up to the Tet Offensive, an oppositional media finally emerged to challenge American foreign policy in Southeast Asia. Former New York *Times* Vietnam correspondent Neil Sheehan earlier offered a prophetic warning: "[I]n the process of waging this war," he wrote a few months after his return to America in 1966, "we are corrupting ourselves."

I wonder, when I look at the bombed out peasant hamlets, the orphans begging and stealing on the streets of Saigon and the women and children with napalm burns lying on the hospital cots, whether the United States or any nation has the right to inflict this suffering and degradation on another people for its own ends. And I hope we will not, in the name of some anti-Communist crusade, do this again.[103]

In the 1960s, America's well-knit fabric of mass-mediated cultural assumptions and comfortable images of itself unraveled, at home and abroad. Smoldering ruins of the urban riots on American television screens were flash points, quick dissolves of the melting pot myth. Media became scapegoats, victims of the failure to communicate a cultural crisis that few, if any, really understood. America was at war with itself, and no one knew how to call a truce. Many blamed LBJ. Bob Greene's generational mea culpa still holds after all these years: "There was much that he did wrong, and many things should not have been. But in the end, the most lasting thing about these years since 1963 will be the dark unhappiness of America."[104]

NOTES

1. James Baldwin, *The Fire Next Time* (New York: Dial Press, 1963), 102.
2. Michael Herr, *Dispatches* (New York: Alfred A. Knopf, 1977), 151.
3. Bob Greene, "Blaming LBJ," in *Johnny Deadline, Reporter* (Chicago: Nelson-Hall, 1976), 114.
4. "Races: Sparks & Tinder," *Time*, 21 July 1967, 15.
5. "Newark Boils Over," *Newsweek*, 24 July 1967, 21.
6. "Races," 15; "Newark," 22; U.S. *News & World Report*, 7 August 1967.
7. "An American Tragedy, 1967–Detroit," *Newsweek*, 7 August 1967, 18.
8. "Races," 15-21; "Newark," 21-22; "Looting, Burning–Now Guerilla War," *U.S. News & World Report*, 7 August 1967, 23-26.
9. "American Tragedy," *Newsweek*, 20.
10. "The Fire This Time," *Time*, 4 August 1967, 13.
11. "You Can't Run Away," *Newsweek*, 31 July 1967, 17.
12. Ibid., 18.
13. "Fire," 13.
14. "American Tragedy," 31.
15. "Run Away," 17.
16. *Report of the National Advisory Commission on Civil Disorders* [Kerner Commission Report] (New York: Bantam Books, 1968), 538-541.
17. Ibid., 536.
18. Ibid.
19. "American Tragedy," 26.
20. Kerner Commission Report, 537.
21. "The News Media and Racial Disorders–A Preliminary Report," *Columbia Journalism Review* (Fall 1967): 3.
22. Ibid.
23. Ibid., 5.
24. Ibid.
25. Kerner Commission Report, 363.
26. Ibid.
27. Ibid., 364.
28. Ibid., 365.
29. Ibid., 366.
30. Ibid., 383.
31. Ibid.

32. Ibid., 389.

33. Bernard Roshco, "What the Black Press Said Last Summer," *Columbia Journalism Review* (Fall 1967): 6.

34. Ibid.

35. Ibid., 7.

36. Ibid., 8.

37. Ibid., 9.

38. Philip Meyer, "Detroit: When Scholars Joined Journalists," *Columbia Journalism Review* (Fall 1967): 10.

39. "What Must Be Done," *Newsweek*, 20 November 1967, 33.

40. New York *Times*, 5 April 1968.

41. New York *Times*, 6 April 1968.

42. "Seven Days in April," *Newsweek*, 15 April 1968, 31.

43. Ibid.

44. Marvin Barrett, "A Time of Assassins," *Columbia Journalism Review* (Summer 1968): 5.

45. Ibid., 6.

46. Ibid.

47. *Rights in Conflict: The Violent Confrontation of Demonstrators and Police in the Parks and Streets of Chicago During the Week of the Democratic National Convention of 1968, A Report Submitted by Danield Walker, Director of the Chicago Study Team, to the National Commission on the Causes and Prevention of Violence* [Walker Report] (New York: Bantam Books, 1968), 1, 7.

48. Ibid., 317.

49. Ibid.

50. Ibid., 5.

51. Jules Whitcover, "The Press and Chicago: The Truth Hurt," *Columbia Journalism Review*, (Fall 1968): 5. Also see: Edwin Diamond, "Chicago Press: Rebellion and Retrenchment," *Columbia Journalism Review* (Fall 1968): 10-17.

52. Whitcover, "The Press and Chicago."

53. Ibid., 8.

54. David Halberstam, *The Making of a Quagmire* (New York: Random House, 1965), 268; James Aronson, *The Press and the Cold War* (New York: Bobbs-Merrill, 1970), 204-205; Phillip Knightly, *The First Casualty* (New York: Harcourt Brace Jovanovich, 1975), 380.

55. "Foreign Correspondents: The Saigon Story," *Time*, 11 October 1963, 55-56.

56. "Foreign Correspondents: The View From Saigon," *Time*, 30 September 1963, 62.

57. John Hohenberg, *Foreign Correspondence: The Great Reporters and Their Times* (New York: Columbia University Press, 1964), 447. Also see Malcolm W. Browne, "Vietnam Reporting: Three Years of Crisis," *Columbia Journalism Review* (Fall 1964): 4-9.

58. Hohenberg, *Foreign Correspondence*, 446.

59. Stanley Karnow, *Vietnam: A History* (New York: Viking Press, 1983), 375.

60. Michael J. Arlen, *Living-Room War* (New York: Viking, 1969).

61. Oscar Patterson III, "An Analysis of Television Coverage of the Vietnam War," *Journal of Broadcasting* 28 (Fall 1984): 397-404, esp. 401; George Bailey, "Television War: Trends in Network Coverage of Vietnam, 1965-1970," *Journal of Broad-*

casting 20 (Spring 1976): 147-159; Daniel C. Hallin, *The "Uncensored War": The Media and Vietnam* (Berkeley: University of California Press, 1986), 103-158.

62. Edward J. Epstein, "The Televised War," in *Between Fact and Fiction: The Problem of Journalism* (New York: New York Vintage Books, 1975), 218.

63. Ibid.

64. Herr, *Dispatches*, 92-93.

65. Epstein, "The Televised War," 215.

66. Peter Braestrup, *The Big Story: How the American Press and Television Reported and Interpreted the Crisis of Tet 1968 in Vietnam and Washington*, 2 vols. (Boulder, CO: Westview Press, 1977), 1: 42-43; Michael Emery and Edwin Emery, *The Press and America: An Interpretive History of the Mass Media*, 6th ed. (Englewood Cliffs, NJ: Prentice-Hall, 1988), 476; Epstein, *Between Fact and Fiction*, 213.

67. Epstein, "The Televised War," p. 213; Martin Gershen, "The Right to Lie," *Columbia Journalism Review* (Winter 1966/1967): 14-15.

68. Harrison E. Salisbury, *Behind the Lines–Hanoi: December 23, 1966-January 7, 1967* (New York: Harper & Row, 1967), 3.

69. New York *Times*, 25 December 1967.

70. James Boylan, "A Salisbury Chronicle," *Columbia Journalism Review* (Winter 1966/1967): 11.

71. New York *Times*, 27 December 1967.

72. Boylan, *Salisbury Chronicle*, 11.

73. Ibid., 12-13.

74. Ibid., 14.

75. Walter Lippmann, "A Sort of Farewell to Washington," Washington *Post*, 19 March 1967.

76. Kathleen J. Turner, *Lyndon Johnson's Dual War: Vietnam and the Press* (Chicago: University of Chicago Press, 1985), 61-62, 117. Also see Elmer E. Cornwell Jr., "The Johnson Press Relations Style," *Journalism Quarterly* 43 (Spring 1966): 3-9.

77. Ronald Steel, *Walter Lippmann and the American Century* (New York: Viking Books, 1981), 572.

78. Walter Lippmann, "The Credibility Gap–I," Washington *Post*, 28 March 1967.

79. Ibid.

80. Walter Lippmann, "The Credibility Gap–II," Washington *Post*, 30 March 1967.

81. New York *Herald Tribune*, 23 May 1965; Turner, *Lyndon Johnson's Dual War*, 140-141.

82. "A Nation at Odds," *Newsweek*, 10 July 1967, 17.

83. Ibid., 19.

84. Ibid., 84.

85. Ibid.

86. "The Presidency: A Failure of Communication," *Time*, 25 August 1967, 13.

87. "Protest: The Banners of Dissent," *Time*, 27 October 1967, 24.

88. Ibid., 23-24; "Dissenters: Rebels with Many Causes," *Newsweek*, 10 July 1967, 29-30, 33; Bill Davidson, "'Hell, No, We Won't Go,'" *Saturday Evening Post*, 27 January 1968, 21-26; Abbie Hoffman, *Soon to Be a Major Motion Picture* (New York: Perigree Books, 1980), 126-129; Todd Gitlin, *The Whole World Is Watching: Mass Media in the Making & Unmaking of the New Left* (Berkeley: University of California Press, 1980); Nancy Aroulis and Gerald Sullivan, *Who Spoke Up?: American Protest*

Against the War in Vietnam 1963-1975 (Garden City, NY: Doubleday, 1984), 149-208.

89. "Newspapers: Editorial Unease," *Time,* 20 October 1967, 57.

90. "Doubts About Vietnam," *Newsweek,* 23 October 1967, 96.

91. Ibid.

92. Ibid.

93. Karnow, *Vietnam,* 523-526.

94. George Bailey and Lawrence Lichty, "Rough Justice on a Saigon Street: A Gatekeeper Study of NBC's Tet Execution Film," *Journalism Quarterly* 49 (Summer 1972): 221-229, 238.

95. Clark Dougan and Stephen Weiss, *Nineteen Sixty-eight: The Vietnam Experience* (Boston: Boston Publishing Co., 1983), 66.

96. Braestrup, *The Big Story,* 2: 188-189.

97. Turner, *Lyndon Johnson's Dual War,* 232.

98. *Wall Street Journal,* 23 February 1968.

99. New York *Times,* 10 March 1968.

100. Dougan and Weiss, *Nineteen Sixty-eight,* 78-79.

101. New York *Times,* 1 April 1968.

102. New York *Times,* 1 April 1968.

103. Neil Sheehan, "Not a Dove, But No Longer a Hawk," *New York Times Magazine,* 9 October 1966, 140.

104. Greene, "Blaming LBJ," 116.

12

DAVID DUKE AND
THE NEW ORLEANS *TIMES-PICAYUNE*

Keith Woods

David Duke, the controversial former Grand Wizard of the Ku Klux Klan (KKK), arrived at the threshold of the Louisiana Governor's Mansion in November 1991. It was a shocking moment in state politics, but the evidence that it could happen, poorly investigated and wrongly interpreted by the media, had been there for some time.

Duke had operated on the fringes of state politics for years, openly advocating white supremacy long after he had traded in his KKK robes for a suit and tie. He ran for president in 1988, switching from Democrat to the ultra-right Populist Party and winning no delegates while scraping together .05 percent of the vote. He ran twice unsuccessfully for state Senate but received 31 percent of the vote in one of those races.

Undeterred, perhaps even encouraged, he signed up as a Republican and stunned the state by winning a seat in the Legislature, upsetting Republican homebuilder John Treen. Treen was a bland opponent for sure, but he, like Duke, was a conservative, leaving Duke's race-baiting appeal as the major distinguishing political difference between the two men.

Duke's sudden ascendance was covered as a political story, not as a race story, and District 81 was widely dismissed as a racist anomaly. In a February 20, 1989, editorial, the New Orleans *Times-Picayune* said it did not attach any significance to Mr. Duke's narrow 227-vote victory over Treen beyond the outcome of this special election to fill a vacant seat in Metairie House District 81.[1]

From his Baton Rouge soapbox, Duke launched himself into the 1990 U.S. Senate race against a confident and powerful incumbent, J. Bennett Johnston. Duke lost, but he surprised many political observers by getting 605,681 votes, 44 percent of the electorate and 60 percent of the white vote.

The constituency was there and the time was right. He was ready for the governor's race.

Even then, he had polled no better than third with a weak 15 percent and was not considered a likely runoff candidate right up to the final week of the primary campaign. At that time, University of New Orleans pollster Susan Howell introduced an index she said could account for the "hidden" Duke vote. Her calculations showed Duke capable of leaping past his opponents to finish first in the voting.[2]

He came only three percentage points short of doing just that.

As the votes were cast, *Times-Picayune* Metro editor Peter Kovacs met with editor Jim Amoss and suggested a political coverage strategy that would be unlike any the newspaper had launched in its history. A meeting was called for the Monday morning after the October 19 primary election, when thousands of Louisiana voters awakened to the unthinkable realization that they would have to choose between a former Grand Wizard of the KKK and Edwin Edwards, the twice-indicted, flamboyant, and cagey former governor.

Gone from the race was one-term reform governor Buddy Roemer, who had been propelled out of obscurity and into the thick of the 1987 gubernatorial race largely on the strength of a page 1 endorsement from the *Times-Picayune*. That extraordinary editorial comment, which attracted immense statewide media interest and financial backing to the largely unknown congressman from northwest Louisiana, would serve as a benchmark for the kind of strategy the newspaper was about to undertake, one centered in a belief among the editors that the paper had to step forward and exercise an aggressive leadership role.

Around the table for the meeting were most of the editors responsible for setting the course of daily coverage in the metropolitan area and state government, along with a few reporters and editorial writers. The question: How could the newspaper, with just four weeks between primary and runoff, launch the kind of comprehensive editorial campaign that could lay out the case against Duke without coming across as an ivory tower preacher and losing the undecided voters?

The newspaper would target those fence-sitters, believed to exist in substantial enough numbers to swing a close election. Those voters felt burned by 12 years of Edwin Edwards, whose tenure could be measured as accurately by the number of indictments he and his friends had earned as by any ordinary economic or social indicator. Disaffected and frustrated, those voters were considered well primed for Duke's government bashing and scapegoating or at risk of sitting the election out altogether. The editorials would have to speak to them.

With Edwards's traditionally loyal voters sure to back him in the runoff and Duke's supporters unlikely to be swayed by a newspaper openly hostile to their candidate, the fence-sitters—supporters of Roemer and fourth-place candidate Congressman Clyde Holloway—would have to be convinced of two equally important things: that a Duke victory would devastate Louisiana in unspeakable ways and that the state's leadership, including the newspaper, would be vigilant in keeping Edwards's hands—and those of his friends—out of the state coffers.

The newspaper decided on a series of five editorials, all to be written by top editors and produced in less than a week. They would begin one week after the election and would set the tone for all remaining editorials and, as it turned out, news coverage as well.

The last time the newspaper sought to so influence the governor's race was in 1987. After the page 1 endorsement of Roemer,[3] the state's largest newspapers followed the *Times-Picayune*'s lead to form a surprising coalition of support. After that, Roemer, polled in fifth place in that race, leaped into a runoff with Edwards who, himself shocked and discouraged by Roemer's showing, would concede defeat shortly thereafter. It was a surprising turn of events. This time around, the newspaper was counting on just such a profound impact.

It had gone on record on October 20, the morning after the primary vote, with an editorial that would be its first volley in an all-out campaign to keep Duke out of Baton Rouge: "This morning finds Louisiana with a bad hangover," the editorial began. "Of all the excesses that have made our state notorious, yesterday's will go into the history books. File it under 's,' for shame. David Duke is in a runoff for governor."[4]

It concluded with this optimistic nudge: "The clear-headed people of this state—and we happen to think there are still many—must now muster their resolve to see that on Nov. 16 Mr. Duke is not elected governor."[5]

Five editors were dispatched to write the editorials as the newspaper's leadership sought to muster its resolve. This unusual mingling of professional roles, demonstrated by the composition of the group in the October 21 meeting, all but obliterated the line between subjective editorials and the objective ideals of the newsroom. The focus of coverage, like the editorials, was aimed at defeating Duke.

The newspaper knew plenty about both men. Edwards, in the public eye for 12 years as governor, had been taken apart and examined by the media. His bent for gambling, his womanizing, his brazen deal-making, his political genius, his confounding wit and charm, all had found their way to the pages of the newspaper since his emergence in statewide politics in 1972.

Duke, an opportunist who often tailored his anti-Semitism and other prejudices to fit the audience, had been dogged by *Times-Picayune* reporter Tyler Bridges as soon as it was clear that Duke would be more than a marginal white leader selling pornography and white supremacy literature from his suburban home.

Much of what would be reported, then, would not be new. Cast now in the context of this governor's race, however, all of it was newly relevant.

The newsroom, like the state, was consumed by the election. Some 40 reporters, editors, artists, and photographers were drawn into the coverage. Employees talked about depression, insomnia, spontaneous arguments with neighbors, coworkers, family, strangers. As if to purge themselves of the campaign's poison, many wrote about the inner turmoil brought on by what columnist James Gill dubbed "the runoff from hell."[6]

Several people wept openly while trying to lend words to the stress that the election had placed upon them. Heated internal debates flared repeatedly over the potential impact of what the newspaper was attempting to do. Give Duke too much coverage, some said, and he would gain support and a sympathy vote. Give him too little, others said, and he would benefit from ignorance and capture the undecided vote.

It was an old debate given new poignancy. Early in Duke's climb to this precarious spot in history, the newspaper had chosen a side in the matter. Former editor Charles A. Ferguson instructed the staff that, unless absolutely necessary, the newspaper would publish no page 1 stories in which Duke was allowed to espouse his racist and anti-Semitic views, lest the newspaper help him to promote his vitriol. As Duke's support emerged, editor Amoss would choose a different tack.

The public weighed in after the publication of the first postprimary editorial and the first story describing the dismay with which Roemer voters greeted the runoff field. Duke's supporters were especially vocal, canceling subscriptions, flooding radio call-in shows, and hitting the newspaper with a barrage of letters to the editor.

Amoss, in an article written for the American Society of Newspaper Editors (ASNE) journal, described the response: "The most vocal were the many anonymous callers who began their complaints with the refrain, 'I'm not a racist, but . . . ' We were told we were being unfair to Duke in focusing so much on him. Why couldn't we forgive a bout of youthful 'intolerance,' the word Duke used to explain his past? On the other hand, some anti-Duke callers accused us of making Duke an underdog and generating a sympathy vote by attacking him so vehemently."[7]

The newspaper wrote stories about all of it: the angst, the anger, the dismay, the glee. During that first week, an editor pointed out that two thirds of the voters were actually happy and that somber stories of fear and loathing did not totally reflect reality. So stories were commissioned to visit the supporters of each candidate, and Duke's fans got their chance to be heard. They were not pressed on his racist past, nor confronted with his lack of job experience. They were just asked how they felt.

"On the night of Oct. 19 this year, as the primary returns made it clear Duke would be in the runoff, 350 people tried to jam into the small shopping-mall storefront that is Duke headquarters in St. Bernard Parish," wrote reporters John C. Hill and Robert Rhoden. "They were chanting Duke's name and buying up every piece of Duke paraphernalia they could get their hands on.

" 'It was a feeling of unitedness,' said Joe Cadwell, an exterminator who is running Duke's campaign in the parish. 'Common people, common workers, getting something done in their government.' "[8]

Jewish and black people in the newsroom talked about the welling anxiety they and their friends felt knowing that Duke might win.

"My daughter expressed concern that so many youngsters in her classroom were supporting Duke and that others were fearful of the election's aftermath," reporter Mark Schleifstein, who is Jewish, wrote two days before the election.

" 'My friends have talked about moving out if he's elected,' she told me. 'That might really happen.' My son is concerned about people moving away, too, but his concerns have gone beyond his own feelings to worries about the future of Louisiana."[9]

Two news stories on the subject were published a week after the primary and included a textbook containing excerpts from Duke's 1985 interview with graduate student Evelyn Rich, who was researching a doctoral dissertation on the Klan:

Duke on black people: "What we really want to do is to be left alone. We don't want Negroes around. We don't need Negroes around. We're not asking, you know, we don't have to have them, you know, for our own culture. We simply want our own country and our own society."[10]

Duke on Jews: "And those Jews who run things, who are producing this mental illness—teen-age suicide—just read the modern novelists, read Philip Roth—all these Jewish sicknesses in there like that. Of course that's nothing new. The Talmud's full of it, like sex with boys and girls. Did you know that?"[11]

Routine speculation in news meetings about the motives of Duke's voters led to the newspaper's first cogent, sophisticated, nonhysterical look at people otherwise easily shrugged away as rabid racists. The story also signaled the newspaper's intent to decode Duke's often veiled racism and force his supporters to talk straight about race.

"Duke's message is structured along racial lines," the November 10 story by assistant Metro editor James O'Byrne and reporters Bill Walsh and Coleman Warner said. "When he says 'we,' he means white people. When he speaks of welfare cheats, he means black people. When he speaks of New York interests, he means Jewish people."[12]

Scheduled for the Sunday before the election, the story quickly became a lightning rod for the charged newsroom debate about how best to challenge Duke's candidacy. In the ASNE article, Amoss told how what he called "the battle for the soul of the electorate" played out in his office on November 8, two days before the story would be read by hundreds of thousands of Louisianians:

Two *Times-Picayune* editors and a reporter had asked to speak to me. . . . The three staff members had a high regard for the authors. Each had seen the piece in our system and thought it outstanding. But they were deeply worried that a story about ordinary people supporting the neo-Nazi and former Klan leader, a story that portrayed them in their frustration and humanity on the eve of the most important election in Louisiana history, would tacitly lend legitimacy to Duke himself. And they were here to suggest that I kill the story or hold it until after the election.
     We deliberated throughout the day. Clearly the three stepped outside the orthodox bounds of journalism, but I understood them perfectly. As citizens with a love of our city and state, we knew that a Duke victory would be a heavy blow. Each of us, to some degree, ached to hold the story, lest we give comfort to the leaning-toward-Duke voter.[13]

So volatile was the story and the concern around it that there was even strenuous debate about whether the headline "The Duke Voters" might inflame and galvanize Duke's supporters because Duke's name was emblazoned in red while the other words in the headline were white. The front-page story was flanked by a two-column editorial that ran the length of the page. By the time that editorial had gotten into the newspaper, the tone of the race had taken an unmistakable change. The newsroom staff never had a meeting akin to the one called to plan the editorials, but it was clear that most stories flowed from the same philosophical bent. Many were published not merely to inform or chronicle but to influence as well.
     The Rich interview, used repeatedly throughout the coverage, was intended to rebut—for the benefit of the undecideds—Duke's contention that his racism and anti-Semitism were long behind him.
     Most of the daily coverage required no theoretical guidance, however. The campaign provided its own direction. The newspaper covered the massive turnout of would-be voters drawn to registrar's offices statewide, turnout that smashed records for the largest leap in registration between primary and runoff. It covered the mobilization of leadership, reminiscent of the civil rights days, to get black people, underrepresented in most elections, registered and to the polls.
     It covered the repudiation of Duke by leadership as diverse as former governors Roemer and Dave Treen, and New Orleans Saints quarterback Bobby Hebert, who cut a commercial to speak out against bigotry. And it covered the rapid-fire release of poll results. They were reported the way meteorologists report on hurricanes, tracking the progress of Duke and Edwards the way scientists look at longitude and latitude, plotting a course to Baton Rouge that, to many people, would mean a catastrophic landfall no matter which man won.
     Three times the newspaper carried full pages of letters from readers,

many of them irate that their hometown paper was stepping so radically into advocacy journalism and stepping on their candidate in the process. The newspaper explained through a blurb announcing the letters page that "because of the extraordinary public interest in the race and the exceptional number of letters we are receiving," it had set aside its policy of not publishing letters in support of or opposition to political candidates. It also pointed out to readers that the letters heavily favored Edwards. "Since the Oct. 19 primary," the third and final blurb on November 15 said, "we have received almost 700 letters on the governor's race and they have been overwhelmingly against David Duke."[14]

The letters pages gave voice to swelling, visceral emotions and allowed readers to talk to each other and to the newspaper: "Louisianians are proud to wave the American flag and profess support for our armed forces," wrote Gary R. Roberts of New Orleans. "On Oct. 19, one-third of them voted for a man who only a short time ago, paraded around with a swastika on his arm, celebrated Adolf Hitler's birthday and claimed the Nazis had the right idea. Are the people of Louisiana that stupid?"[15]

From Duke supporter J. Kanoc of suburban Marrero: "The sheer hypocrisy of *The Times-Picayune* appalls me. The one-sided reporting against David Duke makes me puke! All the politicians endorsing Edwards tells me the quality of politicians Louisiana has. . . . Why don't you publish Edwards' downfalls, of which there are many, as you do Duke's? After all, a newspaper should be unbiased and report both sides of the story equally without prejudice."[16]

By any measure, the media faced a no-win scenario in covering Duke. "You were biased either way," Night Metro editor Jed Horne said after the election. "You covered Duke like a 'normal' candidate, you favored Duke because you treated his past and present views as though there was nothing special about them. If you wrote about his past, you were favoring Edwards."

Nowhere was that philosophical dichotomy clearer than in the five pieces the newspaper produced under the logo "Election '91," a series that aspired to compare the candidates on campaign issues. It was a rare opportunity to treat Duke the way any normal candidate might be treated. It proved to be almost impossible.

Part of the problem was the issues themselves: the economy, the environment, welfare, education, and affirmative action. Long on rhetoric and short on specifics, Duke easily looked like an uninformed political interloper when compared to Edwards's vast knowledge of economic, environmental, and educational issues.

During his three terms as governor, Edwards helped create legislation setting up a $600 million education trust fund, requiring school boards to offer kindergarten and changing the office of state superintendent of education from an elective position to an appointed one, reporter Lisa Frazier wrote in the fourth installment of the series.

Among his new proposals, Edwards said he would support dedicating 75 percent of lottery proceeds to education and full financing of the Louisiana Opportunity Program, a Roemer initiative that would grant low-interest college loans to middle-class families.

Duke said he would work to improve the education system but offered no specifics. "Our educational system has been nowhere near what it could be for the people of our state," Duke said. "We need some changes and I represent that change."[17]

Duke was in his element blasting welfare and affirmative action, but how could the newspaper responsibly report his position on the issues without pointing out Duke's racist agenda in attacking those programs or showing how relatively insignificant the issues were in the first place? Treat them as normal and favor Duke. Thoroughly report them and risk the wrath of his followers.

For the newspaper, it was an easy choice.

"Duke has claimed that welfare is a major drain on state revenues, but statistics show state AFDC (Aid to Families with Dependent Children) spending amounts to about 1 percent of total state spending," Frazier wrote in the third installment.[18]

The editorial series, entitled "The Choice of Our Lives," began on October 27. For many Duke supporters, its appearance verified every suspicion they had held about the newspaper's wanton refusal to meet its basic responsibility as an objective journal. The editorials unleashed a formidable, unapologetic arsenal against Duke, turning his life and words against him at every turn.

"But who is the new David Duke?" the newspaper asked in the first editorial in the series.

Is he the legislator who claims to be pro-life? Or the pamphleteer who, as the father of two children, told Rich, "I don't think the fact that somebody is human necessarily . . . is any great plus in their favor."

Will he reveal himself and, like Mr. Edwards, challenge us to accept him? Or will he continue to lie about himself? Can he unify the state Legislature behind a practical agenda? Or will he remain as impotent there as he is today, having passed one bill in three sessions, a politician so isolated that many of his colleagues will not shake his hand?

Will he help us help each other? Or will he do across the state what he has done in the Legislature, destroying hard-won understanding and turning former colleagues against each other?

Will Mr. Duke attract new business to Louisiana? Or will we continue to get the calls from our dumbfounded business friends around the country: "What's going on down there?"[19]

The editorials, borrowing heavily from the voluminous research of reporter Bridges, attacked Duke's associations with the Klan and Nazi Party, his lack of any job experience save the stint in the legislature, his divisiveness, his lies about military service in Vietnam, his facelift, and his dubious conversion to Christianity.

The editorials consumed the time and attention of the newsroom's top decision-makers and were so rich with current, crucial facts and insights that they sometimes got ahead of the news coverage from which editorials typically flow. The October 29 editorial, the second in the series headlined "Governor Must Be Able to Bring Home the Bacon," raised the specter of a Duke victory destroying tourism in New Orleans and wreaking havoc on the state's economic development.[20]

A Page 1 story on the subject, illustrated with excerpts from letters sent by convention groups threatening to cancel if Duke were elected, followed the editorial by three days. An exhaustive, two-page profile of Duke was published three days after the series concluded, further fleshing out his history. It was not the first time the newspaper would seek to explain Duke to its readers, but there was no doubt that there was a captive audience this time. The Rich tapes, then, would have greater impact now than in 1990, when they were excerpted during Duke's Senate race but buried on Page 7. This time, the excerpts occupied three 21-inch columns.

Bridges' story had a decidedly indicting tone and, though offering little in the way of new information, had the ring of an exposé. It also bore an unsurprising resemblance to one of the newspaper's recent editorials: "Duke has resolutely embraced the Republican Party as he asks voters to elect him governor of Louisiana," Bridges wrote. "But before they pull the Duke lever Nov. 16, voters will be asking themselves two questions: Is this the real David Duke? Or has he merely traded in the Nazi uniform and hooded Klan robe of his past for the guise of a conservative suburban Republican?"[21]

Edwards, certainly among the most-profiled gubernatorial candidates in the country, was treated more kindly by capitol bureau chief Jack Wardlaw, whose story spoke of Edwards's "magic" and dwelled much more on his achievements and political savvy than on his indictments and other flirtations with the courtroom. To match the three-column Rich excerpts, the newspaper published an equal amount of testimony from Edwards's 1985 racketeering trial. If publishing that testimony served any journalistic purpose, it was mostly by coincidence. Conscious of the unrelenting complaints from Duke's supporters that the newspaper's coverage was warped beyond reason, the newspaper decided to find something damaging to print about Edwards to match that written about Duke, thereby giving the appearance of fairness. "An artifice," declared one editor.

Leaders of the city's tourism industry had visited the newspaper and delivered the potential conventioneers' threatening letters after the editorial series began running. Hoping the editorials would provoke just such activism, the newspaper repackaged "The Choice of Our Lives" in a four-page reprint and mailed it to newspapers throughout the state, encouraging them to quote pieces at their discretion.

The visit by tourism leaders and the coalescing of opposition to Duke that was taking place among prominent business leadership throughout the state, particularly in the populous metropolitan New Orleans area, served to focus the *Times-Picayune*'s coverage on Duke's enormous economic liability, the flaw that resonated loudest from north to south, rich and poor, black and white.

The newspaper had simultaneously hooked into another weak spot in what weeks earlier had seemed like an impenetrable armor: Duke's newfound faith. Offering himself as a born-again Christian, Duke sought to lighten the baggage of his past by claiming, as he did during the 1990 Senate race, renewed dedication to God. He also claimed membership in a church—The Evangelical Bible Church. Neither held up to scrutiny, and exposing Duke's hypocrisy would deal his candidacy a staggering blow.

"Duke's Christian fervor contrasts with past views," a November 1 story said. A day later came the headline: "Tourism Leaders: Duke Will Be Costly." It would be a one-two punch the newspaper would throw with great authority and undeniable impact. On November 13, three days before the election, it published three front-page stories contradicting Duke's claim to rebirth. The first recounted a 1990 interview Duke conducted with a Scottish reporter in which he repeated his views that Jews "are trying to destroy all cultures."[22]

The second revealed the defection of one of Duke's top campaign coordinators, former Tennessee state legislator Bob Hawks, who said Duke and his staff used racial slurs during the campaign and that Hawks had "never seen him [Duke] go to church or do anything along the lines of Christianity."[23] The third punch in the barrage quoted a collection of Christian ministers who had their doubts about Duke's sincerity. The next day, a page 1 story told of businesses that were sending letters to their employees warning that a Duke victory could well mean the loss of their jobs.

"Hundreds of business people around New Orleans, shaken by the prospect of David Duke as governor, are responding with a resounding roar," reporter Elizabeth Mullener wrote.

From law firms to restaurants, from manufacturers to hotels, from oil companies to universities, employers are sending out letters to their employees—and sometimes their suppliers and clients—in a last-ditch effort to bar Duke from the Governor's Mansion and prevent the consequent nose dive they fear the New Orleans economy would take. Altogether they are sending tens of thousands of letters.[24]

The reporting, in some respects, had achieved its self-fulfilling goals.

Stories nearly two weeks earlier spoke of tourism industry fears and hidden contradictions of faith. As the election neared, business leaders were all but telling their employees to vote against Duke, and Christian ministers were cutting a commercial telling the faithful, "We can pray for David Duke, but we should not vote for him."[25]

That hardening of opposition was reflected in the unique November 10, page 1 editorial. Where the opening editorial in "The Choice of Our Lives" raised questions about Duke and his past, this editorial, stripped into the space traditionally reserved for the day's most important news story, provided unequivocating answers:

For those who would have us believe that Mr. Duke's past as a Klansman and neo-Nazi were but a youthful lapse into intolerance on the road to maturity, we offer the record. It says otherwise. This was not a long-ago infatuation, but a committed adult's world view, occupying at least 22 years of his grown-up life. It was a fully mature David Duke who, as recently as 1985, called for a South African–like apartheid for Louisiana and into the mid-'80s toasted the birthday of Adolf Hitler. Against such evidence, and with the Governor's Mansion within his grasp, his claim to a Saul-like conversion is lame. There is no "new" David Duke. Only the old to advantage dressed.[26]

For those who might yet be persuaded to hold their noses and vote for Edwards (a metaphor popular among Roemer voters), the editorial addressed Edwards's alleged political conversion:

Edwin Edwards has said that this time he wants to do it right; that he values the mandate of an unprecedented coalition of Louisianians; that he will, as he puts it, "redeem myself." As a newspaper, we pledge to you, our readers, that we will exert all effort and enterprise throughout his governorship to see that this trust is not betrayed.[27]

Since early on in the campaign, Duke had refused interviews with reporters from the *Times-Picayune*, who were not even allowed in his suburban New Orleans headquarters. But until the final week, as polls began showing what would be a huge and devastating voter shift, he had remained cocky and unfettered by the blistering editorials and unrelenting bad press. In that final week, the Teflon wore away and Duke acknowledged the sting by attacking the newspaper: "You might think my election is the worst fear of the *Times-Picayune*'s editors," he said in a television commercial. "It's not. Their worst fear is having a flat tire near their inner-city office."

On the night before the election, Duke basked in the glow of one last outdoor rally while his followers took one last shot at the newspaper, chanting, "Go to hell, T-P, go to hell!"[28]

Duke received 671,009 votes. But that amounted to only 39 percent of the total vote. Thus vanquished, Duke blamed the media and singled out the *Times-Picayune*: "Sometimes David doesn't overcome Goliath," he said. "We were overwhelmed with a lot of negative press—the *Picayune* and its sources."

Edwards's victory was clear to newsroom staff by 4 p.m. on election day. Exit polls commissioned by the newspaper foretold the rout. But the newsroom did not celebrate until Duke appeared on the television screen for a rambling concession speech. As he announced his surrender, champagne corks popped, and the crowd gathered around the newsroom TV erupted in cheers.

NOTES

1. New Orleans *Times-Picayune*, 20 February 1989.
2. New Orleans *Times-Picayune*, 3 October 1991.
3. New Orleans *Times-Picayune*, 20 October 1991.
4. New Orleans *Times-Picayune*, 20 October 1991.
5. New Orleans *Times-Picayune*, 20 October 1991.
6. New Orleans *Times-Picayune*, 11 October 1991.
7. American Society of Newspaper Editors (ASNE) Bulletin, March 1992, 8-9.
8. New Orleans *Times-Picayune*, 31 October 1991.
9. New Orleans *Times-Picayune*, 14 November 1991.
10. New Orleans *Times-Picayune*, 3 November 1991.
11. New Orleans *Times-Picayune*, 3 November 1991.
12. New Orleans *Times-Picayune*, 10 November 1991.
13. ASNE Bulletin, March 1992, 8-9.
14. New Orleans *Times-Picayune*, 15 November 1991.
15. New Orleans *Times-Picayune*, 13 November, 1991.
16. New Orleans *Times-Picayune*, 13 November 1991.
17. New Orleans *Times-Picayune*, 8 November 1991.
18. New Orleans *Times-Picayune*, 7 November 1991.
19. New Orleans *Times-Picayune*, 27 October 1991.
20. New Orleans *Times-Picayune*, 29 October 1991.
21. New Orleans *Times-Picayune*, 3 November 1991.
22. New Orleans *Times-Picayune*, 13 November 1991.
23. New Orleans *Times-Picayune*, 13 November 1991.
24. New Orleans *Times-Picayune*, 14 November 1991.
25. New Orleans *Times-Picayune*, 13 November 1991.
26. New Orleans *Times-Picayune*, 10 November 1991.
27. New Orleans *Times-Picayune*, 10 November 1991.
28. Tyler Bridges, *The Rise of David Duke* (Oxford: University Press of Mississippi, 1994), 234.

13 ⪽

POPULATION: THE ONCE AND FUTURE ENVIRONMENTAL CRISIS

Mike Maher

Once we worried about California condors and bald eagles; now an esti-mated 140 plant and animal species meet extinction each day. Once we worried about smog; now the protective ozone layer is thinning while the atmosphere gains ever-greater concentrations of greenhouse gases. Once we sought to save the redwoods; now earth's forests vanish at a rate of some 17 million hectares per year, an area half the size of Finland.[1]

Experts say these and many other environmental crises originate with three ultimate causes: technology, consumption levels, and human popu-lation growth.[2] Many regard population growth as the ultimate environ-mental problem; indeed, in 1992, three different scientific groups issued appeals urging humanity to stabilize its surging population:

- The National Science Foundation and the British Royal Society drafted a joint statement to world leaders that human population growth and environmental degradation had reached crisis proportions. "If current predictions of population growth prove accurate and patterns of hu-man activity on the planet remain unchanged, science and technology may not be able to prevent either irreversible degradation of the envi-ronment or continued poverty for much of the world."[3]
- The Scientists' Appeal on the Environment, an initiative led by Carl Sagan, called for a halt to population growth.[4]
- The Union of Concerned Scientists gathered the endorsements of 1600 scientists (including 99 Nobel Laureates) for a "Warning to Humanity" that urged a stable population and other environmental measures.[5]

Ironically, also in 1992 a Gallup poll showed that Americans were *less* concerned about population growth than they had been 20 years before![6]

Why are the world's leading scientists so concerned about population, while public interest wanes? How can public concern over population decline while population-driven environmental problems—extinctions, endangered species, deforestation, water shortages, atmospheric changes—become increasingly serious worldwide?

To understand why population declined as a public issue while advancing in its actual impact on the planet, we must look at the media's role not only as agenda-setter, but also as framer of the population issue, from the mid-1960s to the present. This can illuminate not only the population issue itself but also the ability of the news media to explain the cause of events—a task that Harold Lasswell defined as one of three major functions of communication.[7]

Just after World War II, human population growth shifted into high gear. In part this resulted from increased birth rates in the developed countries—the baby boom—but more profoundly from a dramatic reduction in the death rate in developing countries. The postwar spread of epidemiology, roads, law and order, schools, medical clinics, fertilizers and pesticides severely reduced the famine and pestilence that had kept Third World populations in check.[8] For example, the death rate fell so rapidly in Sri Lanka that the nation's average life expectancy at birth gained nine years in a single year![9] This was attributed to DDT, which killed the malaria-carrying mosquitoes that had previously kept death rates high. The world's population growth rate peaked in the 1960s,[10] and about that time concern about population began to grow commensurately. Ecologists and demographers plotted birth rates against agricultural productivity gains and panicked.

The Population Bomb (1968) began with Paul Ehrlich's prediction: "The battle to feed all of humanity is over. In the 1970's the world will undergo famines—hundreds of millions of people are going to starve to death in spite of any crash programs embarked upon now."[11]

Nor was Ehrlich the first or the most apocalyptic visionary of population-driven famine. Georg Borgstrom warned of starvation in *The Hungry Planet*,[12] and in its sequel, *Too Many*, he voiced a resignation similar to Ehrlich's: "Both as a human family and as agriculturists or food scientists we have lost the race between the baby crop and the grain crop."[13] In *The Hunger to Come*, another writer notes that this is "the great problem of the mid-20th century—too many people, too little food and an even more acute lack of appreciation of the problem."[14]

In 1967, William and Paul Paddock predicted an Age of Famines in their book, *Famine—1975!* They advocated the idea of triage: Nations with a food surplus would have to divide the rest of the world into three categories. The first, nations whose populations were dramatically out of balance with the carrying capacity of their agriculture, would be left to starve. The second, those that had enough food to survive and whose populations were relatively stable, would receive no food aid. The third, those nations faced with starvation but whose population/food imbalance was relatively manageable, would receive food. "Waste not the food on the 'can't-be-saved' and the 'walking wounded,' "[15] the Paddocks intoned.

These and many other writers are called neo-Malthusians because they are concerned with the balance between population and food. Their philosophical forebear, Thomas Malthus, had predicted that population, when unchecked, outstrips the growth of food.[16] He also noted that the tendency of man was to fulfill this dire prediction.[17] The neo-Malthusians typically frame the effects of population in terms of subsistence. By the 1970s the news media had accepted this concept, as we see when we examine coverage of the world's first major population conference.

Food and population were the major worry as the first International Conference on Population and Development (ICPD) opened in Bucharest in August 1974. The New York *Times* editorialized that the world was running "perilously short of food and other basic commodities"[18] and that "the growing world scarcity of food and other natural resources makes the choice [of reducing birth rates] tragically and increasingly clear."[19] The *Times* added on August 30 that world population would be prevented from doubling in 30 years "only by starvation, disease and war."[20]

Environmentalist Lester Brown told the assembled ICPD delegates that the world had only 27 days of food reserves. Raising the specter of triage, he said that the United States may soon have to decide "which nations starve and which survive."[21] Food was high on the New York *Times* agenda as the world population conference began. On August 27, alone, the *Times* carried a page 1 story quoting Agriculture Secretary Earl Butz on the adequacy of U.S. food supplies; a long feature on how crop enumerators estimate U.S. agricultural yields; and an article on Green Revolution scientist Norman Borlaug's visit to China. The following day, the *Times* ran a feature titled "Java Is Lush, But Not Rich Enough to Feed All Its 80 Million People,"[22] as well as an editorial, "Why We Fertilize Golf Courses,"[23] accompanied by a drawing of a malnourished African child holding a withered stalk of grain. "Runaway population growth threatens all nations, rich and poor, but especially the poor," the *Times* editorialized on August 21. "The demographic realities of the modern world require responsible, cooperative action by all nations to limit population growth."[24]

The Times of London offered similar coverage. Preparatory to the conference, the *Times* devoted a six-page section to world population problems, as well as a long essay advocating that official policy should allow the British population to shrink from 56 million to around 35 million.[25] The *Times* covered the conference diligently, reporting British delegate Lord Shepherd's offer to aid those countries that wanted to cut their birth rate.

The British, too, were concerned about the effect of population on the world's food supply. *The Times of London* writer Pearce Wright pointed out that "in the past two years major famines have swept several regions." But he also argued that food was a concern for the developed world. For its food supply, he noted, "Europe depends on a 'shadow' continent equal to half the size of its own cultivated lands. This estimate includes an allowance for food from distant fisheries."[26] *The Times of London* also noted growing pressure for a world food bank to help Third World countries.[27]

Ironically, *The Times of India* (Bombay) took little notice of the population conference and carried only brief, sketchy reports of the proceedings. But food was in the news. On August 27, the same day that Earl Butz was assuring Americans they had ample food supplies, the Bombay *Times* carried two page 1 stories about food: problems with "sick" sugar mills and distribution of "edible oil" (seed oil), as well as a page 7 story titled, "Give Food or Face Revolt." The next day, the *Times* headlines reported on page 1, "Polluted Fish Pose Danger," and on page 6, "Food Shortage in West Bengal/Hunger Deaths Reported." That story reported, "Hungry people are said to be eating dried grass seeds and roots."[28]

Thus, as representatives of the earth's many countries gathered in Bucharest to discuss world population, well-fed Americans and English believed that population was outstripping the food supply. Their nations' leading newspapers devoted regular coverage to the conference and impassioned editorials urging population stability—chiefly as a means of averting famine. But in Bombay, the most populous city of the world's second-most-populous country, a country faced not with the *threat* of starvation but with the real thing, a country that was growing by more people than the whole population of Australia every year, population was not a news concern and the population conference was accorded indifferent coverage.

This news coverage presaged the outcome of the population conference, which quickly devolved into an ideological roller derby. The developed countries had proposed measures to promote population stability in a preconference draft of a World Population Plan of Action. The Communist delegations, particularly the People's Republic of China, immediately assailed these measures with adjectives ranging from *pessimistic* to *neocolonialist* to *genocidal*. The Chinese delegation encouraged Third World countries to *grow* in population as a "condition for the fight against imperialism and hegemonism."[29]

India's health minister, Dr. Karan Singh, coined the phrase "development is the best contraceptive,"[30] which, loosely translated, meant that the Third World would do nothing about halting its population growth until the developed world proffered massive economic aid—at which point, development proponents argued, the population problem would take care of itself.

The developing countries ultimately rejected the original formulation of the World Population Plan of Action, bleeding its 93 paragraphs with more than 200 amendments, according to *The Times of London*.[31] *The Times* editorial on August 31 repeated one British delegate's evaluation of the document, "a castrated plan,"[32] but allowed that it was better than nothing at all. The New York *Times* blasted the Marxists for "Demagogy in Bucharest"[33] and editorialized that the conference had adjourned "with the feeble conclusion that countries should try to reduce their birth rates by 1985 if, as sovereign nations, they happen to think they ought to. Much of the delegates' time was spent on propagandistic irrelevancies."[34]

Despite the failure of the first world population conference, media coverage in the United States during the 1960s and early 1970s had placed population on the agenda. Indeed, population was one of the 15 top issues of the 1960s.[35] Paul Ehrlich's name was so well-known that he actually did a *Playboy* interview in 1970.[36] John Laffin claimed that "there is acute anxiety about population figures"[37] in the United States, and David Yaukey's textbook *Demography* says: "Public alarm reached almost the panic stage in about 1969. The mass media publicly aired the problem, searched for solutions, and found none likely."[38]

Further, Gallup Polls done in the 1960s show strong concern about population among the American public. A 1963 poll showed that 68 percent of Americans were aware of the rising population growth rates.[39]

But in retrospect, this concern was misdirected. As a media-reported crisis, population got onto the media agenda in relation to the world potential for famine. The media had taken their cues from neo-Malthusian writers, who had taken their cues from "gloomy parson" Malthus himself. We should be concerned about population, they told us, because population growth is about to cause massive famines that will kill millions.

But they were wrong. Half wrong, anyway. As Malthus postulated, population *can* grow geometrically, and world population currently is doing just that. Any long-term chart of world population growth will show this. But Malthus and his followers were wrong about food. Food reserves jumped well ahead of population, just as population doomsayers were predicting famine. Ironically, the media and their sources scared the public by projecting a Malthusian, population-driven food crisis just as the Green Revolution was outstripping even the record population growth of the 1960s.

Norman Borlaug won the Nobel Prize in 1970 for developing a variety of wheat that doubled or tripled yields. Similar productivity gains were soon developed for rice and maize. Between 1961 and 1980, India tripled its wheat production. From verging on the brink of famine in 1967, India produced enough wheat to feed its population within five years.[40]

However, India hovered near large-scale famine for several years, even as the Green Revolution was improving grain supplies. India came perilously close to disaster,[41] and as late as 1976 the president of the World

Food Council said that for many of "the developing countries the famine hazard is not something of the future, but is there now, at this moment."[42] Nor has the threat of famine wafted away forever. World per-capita grain production peaked in 1984 and has declined ever since, lagging behind population growth, just as Malthus would have predicted.[43]

Nevertheless, the population crisis of the 1970s proved to be a noncrisis when hundreds of millions of people did not starve. The predicted Age of Famines is better remembered today as the Age of Polyester Leisure Suits.

Because they had framed the effects of population growth in terms of food and famine, the news media lost interest in population when the famines didn't happen. Interest in population also waned in magazines. In analyzing the post-World War II population debate in American popular magazines, John Wilmoth and Patrick Ball pointed out:

A gradual decrease in the number of articles addressing population matters is evident after the late 1960s. This decline stands in sharp contrast to the aforementioned increase in the number of periodicals being indexed over this period and to the total number of annual citations in the *Reader's Guide* regardless of subject matter.[44]

By 1989 Paul Ehrlich was complaining that "a conspiracy of silence" was keeping population out of the public discussion.[45]

Agenda-setting theory tells us that when an issue declines in aggregate news coverage, it is nudged down on the public's agenda by other issues that get more coverage.[46] A recent Gallup Poll confirms that just such a decline has occurred, that population is less important an issue in the 1990s than it had been 20 years before. This Gallup Poll shows that the percentage of Americans who perceive population growth to be a problem *diminished*, rather than increased, from 1971 to 1992.[47] That is, in 1971, 41 percent of Americans surveyed by Gallup said that population growth was a serious problem for the United States; but in 1992, only 29 percent felt it was a serious problem. Further, the percentage of Americans who said population growth would *not* become a problem almost doubled during this period. In 1971, only 13 percent of those surveyed felt that population growth would not be a problem in the future, while in 1992, 24 percent said they did not expect population growth to become a problem.

The 1992 Gallup Poll also showed that awareness of population growth as a problem had diminished. A 1963 poll showed that 68 percent of Americans were aware of "the great increase in population which is predicted for the world during the next few decades." In the 1992 poll, the awareness level was 51 percent.

Another national poll, conducted in 1994 for the Pew Global Stewardship Initiative, indicated a somewhat greater concern about population.

Of 2080 American respondents, 60 percent felt the world was very or some-what overpopulated. And when told that "demographers estimate the world's population will increase by three billion people in the next 20 years," a clear majority (73 percent) of respondents said this would have a negative impact. But their response could have been biased by the sur-veyors' introduction of the 3 billion people figure, for only 52 percent of respondents felt population growth would worsen the quality of their lives. And in ranking the seriousness of global environmental issues on a 1-to-10 scale, respondents ranked rapid population growth sixth out of seven issues, behind toxic waste, water pollution, loss of rain forests, air quality, and overconsumption of resources, but ahead of global warming/ozone depletion.[48]

The poll showed no strong consensus that action is necessary to re-duce population growth. Confirming the 1992 Gallup Poll findings of weak support for population control, the 1994 poll found that slightly more than half (51 percent) favored U.S. support for population control pro-grams overseas—although support for family planning (a less coercive-sounding approach) ranked higher (59 percent). Regarding the U.S. popu-lation, respondents were deadlocked on the statement, "It is important that we lower birth rates in the U.S. to help save the environment." Forty-nine percent agreed and 48 percent disagreed, but more disagreed strongly (22 percent) than agreed strongly (18 percent).

This latter point may explain the political reality of recent U.S. popu-lation policy: A dogmatic minority can set policy that thwarts the wishes of a slightly-above-lukewarm majority. Recent political history also con-firms that population is low on Americans' agenda. During the Reagan and Bush administrations, those strongly opposed to population-stabiliz-ing measures dictated U.S. policy, in part because they faced no strong, organized resistance. They were able to forge the Mexico City Policy, which the United States announced at the second U.N.-sponsored Inter-national Conference on Population and Development in 1984. Head U.S. delegate James Buckley declared population a "neutral phenomenon" and told delegates at the Mexico City conference that free enterprise was "the natural mechanism for slowing population growth."[49] The United States also announced it would withdraw support for any program that per-formed or promoted abortion, even if the funds were not used directly for these purposes.

The Reagan administration withdrew U.S. support for the U.N. Popu-lation Fund and for International Planned Parenthood, which estimated that slightly less than one half of 1 percent of its budget went to agencies that offered abortion.[50] Marshall Green, senior State Department adviser, told the New York *Times* that the Mexico City policy arose in part from "the right wing of the right-to-life movement, which has supporters within the White House Staff."[51] *The Times of London* noted "widespread condemnation" of the U.S. policy by delegates to the Mexico City population conference.[52] *Times of London* writer Andrew Lycett noted of the Mexico City policy:

The US statement can be viewed simply as a nicely timed piece of electioneering. A week after the UN conference, the Republican Party Convention begins in Dallas, and President Reagan is eager to allay the fears of right-wingers who think he has been too centrist, particularly on abortion.[53]

George Bush also capitulated to the Religious Right. As a congressman he had been so staunch an advocate of birth control that his colleague Wilbur Mills had nicknamed him "rubbers." In 1969 he chaired a Republican task force on earth resources and population control and later that year said, "Our entire environmental degradations are the result of our inability to manage and accommodate the rapid increase in our population."[54] Yet as president, Bush was so beholden to pronatalists that he continued all of the Reagan-era restrictions on funding family planning programs, and he even issued a gag order prohibiting clinics that get federal money from even offering counseling about abortion.

While the Clinton administration reversed most of the Republican strictures against family planning and abortion, these policy reversals and poll results indicate the same thing: Americans are ambivalent about the population issue. Not enough Americans are concerned about it strongly enough to constitute a bipartisan mandate. The Pew and Gallup Polls indicate no clear consensus for action on population growth. The Pew poll indicates a low-agenda ranking for population growth among other global environmental issues, and the Gallup Poll indicates Americans' diminishing interest in population since the 1960s and early 1970s. Garrett Hardin summarized how far population fell from the U.S. agenda:

During the 1980s compulsive optimists seized the reins of political and media power, thus contributing to the suppression of the discussion of population during Earth Week celebrations of 1990. By this time population was, in some quarters, almost a tabooed subject.[55]

A series of 18 focus group interviews conducted in 10 cities across the United States gives a deeper and more interesting indicator of why various voting groups remain indifferent about population growth. The study found the issue of population "is not invisible but most often it is a weak blip on the radar screens for most of the voting groups."[56]

Focus groups are ideal for getting beneath the surface of public opinion, for finding not merely what people think, but why they think it. And most tellingly, when the focus groups were evaluated on whether respondents could connect population growth with environmental degradation,

environmentalists and some of the internationalists and Jewish men's focus groups could make the connection, "but overall *most of the others do not
make many direct, unaided connections between population and environment*,"
the 1993 Pew report states.[57]

The public's inability to connect population growth to environmental
problems demonstrates what is America's second population crisis. It is
virtually the inverse of the first. The first was a well-reported but false
crisis of the 1960s and early 1970s that connected population to the food
supply. This second crisis is a whole set of population-driven environmental problems—endangered species, habitat loss, urban sprawl, deforestation, and many other issues—but the news media do not connect these
problems to their source in population growth. The public remains
clueless about the connection between population growth and environmental degradation, because media coverage consistently omits mention
of population growth as a source of the problem. We can see why population remains off the agenda when we look closely at how media frame
causality in stories about environmental problems.

Quite a few scholars have begun to use the term *framing* in discussing
media effects, and indeed, the term has escaped into the general parlance
of the media savvy. Framing was first used as a construct for how the
individual organizes experience. Psychological frames organize and explain their contents, much as a picture frame does.[58] Frames also imply
premises for inclusion and exclusion, such that the experience being
framed is separated from the complex infinity of everyday reality.[59]

Framing has been popularized in media analysis[60] and linked to
agenda setting by Wenmouth Williams Jr., Mitchell Shapiro, and Craig
Cutbirth,[61] who showed that stories having an overt political frame have a
much stronger media-to-audience agenda-setting effect than do stories
without a political frame.

While no one is satisfied with the slippery nature of the term *framing*,
Robert Entman synthesized much previous scholarship in attempting to
clarify what he calls a "fractured paradigm." He pointed out that "framing essentially involves selection and salience"[62] and noted that framing
involves promoting a particular definition of a problem, as well as its
causal interpretation and recommended treatment.

Framing and gatekeeping are the two journalistic decision points that
lead to agenda setting. Framing, gatekeeping, and agenda setting all in-
volve winnowing and ranking. In framing a story, a journalist decides
what facts, sources, and quotes to use, and what to exclude. Then the
journalist ranks these elements in descending order of importance within
the story. In gatekeeping, an editor decides what stories to use and what
to omit in a given broadcast or edition; then the editor ranks those stories
by giving prominence to the most important, in terms of layout or airtime.
Over a period of time, these journalistic decisions set the public's agenda,

for the public infers from cumulative journalistic coverage what issues are most important and what issues can be forgotten. More than 200 agenda-setting studies have confirmed that, yes the media does successfully tell the public what to think about.[63]

This is not to say that framing is something journalists do to stories, and stories do to people. Audience members interpret media messages through their own cognitive schema and may arrive at conclusions well beyond what the writer of any given message intended. But as Entman pointed out, "Most frames are defined by what they omit as well as include, and the omission of potential problem definitions, explanations, evaluations, and recommendations may be as critical as the inclusions in guiding the audience."[64] Media framing of environmental problems guides the audience away from concern about population, as we see when we compare media framing to expert framing of causality in population-driven environmental problems.

As noted earlier, environmental writers frequently implicate human population growth as a major general determinant of environmental degradation (along with consumption level and technology). With specific reference to wildlife habitat loss, it has been shown that population growth pushes people into the natural world.[65] In addition, population growth has been tied to water shortages.[66] These citations are illustrative but by no means exhaustive; hundreds of writers have implicated population growth as a source of environmental degradation.

In addition to individual environmental writers, the *Global 2000 Report* to President Jimmy Carter and the Commission on Population Growth and the American Future have demonstrated the negative effects of population growth and recommended policy measures to stabilize growth.

At the international level, many commissions and scientific groups have urged a stable population. In addition to the scientists' groups mentioned earlier, these include the U.N. World Leaders Declaration on Population (1966), the U.N. World Population Plan of Action (1974), the U.N. Brundtland Commission Report *Our Common Future* (1987), the Stockholm Initiative on Global Security and Governance (1991), the Interparliamentary Conference on the Global Environment (1991), and the Bali Declaration on Population and Sustainable Development (1992).

While it is well known that environmentalists and expert commissions connect environmental degradation to population growth, it is less well known that land developers are equally straightforward in implicating population growth as a causal agent for turning wildlife habitat and farmland into subdivisions. The how-to manuals for real estate development are quite specific about the causal role of population growth.[67]

Naturally, they frame the results with different language. What developers might call "conversion of raw land to happy communities" could be the same phenomenon that environmentalists would call "loss of critical wildlife habitat." But both environmentalists and developers agree that population growth is a chief force driving the process of land conversion. Land conversion, in turn, is frequently the chief cause of species decline and urban sprawl.

Some theorists dismiss the negative consequences of population growth.[68] But while pronatalists have justifiably criticized neo-Malthusian doomsaying about famines and resource shortages, they have not successfully explained away the negative effects that population growth has had on wildlife habitat and water resources. Population growth clearly is a chief cause of water shortages, urban sprawl, and the conversion of wildlife habitat to human uses. Experts from environmental science, presidential and international commissions, and even land development economics agree that population is an important variable in these problems. But is this causality indicated in newspaper stories?

When population growth converts forest to farmland, farmland to suburb, suburb to strip mall, strip mall to urban center, frequently this becomes news, because most people *don't like* the effects of population growth. One authority lists "small-town pastoralism" as one of eight enduring values in the news.[69] The Council on Environmental Quality found that 57 percent of a sample of Americans said they preferred to live in a small town or rural area.[70] More recently, in some areas, NIMBY (not in my back yard) has given way to BANANA (build absolutely nothing anywhere near anybody).

Two subgenres of news stories have become common over the past 20 years as a result of population growth: urban sprawl and endangered species. Both frequently occur along the periphery of a city, where population growth has pushed the "envelope" of people habitat deeper into wildlife habitat or farmland, with results that people lament in news stories. Water shortages have become a third common modern population-driven environmental problem. While droughts do occur, the supply of water per capita is inevitably diminished by more capitas. My analysis of how newspapers frame endangered species, urban sprawl, and water shortage stories shows considerable discrepancy between expert framing and news framing. Using a randomized sample of articles from Nexis, I found that only 16 of 150 news stories mentioned population growth as a cause of the environmental problem described in the story. Population growth appeared in 8 urban sprawl stories, 7 water shortage stories, and 1 story on endangered species. Only 1 article in 150 mentioned that policies to stabilize population might be a possible solution.[71]

Instead of framing urban sprawl, water shortages, and endangered species crises as the inevitable consequence of population growth, news media instead direct the public's attention to proximate causes: development, drought, lack of zoning, and so forth. Generally the solutions mentioned in these stories are palliative; they address the effect rather than the cause of the problem. Endangered species stories frequently list as possible solutions federal protection under the Endangered Species Act, habitat acquisition, or captive breeding. Urban sprawl stories commonly mention zoning or growth management as a solution. Such a solution simply dumps the population growth problem on some other community. Water shortage stories generally assume that the water-per-capita problem can only be addressed by gaining new water supplies, rather than by stabilizing capitas.

Searching Nexis for environmental dispute stories is like visiting Dante's Inferno. Each database search turns up thousands of stories, and story after story is the same: People are in conflict because things they value—animal species, natural land, fresh water—are in shorter and shorter supply. People resent that the quality of their lives is diminishing, but rather than see their situation as the inevitable consequence of population growth, they blame others in their community: land developers, highway builders, even other average citizens who are merely engaging in activities that, not long ago, were completely innocuous.

There is considerable pathos in these stories: the Ottawa suburbanite who warns of a "lynching" if the city goes through with plans to turn the city greenbelt into urban development.[72] The Vancouver watershed protection officer who measures the snowpack and, finding it thin, returns home to wash his car because "it may be the last chance I get to do it this year."[73] The Fresno County, California, farmer whose irrigation water has been reallocated to urban centers.[74] The Floridian who says his ponds have lost 14 feet of shoreline to nearby water wells that supply St. Petersburg.[75] The Minnesota dairy farmer who must pay assessments for paved roads he doesn't want, roads that bring development he doesn't want.[76] The Seattle journalist who wonders in his lead: "How many skipped showers equal a green lawn?"[77]

The most pathetic of these microcosms is the Maryland woman who apprehends a small boy trying to catch a turtle in his neighborhood pond and turns him in to the authorities because area wildlife are disappearing. "There's nothing innocuous about a kid with a turtle," she tells the Washington *Post*.[78] A kid with a turtle is the most innocuous thing in the world. Kids have been catching turtles for as long as there have been kids. But suddenly the rules are different: a car wash, a shower, catching a pet turtle, making a living by farming—all are no longer the simple, uncomplicated pleasures of daily life. And no one in these stories seems to know why things have changed. What is not innocuous is the countless ways that population growth adversely affects people's lives. What is particularly not innocuous is the uniformity with which newspapers crop from the story frame any mention of population as an ultimate cause of the problems they report.

Despite the fact that many scientific groups, environmental scientists, and even land development specialists connect land conversion and water shortages to population growth, only about 10 percent of news stories link human population growth to the problems it causes. Even more significantly, only 1 story in a sample of 150 presents the view that limiting population growth might be a solution to environmental problems. From the standpoint of framing environmental problems, the most misleading stories might be those that mention population growth as a source of the problem but ignore population stability as a solution. For these stories effectively tell the reader: *Yes, population growth causes environmental degradation, but population growth is too sacred a cow to be addressed as a policy issue.*

Environmentalist Lester Brown opened a recent New York *Times* article, "When the history of the last half of this century is written, population growth is likely to get far more attention than it does now."[79] His point is that we do not understand the sweeping changes that population growth is wreaking around us, and we will not understand them until it may be too late. Why not? Why do opinion polls and U.S. policy show such indifference toward the population issue? This chapter's examination of the history of media coverage of population problems suggests several answers.

The first population crisis, the "bomb" reported by the media through the 1960s and into the early 1970s, ended not with an explosion but with a Green Revolution. The neo-Malthusians gave a famine and nobody came; hence, the news media and the public gradually lost interest in population. But during the past 25 years, while pronatalists have had good sport kicking the neo-Malthusians for profligate prophesy,[80] while media coverage and public attention waned on the population issue, population has kept growing. And so have its effects. During the past 25 years, world population has grown by about 2 billion people. The effects of this growth have been tremendous—not in terms of human starvation but in terms of the pressure on a finite environment. By one estimate, humans now appropriate 40 percent of the net primary production of photosynthesis on the entire planet.[81]

In the United States, the negative effects of population growth can be seen in thousands of communities, in the form of diminished wildlife habitat, endangered species, water shortages, and many other collisions between expanding human populations and finite nature. These thousands of minicrises do not have the drama of a massive famine, yet they reduce the quality of Americans' lives in tiny nibbles.

One agenda-setting study of the issues of the 1960s shows that news coverage and public awareness of issues frequently bear tenuous relation to the actual severity of the issues reported.[82] Certainly this has been the case with population growth. Since the early 1970s, we have seen virtually an inverse relationship between media coverage (and public concern) about population growth and the actual seriousness of the effects of population growth. As population grew and its effects became more virulent, media coverage and public interest waned. This disparity between perception and reality originates in how the media frame the effects of population growth.

The media and their neo-Malthusian sources mislabeled the population crisis of the early 1970s by framing the effects of population in terms of the food supply. The media and their sources accepted Malthus's premise that the food supply could grow only in a linear fashion, when in fact plant science was able to outstrip even exponential population growth.

The real locus of the population crisis has not been the food supply—which human ingenuity *can* and *did* cause to increase dramatically—but rather environmental quantities that we cannot substantially increase at all: the land, the water, the atmosphere. Viewed in this frame, population growth is not merely the progenitor of future famines in faraway lands but a very American problem, here and now. But population remains low on the agenda for most Americans, and until news framing connects population growth to the problems it causes, population seems likely to remain a crisis for the future, off the agenda for now—despite its significant role in environmental degradation and despite the warnings of the world's leading scientists.

NOTES

1. Sandra Postel, "Denial in the Decisive Decade," in *State of the World, 1992*, Linda Starke, ed. (New York: W.W. Norton Co., 1992), 3-8.

2. Barbara Ward and René Dubos, *Only One Earth* (New York: W. W. Norton Co., 1972); Paul Ehrlich and Anne Ehrlich, *The Population Explosion* (New York: Simon & Schuster, 1990); Barry Commoner, *Making Peace with the Planet* (New York: Pantheon Books, 1990); Paul Harrison, *The Third Revolution* (London: I.B. Tauris, 1992).

3. *Christian Science Monitor, 27 April 1992.*

4. Carl Sagan, "To Avert a Common Danger," *Parade Magazine*, 1 March 1992, 10-14.

5. Jim Detjen, "Scientists: Earth Near Danger Level," Knight-Ridder News Service, in Austin *American-Statesman*, 19 November 1992. The full text of the message can be found in "Warning to Humanity–A Declaration by Scientists on Global Issues," *Population and Development Review* 18 (December 1992): 782-783.

6. Frank Newport and Lydia Saad, "Public Support Mixed for U.S. Efforts to Curb World Overpopulation," *The Gallup Poll Monthly* 320 (May 1992): 34-41.

7. Harold Lasswell, "The Structure and Function of Communication in Society," in *The Communication of Ideas*, L. Bryson, ed. (New York: Harper & Brothers, 1948), 37-51.

8. Jan Hogendorn, *Economic Development*, 2nd ed. (New York: HarperCollins Publishers, 1992), 258-294.

9. William Petersen, "Staying Alive: Some Home Truths About Population," *American Scholar* 57 (Winter 1988): 58.

10. David Yaukey, *Demography: The Study of Human Population* (Prospect Heights, IL: Waveland Press, 1985), 40.

11. Paul Ehrlich, *The Population Bomb* (New York: Ballantine Books, 1968), xi.

12. Georg Borgstrom, *The Hungry Planet* (New York: Macmillan, 1965).

13. Georg Borgstrom, *Too Many: A Study of Earth's Biological Limitations* (New York: Macmillan, 1969), 320.

14. John Laffin, *The Hunger to Come* (London: Abelard-Schuman, 1971), 23.

15. William Paddock and Paul Paddock, *Famine–1975!* (Boston: Little, Brown and Company, 1967), 229.

16. Thomas Malthus, "An Essay on the Principle of Population," in *On Population: Thomas Robert Malthus*, Gertrude Himmelfarb, ed. (New York: Random House, 1960), 9.

17. Ibid., 124.

18. New York *Times*, 21 August 1974.

19. New York *Times*, 26 August 1974.

20. New York *Times*, 30 August 1974.

21. New York *Times*, 21 August 1974.

22. New York *Times*, 28 August 1974.

23. New York *Times*, 28 August 1974.

24. New York *Times*, 21 August 1974.

25. *The Times of London*, 16 August 1974.

26. *The Times of London*, 26 August 1974.

27. *The Times of London*, 28 August 1974.

28. *The Times of India* (Bombay), 28 August 1974.

29. New York *Times*, 26 August 1974.

30. G. Narayana and John F. Kantner, *Doing the Needful: The Dilemma of India's Population Policy* (Boulder, CO: Westview Press, 1992).

31. *The Times of London*, 26 August 1974.

32. *The Times of London*, 31 August 1974.

33. New York *Times*, 26 August 1974.

34. New York *Times*, 28 August 1974.

35. G. Ray Funkhouser, "The Issues of the Sixties: An Exploratory Study in the Dynamics of Public Opinion," *Public Opinion Quarterly* 37 (1973): 62-75.

36. Paul Ehrlich, "Interview," *Playboy* (August 1970); reprinted in *Population: A Clash of Prophets*, Edward Pohlman, ed. (New York: New American Library, 1973), 13-34.

37. Laffin, *The Hunger to Come*, 50.

38. Yaukey, *Demography*, 12.

39. Newport and Saad, "Public Support Mix," 34-41.

40. Bernhard Glaeser, "Agriculture Between the Green Revolution and Ecodevelopment: Which Way to Go?" in *The Green Revolution Revisited: Critique and Alternative*, Bernhard Glaeser, ed. (London: Unwin Hyman, 1987).

41. Sudhir Sen, *Reaping the Green Revolution: Foods and Jobs for All* (Maryknoll, NY: Orbis Books, 1975), 7.

42. Sayed Marei, *The World Food Crisis* (London: Longman, 1976), 15.

43. Lester Brown, "A New Era Unfolds," in *State of the World 1993*, Linda Starke, ed. (New York: W. W. Norton & Co., 1993), 11.

44. John Wilmoth and Patrick Ball, "The Population Debate in American Popular Magazines, 1946-90," *Population and Development Review* 18 (December 1992): 635.

45. Paul Ehrlich, "Speaking Out on Overpopulation: A Conspiracy of Silence is Limiting Action on the World's Most Basic Environmental Problem," *Issues in Science and Technology* 5 (Winter 1989): 36.

46. Jian-Hua Zhu, "Issue Competition and Attention Distraction: A Zero-Sum Theory of Agenda Setting," *Journalism Quarterly* 69 (1992): 825-836.

47. Newport and Saad, "Public Support Mixed," 34.

48. Pew Global Stewardship Initiative, *Pew Global Stewardship Initiative Survey* (Washington, DC: Belden & Russonello Research and Communications, Project 93-68, February 2-15, 1994), 6-18.

49. New York *Times*, 9 August 1984.

50. *The Times of London*, 6 August 1984.

51. New York *Times*, 11 August 1984.

52. *The Times of London*, 10 August 1984.

53. *The Times of London*, 6 August 1984.

54. Austin *American-Statesman*, 18 August 1992.

55. Garrett Hardin, "From Shortage to Longage: Forty Years in the Population Vineyards," *Population and Environment* 12 (1991), 342.

56. Pew Global Stewardship Initiative, "Report of Findings from Focus Groups on Population, Consumption, and the Environment," (Washington, DC: Belden & Russonello Research and Communications, 1993), 22.

57. Ibid., 26; italics in the original report.

58. Gregory Bateson, *Steps to an Ecology of Mind: Collected Essays in Anthropology, Psychiatry, Evolution, and Epistemology* (San Francisco: Chandler Publishing Co., 1972), 177-193.

59. Erving Goffman, *Frame Analysis: An Essay on the Organization of Experience* (Boston: Northeastern University Press, 1974).

60. See Gaye Tuchman's *Making News: A Study in the Construction of Reality* (New York: Free Press, 1978); and Todd Gitlin's *The Whole World Is Watching: Mass Media in the Making & Unmaking of the New Left* (Berkeley: University of California Press, 1980).

61. Wenmouth Williams, Jr., Mitchell Shapiro, and Craig Cutbirth, "The Impact of Campaign Agendas on Perception of Issues," *Journalism Quarterly* 60 (1983): 226-232.

62. Robert Entman, "Framing: Toward Clarification of a Fractured Paradigm," *Journal of Communication* 43 (1993): 51-58. For in-depth discussion of framing, see William Gamson and Andre Modigliani, "Media Discourse and Public Opinion on Nuclear Power: A Constructionist Approach," *American Journal of Sociology* 95 (1989): 1-37; Zhongdang Pan and Gerald Kosicki, "Framing Analysis: An Approach to News Discourse," *Political Communication* 10 (January-March 1993): 55-76; James Tankard, Jr., Laura Hendrickson, Jackie Silberman, Kris Bliss and Salma Ghanem, "Media Frames: Approaches to Conceptualization and Measurement" (paper delivered at the meeting of the Communication Theory and Methodology Division, Association for Education in Journalism and Mass Communication, Boston, August 1991); Laura Hendrickson, "Multi-Frame News: Identifying Multiple Frames Through Microcoding," *Southwestern Mass Communication Journal* 8 (1993):

17-29; Shanto Iyengar, "How Citizens Think About National Issues: A Matter of Responsibility," *American Journal of Political Science* 33 (November 1989): 878-900; idem, *Is Anyone Responsible? How Television Frames Political Issues* (Chicago: University of Chicago Press, 1991).

63. Maxwell McCombs, "Explorers and Surveyors: Expanding Strategies for Agenda-Setting Research," *Journalism Quarterly* 69 (1992): 813-824. See also Mark Benton and P. Jean Frazier, "The Agenda-Setting Function of Mass Media at Three Levels of Information-Holding," *Communication Research* 3 (1976): 261-274.

64. Robert Entman, *Democracy Without Citizens: Media and the Decay of American Politics* (New York: Oxford University Press, 1989), 54.

65. Paul Sears, "The Process of Environmental Change by Man"; originally published in *Man's Role in Changing the Face of the Earth*, W. E. Thomas, ed. (Chicago: University of Chicago Press, 1956); reprinted in *The Ecology of Man: An Ecosystems Approach*, R. L. Smith, ed. (New York: Harper & Row, 1972), 129-138. See also Richard Jackson, *Land Use in America* (New York: John Wiley & Sons, 1981); Norman Myers, *The Primary Source: Tropical Forests and Our Future* (New York: W. W. Norton & Company, 1992); Ehrlich and Ehrlich, *The Population Explosion*, 129-134; Harrison, *The Third Revolution*, 107-114, 242.

66. Robert McConnell, "The Real Environmental Crisis, or What Happened to Government by the People, for the People?" *Population and Environment* 12 (1991): 407-416. See also Sandra Postel, "Facing Water Scarcity." In *State of the World, 1993*, Linda Starke, ed. (New York: W.W. Norton, 1993), 22-41; Thomas Homer-Dixon, Jeffrey Boutwell, and George Rathjens, "Environmental Change and Violent Conflict," *Scientific American* (February 1993): 38-45.

67. See Lewis Goodkin, *When Real Estate and Home Building Become Big Business: Mergers, Acquisitions and Joint Ventures* (Boston: Cahners Books, 1974), 14; Ira Cobleigh, *All About Investing in Real Estate Securities* (New York: Weybright and Talley, 1971), 10; John McMahan, *Property Development: Effective Decision Making in Uncertain Times* (New York: McGraw-Hill, 1976), 76.

68. See Ester Boserup, *The Conditions of Agricultural Growth: The Economics of Agrarian Change Under Population Pressure* (Chicago: Aldine, 1965); Piers Blaikie and Harold Brookfield, *Land Degradation and Society* (London: Methuen & Co., 1987), 34; Julian Simon, *Population Matters* (New Brunswick, NJ: Transaction Publishers, 1990), 50.

69. Herbert Gans, *Deciding What's News* (New York: Vintage Books, 1979), 48-50.

70. Council on Environmental Quality, *Environmental Quality–1976* (Washington, DC: Government Printing Office, 1976), 297; cited in Richard Jackson, *Land Use in America* (New York: John Wiley & Sons, 1981), 129.

71. Mike Maher, "How News Media Frame the Population-Environment Connection." (Paper delivered to the Media and the Environment Conference, Association for Education in Journalism and Mass Communication, Reno, NV, April 1994), 13-14.

72. Ottawa *Citizen*, 21 February 1993.

73. Vancouver *Sun*, 27 February 1993.

74. Sacramento *Bee*, 6 February 1993.

75. St. Petersburg *Times*, 11 January 1993.

76. St. Paul *Star Tribune*, 6 April 1993.

77. Seattle *Times*, 9 December 1992.

78. Washington *Post*, 22 June 1993.

79. Lester Brown, "Natural Limits," *The New York Times*, 24 July 1993.

80. See, for example, Julian Simon and Herman Kahn, eds., *The Resourceful Earth: A Response to Global 2000* (New York: Basil Blackwell, 1984); Ben Wattenberg, *The Birth Dearth* (New York: Pharos Books, 1987); Ronald Bailey, *Eco-Scam: The False Prophets of Ecological Apocalypse* (New York: St. Martin's Press, 1993); Ben Bolch and Harold Lyons, *Apocalypse Not! Science, Economics, and Environmentalism* (Washington, DC: Cato Institute, 1993).

81. Ehrlich and Ehrlich, *The Population Explosion*, 36.

82. Funkhouser, "The Issues of the Sixties," 62-75.

14 ↝

THE PRESS AND CRISIS:
WHAT HAVE WE LEARNED?

Mike Maher and Lloyd Chiasson Jr.

Harold Lasswell once wrote that the three functions of communication are surveillance, correlation, and transmission of culture.[1] More than 200 agenda setting studies have confirmed that the media generally succeed in surveillance; that is, those issues that get the most media coverage become the issues the public thinks are most important.[2]

But few studies have asked: Are the media telling us to think about *the right things*? And further, how well do the media perform the task of correlation? Do media stories about problems give us an accurate picture of what is causing those problems?

Media critics have noted the inherent weaknesses in how news portrays reality. Walter Lippmann showed that the press had to rely on stereotypes, and that news could merely "signalize events" rather than convey a broader truth that would allow people to take responsible action.[3] Recent critics have shown that media portrayals consistently emphasize people rather than issues, crisis rather than continuity, the present rather than the past or the future. News stories fragment reality into isolated, decontextualized units; but they usually contain official assurance of normalcy, so that the public concludes "the system worked."[4]

Previous scholarship about crisis coverage has noted similar weaknesses–that the media have a tendency to ignore causes and to avoid long-term solutions to the AIDS crisis;[5] that the media do well at disseminating warnings of disaster, but are ineffective in conveying a sense of risk;[6] that media images of famine in Africa tend to portray victims as passive and helpless. This reinforces negative stereotypes and normally emphasizes quick-fix aid rather than genuine relief of the causes of famine.[7] The media spotlight frequently does not fall on the most severe disasters, but media coverage does influence relief aid.[8]

The preceding chapters of this book have shown that media coverage of crises has fallen into these patterns for more than 200 years. For example, after the Japanese attack at Pearl Harbor, newspapers on the West Coast stereotyped the Japanese Americans, and reality became buried under a landslide of misinformation. At a time when the public needed a responsible press, the press failed dismally. Newspapers pointed to isolated incidents, many of which were unsubstantiated rumors, to justify their positions. Problem: Japanese Americans represent a threat. Solution: Remove them. Result: The internal safety of the West Coast will not be compromised, thus guaranteeing a return to normalcy. The press's focus was on the here and now, not on injustices in the past, nor what mass evacuation might mean to constitutional guarantees in the future. Isolated from the real problem, the Japanese-Americans had no chance. It mattered little that the country was at war; that normalcy was an impossibility; that internal security had nothing to do with mass removal of people with a yellow tint to their skin.

Crisis was the anthem of yellow journalism and, in fact, seems to have been the theme of the entire period. No chapter better illustrates the power of the press, its lapses in applying ethical standards to itself, and its tendency to be ruled by monetary impulses. At no time in American history has the press been more rambunctious in its portrayal of reality.

There's a chicken-and-egg aspect to evaluating Joe McCarthy's relationship with the press. What came first: objectivity or the Big Lie? The press created an ideology upon which it functioned for more than a century. McCarthy certainly wasn't the first to see objectivity could be used against the press to personal benefit. He just did it better than anyone else. What the press did wonderfully well during the McCarthy years was to signalize events: a press conference here, a news leak there. Reports of unsubstantiated claims were the fuel to McCarthy's engine, and he, along with the press, kept it running for four long years.

The civil rights movement in the 1960s represented stereotypical coverage dominated by faces, names, and conflicts. But what was behind the faces, the names and the conflicts? What fostered the desire for change? The press covered isolated events, attempted to synthesize, and was efficient in keeping the public informed as to what happened. Unfortunately the press, and the rest of us, rarely grasped why.

We know about the deforestation of Amazon rain forests, about acid rain in the northeastern United States, about the effects of radioactivity on people near Chernobyl. But the press has provided no synthesis of environmental problems, causes, and effects. Instead, the public is fed bits and pieces, fragmented glimpses that fail to bring into focus *the most important story* of the 21st century. At no other time in the history of our species has our population doubled in a single human lifetime. Yet in this century human numbers will double twice in a single lifetime. Neo-Malthusians scared us with the specter of massive starvation during the 1960s, but the Green Revolution allowed us to avert that crisis. The real effects of human population growth have been more subtle, yet more pervasive: loss of wildlife habitat, crowding, water shortages, atmospheric changes, endangered species. But media coverage of these crises consistently fails to tie the problems to their source in population growth. As a result, the American public is less concerned about population than it was a generation ago—yet we add about 90 million people to world population every year. This virtually guarantees that future environmental crises will be even more severe, while population growth remains off the agenda of public concern.

It would be unfair to portray the press as an undermining agent throughout history or to criticize it for what it might not do in the future. The press has often covered events with remarkable fairness and depth, and it has sometimes led public opinion in positive ways. Throughout the party press period, newspapers served as the voices of the fledging parties, and, in doing so, essentially wrote the first party platforms. More than 200 years later, the New Orleans *Times-Picayune* decided to follow its own beliefs, to ignore the prevailing attitude concerning ethical considerations, and to take a stand in a gubernatorial election it considered too important to cover in traditional fashion.

At times, the press has been on the defensive. The Alien and Sedition Acts clearly were attempts at political control through press control. It took less than two decades for the country, and its newspapers, to face its first significant crisis involving freedom of expression. It would not be the last. During the Civil War, the president and the press were in uncharted waters, and the press faced a reduction in freedom of expression, first by the president, then by the military, and to a lesser degree, by itself.

So what is the final verdict about the press in conflict? The press, in short, often can't see the crisis for all the crises. It continues to spend a great deal of time describing the most prominent trees, but we never get more than a fleeting glimpse of what the forest looks like.

W. Lance Bennett once said that media coverage of crises are resolved "when situations return to 'manageable' levels of difficulty. Seldom if ever are underlying problems treated and eliminated at their source. The news is certainly not the cause of these problems, but it could become part of the solution if it dropped dramatic coverage of symptoms in favor of continuing illumination of causes."[9]

Have the media been part of the solution in covering past crises? This historical survey confirms that during 200 years of press reportage of American crises the media have generally neglected underlying causes in favor of covering the spectacular effect. Yet, oddly enough, history has sometimes vindicated this inherent shallowness of media coverage. The colonial press helped maintain morale and sustain indignation about the British by propagandizing for the war effort. The abolitionist press arguably brought slavery to an earlier end—although at a horrible and possibly avoidable cost in human lives. The New Orleans *Times-Picayune* abandoned the traditional press role of impartiality in the 1992 election, to keep Louisiana from electing a neofacist governor. At other times, history has shown that the press penchant to stereotype has served evil ends. The media fomented war fever against Spain at the end of the 19th century. They fostered Communist hysteria in 1919 and 1920. They supported suspension of civil liberties for Japanese Americans during World War II. And knowing the media weakness for sensation, Senator Joe McCarthy was able to manipulate American public opinion by fabulating Communist presence.

What can this kind of coverage mean for agenda setting? It has been shown that agenda setting could extend beyond the level of issue salience and into the realm of causes and solutions.[10] In this light, media coverage of crises arguably sets a palliative agenda. If media stories mention causes at all—and frequently they do not—they tend to mention proximate causes but neglect ultimate causes. Such coverage implies quick-fix solutions: War with Spain means a better Cuba; reporting rumors of Communists in every level of the government will somehow improve the government; supporting exceptions to the Constitution is for Americans', even Japanese Americans' own good; turning murderers like John Brown into martyrs is acceptable for a higher good; making people acquainted with, rather than knowledgeable about, the problems facing the environment is acceptable reportage.

Is this media myopia curable? Or do the media merely give the public what it wants: drama instead of substance? We should acknowledge that many media professionals try to do the best job of reportage they can, given the resources at their disposal. But the forces of media economics, audience wishes, deadlines, and accepted journalistic work routines imply that media performance is unlikely to improve dramatically in coverage of future crises. If nothing else, we can learn from these chapters the dangers of relying on the media to be our agenda setters in times of crisis.

NOTES

1. Harold Lasswell, "The Structure and Function of Communication in Society," in *The Communication of Ideas*, Lyman Bryson, ed. (New York: Harper & Brothers, 1948), 37-51.

2. Everett Rogers, Dearing, J., and Bregman, D. "The Anatomy of Agenda-setting Research," *Journal of Communication 43* (1993): 68-85. *See also* Maxwell McCombs, "Explorers and Surveyors: Expanding Strategies for Agenda-Setting

Research," *Journalism Quarterly* 69 (1992): 813-824; and Maxwell McCombs and Donald Shaw, "The Evolution of Agenda-Setting Research: Twenty-Five Years in the Marketplace of Ideas" *Journal of Communication* 43 (1993): 58-68.

3. Walter Lippmann, *Public Opinion*. (New York: The Free Press, 1922), 226.

4. W. Lance Bennett, *News: The Politics of Illusion* (New York: Longman, 1988), 7-27; see also Robert Entman, *Democracy Without Citizens: Media and the Decay of American Politics* (New York: Oxford University Press, 1989), 49-50.

5. Gene Burd, "Preventive Journalism and AIDS Editorials: Dilemmas for Private and Public Health," in *Bad Tidings: Communication and Catastrophe*, Lynne Masel Walters, Lee Wilkins, and Tim Walters, eds., (Hillsdale, NJ: Lawrence Erlbaum, 1989), 85-113.

6. Ford Burkhart, *Media, Emergency Warnings, and Citizen Response* (Boulder, CO: Westview Press, 1991), 120.

7. Jonathan Benthall, *Disasters, Relief and the Media* (London: I. B. Tauris, 1993), 36-42.

8. Lewis Aptekar, *Environmental Disasters in Global Perspective* (New York: G.K. Hall, 1994), 128-132; for a summary of the history of scholarship on mass communication and disaster, see E.L. Quarantelli, "The Social Science Study of Disasters and Mass Communication," in *Bad Tidings: Communication and Catastrophe*.

9. Bennett, *News: The Politics of Illusion*, 24.

10. Mark Benton and P. Jean Frazier, "The Agenda-Setting Function of Mass Media at Three Levels of Information-Holding," *Communication Research* 3 (1976): 261-274.

REFERENCES

Adams, Alice D. *The Neglected Period of Anti-Slavery in America*. Gloucester, MA: Peter Smith, 1964.

Allport, Gordon W. *The Nature of Prejudice*. London: Addison-Wesley Publishing Company, 1954.

American Society of Newspaper Editors Bulletin, March 1992.

"An American Tragedy, 1967—Detroit." *Newsweek,* 7 August 1967, 18-34. and Clarke, Ltd.,1929.

Ames, William E. *A History of the National Intelligencer*. Chapel Hill: University of North Carolina Press, 1972.

Ames, William E., and Gerald J. Baldasty. "The Washington, D.C., Political Press: A Developmental History of Functions." Paper presented to the Association for Education in Journalism, University of Washington, Seattle, WA, 1978.

Anderson, Jack, and Ronald W. May. *McCarthy: The Man, The Senator, the "Ism."* Boston: Beacon Press, 1952.

Andrews, J. Cutler. "The Confederate Press and Public Morale." *Journal of Southern History* 32 (November 1966): 445–465.

_____. *The North Reports the Civil War*. Pittsburgh, PA: University of Pittsburgh Press, 1955.

_____. *The South Reports the Civil War*. Princeton, NJ: Princeton University Press, 1970.

Aptekar, Lewis. *Environmental Disasters in Global Perspective*. New York: G. K. Hall, 1994.

Aptheker, Bettina. *Woman's Legacy: Essays on Race, Sex, and Class in American History*. Amherst: University of Massachusetts Press, 1982.

Aptheker, Herbert. *Abolitionism: A Revolutionary Movement*. Boston: Twayne Publishers, 1989.

_____. *One Continual Cry*. New York: Humanities Press, 1965.

Arlen, Michael J. *Living-Room War*. New York: Viking, 1969.

Aronson, James. *The Press and the Cold War*. New York: Bobbs-Merrill, 1970.

Avery, Donald R. "The Newspaper on the Eve of the War of 1812: Changes in Content Patterns, 1808-1812." Ph.D. diss., Southern Illinois University, 1982.

Bailey, George. "Television War: Trends in Network Coverage of the Vietnam War," *Journal of Broadcasting* 20 (Spring 1976): 147-159.

Bailey, George, and Lawrence Lichty. "Rough Justice on a Saigon Street: A Gatekeeper Study of NBC's Tet Execution Film." *Journalism Quarterly,* 49 (Summer 1972): 221–229, 238.

Bailey, Ronald. *Eco-Scam: The False Prophets of Ecological Apocalypse.* New York: St. Martin's Press, 1993.

Bailyn, Bernard, David Brion Davis, David Herbert Donald, John L. Thomas, Robert H. Wiebe, and Gordon S. Wood. *The Great Republic: A History of the American People.* Boston: Little, Brown & Co., 1977.

Baldwin, James. *The Fire Next Time.* New York: Dial Press, 1963.

Barney, Ralph, Jay Black, and Bob Steele. *Doing Ethics in Journalism.* Greencastle, IN: Sigma Delta Chi Foundation, 1993.

Barrett, Marvin. "A Time of Assassins." *Columbia Journalism Review,* (Summer 1968): 5–9.

Bartlett, Irving H. "The Persistence of Wendell Phillips," in *The Antislavery Vanguard: New Essays on the Abolitionists.* Princeton, edited by Martin Duberman. NJ: Princeton University Press, 1965.

Basler, Roy P. *The Collected Works of Abraham Lincoln.* 8 vols. New Brunswick, NJ: Rutgers University Press, 1953.

Bassett, John Spencer. *A Short History of the United States: 1492–1920.* New York: Macmillan, 1910.

Bateson, Gregory. *Steps to an Ecology of Mind: Collected Essays in Anthropology, Psychiatry, Evolution, and Epistemology.* San Francisco: Chandler Publishing Co., 1972.

Bayley, Edwin. *Joe McCarthy and the Press.* New York: Pantheon Books, 1981.

Bennett, W. Lance. *News: The Politics of Illusion.* New York: Longman, 1988.

Benthall, Jonathan. *Disasters, Relief and the Media.* London: I.B. Tauris, 1993.

Benton, Mark, and P. Jean Frazier. "The Agenda-Setting Function of Mass Media at Three Levels of Information-Holding." *Communication Research* 3 (1976): 261–274.

Blaikie, Piers, and Harold Brookfield. *Land Degradation and Society.* London: Methuen & Co., 1987.

Blanchard, Margaret A. "Free Expression and Wartime: Lessons from the Past, Hopes for the Future." *Journalism Quarterly* 69 (Spring 1992): 5–17.

Bleyer, Willard Grosvenor. *Main Currents in the History of American Journalism.* Boston: Houghton Mifflin Company, 1927.

Bliven, Bruce. *Five Million Words Later: An Autobiography.* New York: John Day Co., 1970.

Bolch, Ben and Harold Lyons. *Apocalypse Not! Science, Economics, and Environmentalism.* Washington, DC: Cato Institute, 1993.

Bongaarts, John. "Population Growth and Global Warming." *Population and Development Review* 18 (1992): 299–319.

Boorstin, Daniel. *The Americans: The Colonial Experience.* New York: Random House, 1958.

_____. *The Image: A Guide to Pseudo-Events in America.* New York: Atheneum, 1980.

Borgstrom, Georg. *The Hungry Planet.* New York: Macmillan, 1965.

_____. *Too Many: A Study of Earth's Biological Limitations.* New York: Macmillan, 1969.

Boserup, Ester. *The Conditions of Agricultural Growth: The Economics of Agrarian Change Under Population Pressure.* Chicago: Aldine, 1965.

Boughey, Arthur. *Ecology of Populations.* 2nd ed. New York: Macmillan Publishing Co., 1973.

Bowles, Dorothy. "Newspaper Support for Free Expression in Times of Alarm, 1920 and 1940." *Journalism Quarterly* 54 (Summer 1977): 271–279.

Boyce, D. G. "Public Opinion and Historians," *The Journal of the Historical Association* 63 (September 1978): 222.

Boyer, Richard O. *The Legend of John Brown, a Biography and a History.* New York: Alfred A. Knopf, 1973.

Boylan, James. "A Salisbury Chronicle." *Columbia Journalism Review* (Winter 1966-1967): 10–14.

Braestrup, Peter. *The Big Story: How the American Press and Television Reported and Interpreted the Crisis of Tet 1968 in Vietnam and Washington.* 2 vols. Boulder, CO: Westview Press, 1977.

Brant, Irving. *The Bill of Rights: Its Origin and Meaning.* New York: Bobbs-Merrill, 1965; Signet Classics, 1967.

Brantley, Raburn L. *Georgia Journalism of the Civil War Period.* Nashville, TN: George Peabody College for Teachers, 1929.

Bridges, Tyler. *The Rise of David Duke.* Oxford: University Press of Mississippi, 1994.

Brigham, Clarence S. *History and Bibliography of American Newspapers, 1690–1820.* Vols. 23-37. Worcester, MA: American Antiquarian Society, 1947.

Brown, Lester. "Natural Limits." New York *Times*, 24 July 1993.

_____. "A New Era Unfolds." In *State of the World 1993*, edited by Linda Starke, 3-21. New York: W. W. Norton & Co., 1993.

Brown, Roger H. *The Republic in Peril: 1812.* New York: Columbia University Press, 1964.

Browne, Malcolm W. "Vietnam Reporting: Three Years of Crisis," *Columbia Journalism Review* (Fall 1964): 4–9.

Bryan, Carter R. "Negro Journalism in America Before Emancipation," *Journalism Monographs* 12 (1969).

Buchstein, Frederick D. "The Anarchist Press in American Journalism." *Journalism History* 1 (Summer 1974): 43–45.

Burd, Gene. "Preventive Journalism and AIDS Editorials: Dilemmas for Private and Public Health," in *Bad Tidings: Communication and Catastrophe*, edited by Lynne Masel Walters, Lee Wilkins, and Tim Walters. Hillsdale, NJ: Lawrence Erlbaum, 1989.

Burkett, Ford. *Media, Emergency Warnings, and Citizen Response.* Boulder, CO: Westview Press, 1991.

Burns, James MacGregor. *Roosevelt—The Soldier of Freedom.* New York: Harvest/ Harcourt Brace Jovanovich, 1970.

Burt, A.L. "The Nature of the Maritime Issues." In *The Causes of the War of 1812* , edited by Bradford Perkins. New York: Holt, Rinehart & Winston, 1962.

_____. *The United States, Great Britain, and British North America from the Revolution to the Establishment of Peace After the War of 1812.* New Haven, CT: Yale University Press, 1940.

Cappon, Lester J., and Stella F. Duff. *Virginia Gazette Index, 1736–1780.* 2 vols. Williamsburg, VA: Institute of Early American History and Culture, 1950.

Carlson, Oliver and Erest Sutherland Bates. *Hearst, Lord of San Simeon.* New York: Viking, 1937.

Carroll, Peter N., and David W. Noble. *The Free and the Unfree: A New History of the United States.* 2nd ed. New York: Penguin, 1988.

_____. *The Restless Centuries: A History of the American People.* 2nd ed. Minneapolis, MN: Burgess Publishing Co., 1979.

Carter, Hodding. *The Words Were Bullets: The Southern Press in War, Reconstruction, and Peace.* Athens: University of Georgia Press, 1969.

Cater, Douglass. "The Captive Press." *The Reporter* 2 (6 June 1950): 18.

Chafee, Zechariah Jr. *The Blessings of Liberty.* Philadelphia: J.B. Lippincott Co., 1956.

_____. *Free Speech in the United States.* Cambridge: Harvard University Press, 1941; Atheneum Books, 1969.

Channing, Steven. *Crisis of Fear.* New York: Simon and Schuster, 1970.

Cheyney, Edward P. *An Introduction to the Industrial and Social History of England.* New York: Macmillan, 1910.

Chiasson, Lloyd Jr. "An Editorial Analysis of the Japanese-American Evacuation and Encampment, 1941-1942," *Journalism Quarterly* 68, Nos. 1-2 (Spring-Summer 1991).

_____. "The Japanese-American Encampment: An Editorial Analysis of Twenty-seven Newspapers," *Newspaper Research Journal* 12, no. 2 (Spring 1991).

Clark, Mary Elizabeth. *Peter Porcupine in America: The Career of William Cobbett, 1792–1800.* Philadelphia: Beekman Publishers, 1939.

Cobb-Reiley, Linda. "Aliens and Alien Ideas: The Suppression of Anarchists and the Anarchist Press in America, 1901-1914." *Journalism History* 15 (Summer-Autumn 1988): 50–59.

Coben, Stanley. *A. Mitchell Palmer: Politician.* New York: Columbia University Press, 1963.

Cobleigh, Ira. *All About Investing in Real Estate Securities.* New York: Weybright and Talley, 1971.

Commoner, Barry. *Making Peace with the Planet.* New York: Pantheon Books, 1990.

Communist Infiltration in the Army, 83rd Cong., 2d sess., 1954, 107–108.

Cong. Record, 97 (21 April 1951): 4259–4270.

Cong. Record, 97 (14 June 1951): 6556–6603.

Conrat, Richard and Maisie, *Executive Order 9066, the Internment of 110,000 Japanese Americans.* Cambridge, MA: MIT Press, 1972.

Cornwell, Elmer E., Jr. "The Johnson Press Relations Style," *Journalism Quarterly* 43 (Spring 1966): 3–9.

Council on Environmental Quality. *Environmental Quality—1976.* Washington, DC: Government Printing Office, 1976. Cited in Richard Jackson, *Land Use in America.* New York: John Wiley & Sons, 1981.

Craven, Avery. *The Coming of the Civil War.* Chicago: University of Chicago Press, 1942.

Crosby, Donald F. *God, Church and Flag: Senator Joseph R. McCarthy and the Catholic Church, 1950–1957.* Chapel Hill: University of North Carolina Press, 1978.

Crozier, Emmet. *Yankee Reporters, 1861–65.* New York: Oxford University Press, 1956.

Dauer, Manning J. *The Adams Federalists.* Baltimore, MD: Johns Hopkins Press, 1953, 1968.

Davidson, Bill. "'Hell, No, We Won't Go.'"*Saturday Evening Post,* 27 January 1968, 21–26.

Davidson, Philip. *Propaganda and the American Revolution, 1763–1783.* Chapel Hill: University of North Carolina Press, 1941.

Davis, David Brion. *The Slave Power Conspiracy and the Paranoid Style.* Baton Rouge: Louisiana State University Press, 1969.

DeBow, J.D.B. *The Interest in Slavery of the Southern Non-Slave Holder. The Right of Peaceful Secession. Slavery in the Bible.* Charleston, SC: Evans & Cogswell, 1860.

Dementyev, I. *USA: Imperialists and Anti-Imperialists.* Moscow: Progress Publishers, 1979.

Dew, Thomas R. *Review of the Debate in the Virginia Legislature of 1831 and 1832.* Richmond, VA: T.W. White, 1832.

Diamond, Edwin. "Chicago Press: Rebellion and Retrenchment." *Columbia Journalism Review* (Fall 1968): 10–17.

Dictionary of American Biography. Vol. 3. New York: Scribner's Sons, 1929.

Dictionary of American Biography. Supplement Six, 1956–1960. New York: Charles Scribner & Sons, 1980.

Dillon, Merton L. *Benjamin Lundy and the Struggle for Negro Freedom.* Urbana: University of Illinois Press, 1966.

_____. *Elijah P. Lovejoy, Abolitionist Editor.* Urbana: University of Illinois Press, 1961.

"Dissenters: Rebels with Many Causes." *Newsweek,* 10 July 1967, 29–30, 33.

Donald, David. "The Pro-Slavery Argument Reconsidered." *Journal of Southern History* 37 (February 1971): 3–18.

Donovan, Josephine. *Uncle Tom's Cabin: Evil, Affliction, and Redemptive Love.* Boston: Twayne Publishers, 1991.

"Doubts About Vietnam." *Newsweek,* 23 October 1967, 96.

Dougan, Clark and Stephen Weiss. *Nineteen Sixty-eight: The Vietnam Experience.* Boston: Boston Publishing Co., 1983.

Douglass, Frederick. *Life and Times of Frederick Douglass.* Hartford, CT: Park Publishing Co., 1882.

_____. *Narrative of the Life of Frederick Douglass.* Boston: Anti-Slavery Office, 1845.

_____. *My Bondage and My Freedom.* New York: Miller, Orton & Mulligan, 1855.

Duberman, Martin. "The Northern Response." In *The Antislavery Vanguard: New Essays on the Abolitionists,* edited by Martin Duberman. Princeton, NJ: Princeton University Press, 1965.

Eaton, Clement. *The Freedom-of-Thought Struggle in the Old South.* Rev. ed. New York: Harper Torchbooks, 1964.

Ehrlich, Paul. "Interview." *Playboy* (August 1970). Reprinted in *Population: A Clash of Prophets.* Edited by Edward Pohlman, 13–34. New York: New American Library, 1973.

_____. *The Population Bomb*. New York: Ballantine Books, 1968.

_____. "Speaking Out on Overpopulation: A Conspiracy of Silence Is Limiting Action on the World's Most Basic Environmental Problem." *Issues in Science and Technology* 5 (Winter 1989): 36–37.

Ehrlich, Paul, and Anne Ehrlich. *The Population Explosion*. New York: Simon & Schuster, 1990.

Emerson, Thomas I. *The System of Freedom of Expression*. New York: Random House, 1970; Vintage Books, 1971.

Emery, Edwin and Michael Emery. *The Press and America*. 4th ed. Englewood Cliffs, NJ: Prentice-Hall, 1974.

_____. *The Press and America*, 5th ed. Englewood Cliffs, NJ: Prentice-Hall, 1984.

_____. *The Press and America*. 6th ed. Englewood Cliffs, NJ: Prentice-Hall, 1988.

_____. *The Press and America*. 7th ed. Englewood Cliffs, NJ: Prentice-Hall, 1993.

Entman, Robert. *Democracy Without Citizens: Media and the Decay of American Politics*. New York: Oxford University Press, 1989.

_____. "Framing: Toward Clarification of a Fractured Paradigm." *Journal of Communication* 43 (1993): 51–58.

Epstein, Edward J. *Between Fact and Fiction: The Problem of Journalism*. New York: Vintage Books, 1975.

Ex parte Endo, 323 U.S. 283 (1944).

Fehrenbacher, Don E. "The Paradoxes of Freedom." In *Freedom in America: A 200-Year Perspective*, edited by Norman A. Graebner. University Park: Pennsylvania State University Press, 1977.

Filler, Louis. *The Crusade Against Slavery, 1830–1860*. New York: Harper & Brothers, 1960.

"The Fire This Time." *Time*, 4 August 1967, 13–19.

Fisher, Anne Reeploeg. *Exile of a Race*. Seattle, WA: F and T Publishers, 1965.

Foner, Eric. *Nat Turner*. Englewood Cliffs, NJ: Prentice-Hall, 1971.

Foner, Eric, and John A. Garraty, eds. *The Reader's Companion to American History*. New York: Houghton Mifflin Co., 1991.

Foner, Philip S. *The Life and Writings of Frederick Douglass*, Vol. 2. New York: International Publishers, 1950–1955.

"Foreign Correspondents: The Saigon Story." *Time*, 11 October 1963, 55–56.

"Foreign Correspondents: The View from Saigon." *Time*, 30 September 1963, 62.

Franklin, Benjamin. *Writings*. Edited by J. A. Leo Lemay. New York: Library of America, 1987.

Freeman, Harrop A. "Genesis, Exodus and Leviticus—Genealogy, Evacuation and Law." *Cornell Law Quarterly* 28 (June 1943): 414–458.

Fried, Albert. *John Brown's Journey: Notes and Reflections on His America and Mine*. Garden City, NY: Anchor Press, 1978.

Fried, Richard M. *Men Against McCarthy*. New York: Columbia University Press, 1976.

_____. *Nightmare in Red: The McCarthy Era in Perspective*. New York: Oxford University Press, 1990.

Funkhouser, G. Ray. "The Issues of the Sixties: An Exploratory Study in the Dynamics of Public Opinion." *Public Opinion Quarterly* 37 (1973): 62–75.

Furnas, J. C. *Goodbye to Uncle Tom*. New York: William Sloane Associates, 1956.

_____. *Great Times: An Informal Social History of the United States, 1914–1929.* New York: G.P. Putnam's Sons, 1974.

Gamson, William, and Andre Modiglianai. "Media Discourse and Public Opinion on Nuclear Power: A Constructionist Approach." *American Journal of Sociology* 95 (1989): 1-37.

Gans, Herbert. *Deciding What's News.* New York: Vintage Books, 1979.

Gara, Larry. "Who Was An Abolitionist?" in *The Antislavery Vanguard: New Essays on the Abolitionists,* edited by Martin Duberman. Princeton, NJ: Princeton University Press, 1965.

Garrison, William Lloyd. *Thoughts on African Colonization.* Boston: Garrison and Knapp, 1832.

Garrison, W.P. and F.J. *William Lloyd Garrison, 1805–1879; The Story of his Life as told by his Children,* Vol. 1. New York: The Century Co., 1885–1889.

Genovese, Eugene E. *Rebellion to Revolution: Afro-American Slave Revolts in the Making of the Modern World.* Baton Rouge: Louisiana State University Press, 1979.

Gershen, Martin. "The Right to Lie," *Columbia Journalism Review* (Winter 1966-1967): 14–15.

Gitlin, Todd. *The Whole World Is Watching: Mass Media in the Making & Unmaking of the New Left.* Berkeley: University of California Press, 1980.

Glaeser, Bernhard, ed. *The Green Revolution Revisited: Critique and Alternative.* London: Unwin Hyman, 1987.

Glazer, Nathan. "The Methods of Senator McCarthy." In *McCarthyism,* edited by Thomas C. Reeves. Hinsdale, IL: Dryden Press, 1973.

Gleason, Timothy W. "Historians and Freedom of the Press Since 1800." *American Journalism* 5 (1988): 230–248.

The Global 2000 Report to the President: Entering the Twenty-First Century. Washington, DC: U.S. Government Printing Office, 1980.

Goffman, Erving. *Frame Analysis: An Essay on the Organization of Experience.* Boston: Northeastern University Press, 1974.

Goodkin, Lewis. *When Real Estate and Home Building Become Big Business: Mergers, Acquisitions and Joint Ventures.* Boston: Cahners Books, 1974.

Greene, Bob. *Johnny Deadline, Reporter.* Chicago: Nelson-Hall, 1976.

Greenwood, Grace. "An American Salon," *Cosmopolitan* 8 (1890), 437–447.

Griffith, Robert. "The Making of a Demagogue." In *McCarthyism,* edited by Thomas C. Reeves. Hinsdale, IL: Dryden Press, 1973.

_____. *The Politics of Fear.* Lexington: University Press of Kentucky, 1970.

Grodzins, Morton. *Americans Betrayed.* Chicago: University of Chicago Press, 1949.

Halberstam, David. *The Fifties.* New York: Villard Press, 1993.

_____. *The Making of a Quagmire.* New York: Random House, 1965.

Hallin, Daniel C. *The '"Uncensored War": The Media and Vietnam.* Berkeley: University of California Press, 1986.

Hamilton, S. M. *The Writings of James Monroe.* New York: Macmillan, 1898.

Hansen Arthur A. and Betty E. Mitson, eds. *Voice Long Silent, An Oral Inquiry Into the Japanese American Evacuation.* Fullerton: California State University, 1974.

Hardin, Garrett. "From Shortage to Longage: Forty Years in the Population Vineyards," *Population and Environment* 12 (1991): 339–349.

Harding, D. W. "General Conceptions in the Study of the Press and Public Opinion." *Sociological Review* 29 (October 1937): 390.

Harper, Robert. *Lincoln and the Press.* New York: McGraw-Hill, 1951.

Harrison, Paul. *The Third Revolution.* London: I. B. Tauris, 1992.

Harrold, Stanley. *Gamaliel Bailey and Antislavery Union.* Kent, OH: Kent State University Press, 1986.

Hart, Jim Allee. *Views on the News: The Developing Editorial Syndrome, 1500–1800.* Carbondale: Southern Illinois University Press, 1970.

Helper, Hinton R. *The Impending Crisis of the South.* New York: Burdick Brothers, 1857.

Hendrickson, Laura. "Multi-Frame News: Identifying Multiple Frames Through Microcoding." *Southwestern Mass Communication Journal* 8 (1993): 17–29.

Herr, Michael. *Dispatches.* New York: Alfred A. Knopf, 1977.

Higginbotham, Don. *The War of American Independence: Military Attitudes, Policies, and Practice, 1763–1789.* New York: Macmillan Company, 1971.

Hoffman, Abbie. *Soon to Be a Major Motion Picture.* New York: Perigree Books, 1980.

Hofstadter, Richard. *The American Political Tradition.* New York: Knopf, 1948; Vintage Books, 1948.

Hogendorn, Jan. *Economic Development.* 2nd ed. New York: HarperCollins Publishers, 1992.

Hohenberg, John. *Foreign Correspondence: The Great Reporters and Their Times.* New York: Columbia University Press, 1964.

Holden, James Austin. "Influence of Death of Jane McCrea on Burgoyne Campaign." *Proceedings of the New York Historical Association* 12 (1913): 249–310.

Holland, Dewitte. *America in Controversy: History of American Public Address.* Dubuque, IA: William C. Brown, 1973.

Homer-Dixon, Thomas, Jeffrey Boutwell, and George Rathjens. "Environmental Change and Violent Conflict." *Scientific American* (February 1993): 38–45.

Hosokawa, Bill. *Thirty-Five Years in the Frying Pan.* San Francisco, CA: McGraw-Hill, 1978.

Houston, James, and Jean Wakatsuki Houston. *Farewell to Manzanar.* Boston: Houghton Mifflin Company, 1973.

Humes, Joy D. *Oswald Garrison Villard: Liberal of the 1920's.* Syracuse, NY: Syracuse University Press, 1960.

Huntzicker, William E and James Mackey. "Racism and Relocation:" Telling the Japanese-American Experience." *Social Education* 55, no. 7 (November-December 1991): 415–418.

Iyengar, Shanto. "How Citizens Think About National Issues: A Matter of Responsibility." *American Journal of Political Science* 33 (November 1989): 878–900.

_____. *Is Anyone Responsible? How Television Frames Political Issues.* Chicago: University of Chicago Press, 1991.

Jackson, Richard. *Land Use in America.* New York: John Wiley & Sons, 1981.

James, Marguis. *The Life of Andrew Jackson.* Indianapolis, IN: Bobbs-Merrill, 1938.

Jenkins, William Sumner. *Pro-Slavery Thought in the Old South.* Chapel Hill: University of North Carolina, 1935.

Johnson, Gerald. *The Secession of the Southern States.* New York: G.P. Putnam's Sons, 1933.

Johnson, Oliver. *William Lloyd Garrison and His Times, or Sketches of the Anti-Slavery Movement in America, and of the Man Who Was Its Founder and Moral Leader.* Boston: B.B. Russell and Co., 1880.

Jones, Robert W. *Journalism in the United States.* New York: E. P. Dutton & Company, 1947.

Kaplan, Justin. *Lincoln Steffens: A Biography.* New York: Simon and Schuster, 1974.

Karnow, Stanley. *Vietnam: A History.* New York: Viking Press, 1983.

Kennedy, John F. *A Nation of Immigrants.* Rev. ed. New York: Harper Torchbooks, 1964.

Knightly, Phillip. *The First Casualty.* New York: Harcourt Brace Jovanovich, 1975.

Knudson, Jerry W. "The Jefferson Years; Response by the Press, 1801–1809." Ph.D. diss., University of Virginia, 1974.

Kobre, Sidney. *Development of American Journalism.* Dubuque, IA: William C. Brown, 1969.

_____. *The Yellow Press and Gilded Age Journalism.* Tallahassee: Florida State University Press, 1964.

Korematsu v. United States, 323 U.S. 214 (1944).

Kraditor, Aileen S. *Means and Ends in American Abolitionism: Garrison and His Critics on Strategy and Tactics, 1834–1850.* New York: Pantheon Books, 1967.

Laffin, John. *The Hunger to Come.* London: Abelard-Schuman, 1971.

Lasswell, Harold. "The Structure and Function of Communication in Society." In *The Communication of Ideas,* edited by Lyman Bryson. New York: Harper & Brothers, 1948.

Leary, Lewis. *That Rascal Freneau: A Study in Literary Failure.* New Brunswick, NJ: Rutgers University Press, 1941.

Lee, Alfred M. *The Daily Newspaper in America.* New York: The Macmillan Company, 1937.

Lee, James Melvin. *History of American Journalism.* New ed., Rev. Garden City, NY: Garden City Publishing, 1917, 1923.

Levy, Leonard W. *Emergence of a Free Press.* New York: Oxford University Press, 1985.

Limerick, Patricia Nelson. *The Legacy of Conquest.* New York: W.W. Norton, 1987.

Linderman, Gerald F. *The Mirror of War.* Ann Arbor: University of Michigan Press, 1974.

Lippmann, Walter. "A Sort of Farewell to Washington." Washington *Post,* 19 March 1967.

_____. *Public Opinion.* New York: Harcourt, Brace & Company, 1922.

Lippmann, Walter. "The Credibility Gap–I." Washington *Post,* 28 March 1967.

_____. "The Credibility Gap–II." Washington *Post,* 30 March 1967.

Lipset, Symour Martin. "An Instrument Rather Than Creator." In *McCarthyism,* edited by Thomas C. Reeves. Hinsdale, Il: Dryden Press, 1973.

Lofton, John. *Justice and the Press.* Boston: Beacon Press, 1966; Beacon Paperbacks, 1968.

_____. *The Press as Guardian of the First Amendment.* Columbia: University of South Carolina Press, 1980.

Loggins, Vernon. *The Negro Author; His Development in America to 1900*. Port Washington, NY: Kennikat Press, 1964.

"Looting, Burning—Now Guerilla War." *U.S. News & World Report*, 7 August 1967, 23–27.

Lovejoy, Joseph C., and Owen Lovejoy. *Memoir of the Rev. Elijah P. Lovejoy; Who Was Murdered in Defence of the Liberty of the Press, at Alton, Illinois, Nov. 7, 1837*. New York: J.S. Taylor, 1838.

Ludlum, David L. *Social Ferment in Vermont, 1791–1800*. New York: Columbia University Press, 1939.

Maher, Mike. "How News Media Frame the Population-Environment Connection." Paper delivered to the Media and the Environment Conference, Association for Education in Journalism and Mass Communication, Reno, NV, April 1994.

Malone, Dumas. *Thomas Jefferson and the Ordeal of Liberty*. Boston: Little, Brown, 1962.

Malthus, Thomas. "An Essay on the Principle of Population." In *On Population: Thomas Robert Malthus*, edited by Gertrude Himmelfarb, 3–143. New York: Random House, 1960.

Marei, Sayed. *The World Food Crisis*. London: Longman, 1976.

Marszalek, John F. *Sherman's Other War: The General and the Civil War Press*. Memphis, TN: Memphis State University Press, 1981.

Martineau, Harriet. *The Martyr Age of the United States*. Boston: Weeks, Jordan and Co., 1839.

Marvel, William. *Burnside*. Chapel Hill: University of North Carolina Press, 1991.

Mathis, Robert N. "Freedom of the Press in the Confederacy: A Reality." *Historian* 37 (August 1975): 633–648.

Matthews, Joseph J. *Reporting the Wars*. Minneapolis: University of Minnesota Press, 1957.

May, Samuel J. *Some Recollections of Our Anti-Slavery Conflict*. Boston: Fields and Osgood, 1869.

Mayes, Martin. *An Historical-Sociological Inquiry Into Certain Phases of the Development of the Press in the United States*. Richmond: Missourian Press, 1935.

Mazur, Laurie, ed. *Beyond the Numbers: A Reader on Population, Consumption, and the Environment*. Covelo, CA: Island Press, 1994.

McCarthy, Joseph. "Communists in Government—Wheeling Speech." In *Major Speeches and Debates of Senator McCarthy: 1950–1951*. Washington, DC: U.S. Government Printing Office, 1953.

McCombs, Maxwell, and Donald Shaw. "The Evolution of Agenda-Setting Research: Twenty-five years in the Marketplace of Ideas." *Journal of Communication* 43 (1993): 58–68.

McCombs, Maxwell. "Explorers and Surveyors: Expanding Strategies for Agenda-Setting Research." *Journalism Quarterly* 69 (1992): 813–824.

McConnell, Robert. "The Real Environmental Crisis, or What Happened to Government by the People, for the People?" *Population and Environment* 12 (1991): 407–416.

McMahan, John. *Property Development: Effective Decision Making in Uncertain Times*. New York: McGraw-Hill, 1976.

McWilliams, Carey. *Prejudice: Japanese-Americans, Symbol of Racial Intolerance*. Boston: Little, Brown and Company, 1945.

Merritt, Richard L. "Public Opinion in Colonial America: Content-Analyzing the Colonial Press." *Public Opinion Quarterly* 27 (1963): 356–371.

Meyer, Philip. "Detroit: When Scholars Joined Journalists." *Columbia Journalism Review* (Fall 1967): 10.

Middlekauf, Robert. *The Glorious Cause: The American Revolution, 1763–1789*. New York: Oxford University Press, 1982.

Milbrath, Lester. "Environmental Values and Beliefs of the General Public and Leaders in the United States, England, and Germany." In *Environmental Policy Formation: The Impact of Values, Ideology, and Standards*, edited by D. Mann, 43–61. Lexington, MA: Lexington Books, 1981.

Miller, John C. *Crisis in Freedom*. Boston: Little, Brown and Company, 1931.

———. *Toward a More Perfect Union*. Glenview, IL: Scott, Foresman and Company, 1970.

Millis, Walter. *The Martial Spirit*. Boston: Houghton Mifflin Company, 1931.

Miyamoto, Frank S. "The Forced Evacuation of the Japanese Minority During World War II." *Journal of Social Issues* 29 (1973): 11–31.

Morison, Samuel Eliot. *The Oxford History of the American People*. New York: Oxford University Press, 1965.

Morris, Richard B., ed. *Encyclopedia of American History*, 5th ed. (Bicentennial edition). New York: Harper & Row, 1976.

Mott, Frank Luther. *American Journalism: A History of Newspapers in the United States Through 250 Years, 1690 to 1940*. New York: Macmillan Co., 1941.

———. *American Journalism*. Rev. ed. New York: Russell & Russell, 1968.

———. *Jefferson and the Press*. Baton Rouge: Louisiana State University Press, 1943.

———. "The Newspaper Coverage of Lexington and Concord." *New England Quarterly* 17 (1944): 489–505.

Mulcrone, Mick. "'Those Miserable Little Hounds': World War I Postal Censorship of the Irish World." *Journalism History* 20 (Spring 1994): 15–24.

Murphy, Paul L. "Communities in Conflict." In The Pulse of Freedom: *American Civil Liberties, 1920-1970s*, edited by Alan Reitman. 23–65. New York: W.W. Norton and Co., 1975.

———. *The Constitution in Crisis Times, 1918–1969*. New York: Harper Torchbooks, 1972.

Murray, Robert K. *Red Scare: A Study of National Hysteria, 1919–1920*. New York: McGraw-Hill, 1955.

Myers, Norman. *The Primary Source: Tropical Forests and Our Future*. New York, W. W. Norton & Company, 1992.

Nagata, Donna. "The Japanese-American Internment: Perceptions of Moral Community, Fairness, and Redress." *Journal of Social Issues* 46 (Spring 1990):133–146.

Narayana, G., and John F. Kantner, *Doing the Needful: The Dilemma of India's Population Policy*. Boulder, CO: Westview Press, 1992.

"A Nation at Odds." *Newsweek*, 10 July 1967, 16-20.

Neely, Ives. "The Press Was an Accessory." *The Quill* 64 (April 1976), 19–20.

Neely, Mark E., Jr. *The Fate of Liberty: Abraham Lincoln and Civil Liberties.* New York: Oxford University Press, 1991.

Nelson, Truman. *The Old Man: John Brown at Harper's Ferry.* New York: Holt, Rinehart and Winston, 1973.

Nerone, John. *Violence Against the Press: Policing the Public Sphere in U.S. History.* New York: Oxford University Press, 1994.

Nevins, Allan. *American Press Opinion, Washington to Coolidge.* Boston: Ross Hargreaves, 1928.

_____. *The Evening Post.* New York: Boni & Liveright, 1922.

"Newark Boils Over." *Newsweek,* 24 July 1967, 21–24.

Newport, Frank, and Lydia Saad. "Public Support Mixed for U.S. Efforts to Curb World Overpopulation." *The Gallup Poll Monthly* 320 (May 1992): 34–41.

"The News Media and Racial Disorders–A Preliminary Report." *Columbia Journalism Review,* Fall 1967, 3-5.

"Newspapers: Editorial Unease." *Time,* 20 October 1967, 57.

Nordin, Kenneth D. "In Search of Black Unity: An Interpretation of the Content and Function of *Freedom's Journal,*" *Journalism History* 4 (Winter 1977–78):123–128.

North, S. N. D. *History and Present Condition of the Newspapers and Periodical Press of the United States with a Catalogue of the Publications of the Census Year.* Washington, DC: Government Printing Office, 1909.

Nye, Russel B. "Freedom of the Press and the Antislavery Controversy," *Journalism Quarterly* 22 (1945): 1–11.

Oates, Stephen. *To Purge This Land with Blood: A Biography of John Brown.* New York: Harper & Row, 1970.

Okamura, Raymond Y. "The American Concentration Camps: A Cover-Up Through Euphemistic Terminology." *Journal of Ethnic Studies* 10 (Fall 1982): 102.

Ophuls, William. *Ecology and the Politics of Scarcity.* San Francisco, CA: W. H. Freeman and Co., 1977.

Oshinsky, David M. *Senator Joseph McCarthy and the American Labor Movement.* Columbia: University of Missouri Press, 1976.

O'Toole, G.J.A. *The Spanish War.* New York: W. W. Norton & Company, 1984.

Paddock, William, and Paul Paddock. *Famine—1975!* Boston: Little, Brown and Company, 1967.

Pan, Zhongdang, and Gerald Kosicki. "Framing Analysis: An Approach to News Discourse." *Political Communication* 10 (January-March 1993): 55–76.

Patterson III, Oscar. "An Analysis of Television Coverage of the Vietnam War," *Journal of Broadcasting* 28 (Fall 1984): 397–404.

Perkins, Bradford. *Prologue to War.* Berkeley: University of California Press, 1981.

Perkins, Bradford, ed. *The Causes of the War of 1812.* New York: Holt, Rinehart & Winston, 1962.

Perry, Lewis. *Radical Abolitionism, Anarchy and the Government of God in Antislavery Thought.* Ithaca, NY: Cornell University Press, 1973.

Petersen, William. "Staying Alive: Some Home Truths About Population." *American Scholar* 57 (Winter 1988): 51–69.

Pew Global Stewardship Initiative. *Pew Global Stewardship Initiative Survey.* Washington, DC: Belden & Russonello Research and Communications, Project 93–68, 2–15, February 1994.

_____. "Report of Findings from Focus Groups on Population, Consumption, and the Environment." Washington, DC: Belden & Russonello Research and Communications, 1993.

Phillips, Wendell. *Speeches, Lectures, and Letters.* Boston: Lee and Shepard, 1863.

Polenberg, Richard. *War and Society.* New York: J. P. Lippincott, 1972.

Population and the American Future: The Report of the Commission on Population Growth and the American Future. New York: New American Library, 1972.

Postel, Sandra. "Denial in the Decisive Decade." In *State of the World, 1992,* Linda Starke, ed., 3–8. New York: W.W. Norton Co., 1992.

_____. "Facing Water Scarcity." In *State of the World, 1993,* Linda Starke, ed., 22–41. New York: W.W. Norton Co., 1993.

Prato, Lou. *Covering the Environmental Beat: An Overview for Radio and TV Journalists.* Washington, DC: The Media Institute, 1991.

"The Presidency: A Failure of Communication." *Time,* 25 August 1967, 13–14.

Preston, William, Jr. *Aliens and Dissenters: Federal Suppression of Radicals, 1903–1933.* New York: Harper & Row, 1963.

"Protest: the Banners of Dissent."*Time,* 27 October 1967, 23–29.

Quarantelli, E.L. "The Social Science Study of Disasters and Mass Communication," in *Bad Tidings: Communication and Catastrophe,* edited by Lynne Masel Walters, Lee Wilkins, and Tim Walters. Hillsdale, NJ: Lawrence Erlbaum, 1989.

Quarles, Benjamin. *Black Abolitionists.* New York: Oxford University Press, 1969.

_____. "Lord Dunmore as Liberator." *William and Mary Quarterly,* 3rd Series, 15 (1958): 494–507.

"Races: Sparks & Tinder." *Time,* 21 July 1967, 15–21.

Randall, James G. *Constitutional Problems Under Lincoln.* Urbana: University of Illinois Press, 1951.

_____. "The Newspaper Problem in Its Bearing Upon Military Secrecy during the Civil War." *American Historical Review* 33 (January 1918): 303–323.

Raper, Horace W. "William W. Holden and the Peace Movement in North Carolina." *North Carolina Historical Review* 31 (October 1954): 493–516.

Reeves, Thomas C., ed. *McCarthyism.* Hinsdale, IL: Dryden Press, 1973.

Report of the National Advisory Commission on Civil Disorders [Kerner Commission Report]. New York: Bantam Books, 1968.

Report of the Select Committee Investigation on National Defense Migration. John H. Tolan, chairman. Washington, DC: Government Printing Office, 1942.

Reynolds, Donald. *Editors Make War: Southern Newspapers in the Secession Crisis.* Nashville, TN: Vanderbilt University Press, 1970.

Rhoodie, N.C. *Intergroup Accommodation in Plural Societies.* London: St. Martin's Press, 1978.

Rights in Conflict: The Violent Confrontation of Demonstrators and Police in the Parks and Streets of Chicago During the Week of the Democratic National Convention of 1968, A Report Submitted by Daniel Walker, Director of the Chicago Study Team, to the National Commission on the Causes and Prevention of Violence [Walker Report]. New York: Bantam Books, 1968.

Ripley, C. Peter, ed. *The Black Abolitionist Papers, Vol. III, The United States, 1830–1846.* Chapel Hill: University of North Carolina Press, 1991.

Robbins, John B. "The Confederacy and the Writ of Habeas Corpus." *Georgia Historical Quarterly* 55 (Spring 1971): 83–101.

Roberts, Chalmers M. *The Washington Post: The First 100 Years.* Boston: Houghton Mifflin, 1977.

Rogers, Everett, Dearing, J., and Bregman, D. "The Anatomy of Agenda-setting Research," *Journal of Communication* 43 (1993): 68–85.

Rogin, Michael Paul. "Pluralists and Agrarian Radicalism." In *McCarthyism*, edited by Thomas C. Reeves. Hinsdale, IL: Dryden Press, 1973.

Roshco, Bernard. "What the Black Press Said Last Summer." *Columbia Journalism Review* (Fall 1967): 6–9.

Rovere, Richard. *Senator Joe McCarthy.* New York: Harper & Row, 1959.

Saalberg, Harvey. "The Westliche Post of St. Louis: German Language Daily, 1857–1938." *Journalism Quarterly* 45 (Autumn 1968): 452–456.

Sagan, Carl. "To Avert a Common Danger." *Parade Magazine*, 1 March 1992, 10–14.

Salisbury, Harrison E. *Behind the Lines—Hanoi: December 23, 1966–January 7, 1967.* New York: Harper & Row, 1967.

Sanborn, Franklin. *The Life and Letters of John Brown.* Boston: Roberts Brothers, 1891.

Schlesinger, Arthur M. *Paths to the Present.* Rev. ed. Cambridge: Riverside Press, 1964.

————. *Prelude to Independence: The Newspaper War on Britain, 1764–1776.* New York: Alfred A. Knopf, 1958.

Sears, Paul. "The Process of Environmental Change by Man." Originally published in *Man's Role in Changing the Face of the Earth*, edited by W. E. Thomas, Chicago: University of Chicago Press, 1956. Reprinted in *The Ecology of Man: An Ecosystems Approach*, edited by R. L. Smith, 129–138. New York: Harper & Row, 1972.

Second Interim Report of the Select Committee Investigation National-Defense Migration. John H. Tolan, chairman. Washington, DC: Government Printing Office, 1942.

Sekora, John, and Darwin Turner, eds. *The Art of Slave Narrative: Original Essays in Criticism and Theory.* Essays in Literature Series. Western Illinois University, 1982.

Sen, Sudhir. *Reaping the Green Revolution: Foods and Jobs for All.* Maryknoll, NY: Orbis Books, 1975.

Senate Resolution 301, 2 December 1954.

"Seven Days in April." *Newsweek*, 15 April 1968, 26–38.

Shanks, Caroline L. "The Biblical Anti-Slavery Argument of the Decade 1830-1840," *Journal of Negro History*, 16 (1931): 132–137.

Shaw, Donald L., and Maxwell E. McCombs. *The Emergence of American Political Issues: The Agenda-Setting Function of the Press.* St. Paul, MN: West Publishing Co., 1977.

Sheehan, Neil. "Not a Dove, But No Longer a Hawk." *New York Times Magazine*, 9 October 1966, 27, 132–134, 139–140.

Simon, Julian, and Herman Kahn, eds. *The Resourceful Earth: A Response to Global 2000.* New York: Basil Blackwell, 1984.

Simon, Julian. *Population Matters*. New Brunswick, NJ: Transaction Publishers, 1990.

Skaggs, David C. "Editorial Policies of the *Maryland Gazette*, 1765–1783." *Maryland Historical Magazine* 59 (1964): 341–349.

Sloan, William David, Stovall, James G., and Startt, James D, eds. *The Media in America*. 2nd ed. Scottsdale, AZ: Publishing Horizons, 1993.

_____. "Scurrility and the Party Press, 1789–1816." *American Journalism*, 5, no. 2 (1988): 97–112.

_____. "The Federalist-Republican Press: Newspaper Functionsin America's First Party System, 1789–1816." Paper presented to Southwest Symposium for Mass Communication, Fort Worth, TX, 1981.

_____. "The Party Press 1783–1833," in *The Media in America*. 2nd ed., edited by William David Sloan, James G. Stovall, and James D. Startt, Scottsdale, AZ: Publishing Horizons, 1989, 1993.

_____. "Freedom of the Press," *The Media and America*, 2nd ed., edited by William David Sloan, James G. Stovall, and James D. Startt, Scottdale, AZ: Publishing Horizons, 1989, 1993.

Smith, James M. *Freedom's Fetters: The Alien and Sedition Laws and American Civil Liberties*. Ithaca, NY: Cornell University Press, 1956.

Spiller, Robert, Willard Thorpe, Thomas Johnson, Henry Seidel Canby, and Richard Ludwig, eds. *Literary History of the United States*. 3rd ed., rev. New York: Macmillan, 1963.

Spivak, Burton. *Jefferson's English Crisis*. Charlottesville: University of Virginia, 1979.

Starr, Louis M. *Bohemian Brigade: Civil War Newsmen in Action*. New York: Alfred A. Knopf, 1954.

Startt, James D. "The Media and National Crises, 1917–1945." In *The Media in America: A History*, edited by William David Sloan, James G. Stovall, and James D. Startt, 281–310. Worthington, OH: Publishing Horizons, 1989.

Steel, Ronald. *Walter Lippmann and the American Century*. New York: Viking Books, 1981.

Stevens, John D. "Press and Community Toleration: Wisconsin in World War I." *Journalism Quarterly* 46 (Summer 1969): 255–259.

_____. *Shaping the First Amendment: The Development of Freedom of Expression*. Beverly Hills: Sage, 1983.

Stewart, Donald H. *The Opposition Press of the Federalist Period*. Albany: State University of New York Press, 1969.

Stoler, Mark A. *George C. Marshall: Soldier-Statesman of the American Century*. Boston: Twayne Publishers, 1989.

Tankard, James W., Jr. "The Theorists," in *Makers of the Media Mind*, edited by William David Sloan. Hillsdale, NJ: Lawrence Erlbaum Associates, 1990.

Tankard, James, Jr., Laura Hendrickson, Jackie Silberman, Kris Bliss and Salma Ghanem. "Media Frames: Approaches to Conceptualization and Measurement." Paper delivered at the meeting of the Communication Theory and Methodology Division, Association for Education in Journalism and Mass Communication, Boston, August 1991.

Tappan, Lewis. *The Life of Arthur Tappan*. New York: Hurd and Houghton, 1870.

Tebbel, John. *The Compact History of the American Newspaper*. New York: Hawthorn Books, 1963.

_____. *The Compact History of the American Newspaper.* New York: Hawthorn Books, 1966.

_____. *The Media in America.* New York: Mentor Books, 1974.

Tennery, Craig. "To Suppress or Not to Suppress: Abraham Lincoln and the *Chicago Times.*" *Civil War History* 27 (September 1981): 248–259.

Thomas, Isaiah. *The History of Printing in America with a Biography of Printers & an Account of Newspapers.* 2nd ed. Albany, NY: American Antiquarian Society, 1874; reprint ed., Barre, MA: Imprint Society, 1970.

Towery, Patricia. "Censorship of South Carolina Newspapers, 1861–1865." In *South Carolina Journals and Journalists,* edited by James B. Meriwether, Spartanburg, SC: The Reprint Co., 1975.

Track, David F. *The War with Spain in 1898.* New York: Macmillan Publishing Co., 1981.

Trexler, Harrison A. "The Davis Administration and the Richmond Press, 1861–1865." *Journal of Southern History* 16 (May 1950): 177–195.

Trilling, Diana. "How McCarthy Gave Anti-Communism a Bad Name." *Newsweek,* 11 January 1993, 32–33.

Tripp, Bernell. "The Media and Community Cohesiveness: The Black Press and the Colonization Issue" in *The Significance of the Media in American History* , edited by James D. Startt and William David Sloan, Northport, AL: Vision Press, 1993.

_____. *Origins of the Black Press, 1827–1847.* Northport, AL: Vision Press, 1992.

Trowbridge, John Townsend. *Neighbor Jackson.* Boston: Phillips, Sampson, 1857.

Tuchman, Gaye. *Making News: A Study in the Construction of Reality.* New York: Free Press, 1978.

Turner, Kathleen J. *Lyndon Johnson's Dual War: Vietnam and the Press.* Chicago: University of Chicago Press, 1985.

Union of Concerned Scientists. "Warning to Humanity—A Declaration by Scientists on Global Issues." *Population and Development Review* 18 (December 1992): 782–783.

Usher, Roland G. *Pan-Americanism.* New York: Century, 1915.

Van Deusen, Glydon G., and Dexter Perkins. *The United States of America: A History.* Vol. 1. New York: Macmillan Company, 1962.

Villard, Oswald Garrison. *The Disappearing Daily.* New York: Levered A., 1944.

_____. *Fighting Years: Memoirs of a Liberal Editor.* New York: Harcourt, Brace and Co., 1939.

_____. *John Brown: A Biography Fifty Years After.* Gloucester, MA: Peter Smith, 1965.

Ward, Barbara, and René Dubos. *Only One Earth.* New York: W. W. Norton Co., 1972.

Warren, Robert Penn. *John Brown, The Making of a Martyr.* New York: Payson and Clarke, Ltd, 1929.

Watkins, William J. *Our Rights as Men. An Address Delivered in Boston, Before the Legislative Committee on the Militia, February 24, 1853.* Boston: Benjamin F. Roberts, 1853.

Wattenberg, Ben. *The Birth Dearth.* New York: Pharos Books, 1987.

Watterson, Henry. *History of the Spanish-American War.* Richmond, VA: B. F. Johnson Publishing Co., 1898.

Weisberger, Bernard A. *The American Newspaperman*. Chicago: The University of Chicago Press, 1961.

Weisberger, Bernard A. *Reporters for the Union*. Boston: Little, Brown and Co., 1953.

"What Must Be Done." *Newsweek*, 20 November 1967, 33–65.

Whitcover, Jules. "The Press and Chicago: The Truth Hurt." *Columbia Journalism Review* (Fall 1968): 5–9.

White, David Manning. "The Gatekeeper: A Case Study in the Selection of News," *Journalism Quarterly* 27 (Fall 1950): 383–390.

White, Leonard D. "The Embargo," in *The Causes of the War of 1812*, edited by Bradford Perkins. New York: Holt, Rinehart & Winston, 1962.

Whitridge, Arnold. "Canada: The Struggle for the Fourteenth State." *History Today* 17 (1967): 13–21.

Wiebe, Robert H. *The Search for Order, 1877–1920*. New York: Hill & Wang, 1967.

Wilkerson, Marcus W. *Public Opinion and the Spanish-American War*. Baton Rouge: Louisiana State University Press, 1932.

Williams, Wenmouth, Jr., Mitchell Shapiro, and Craig Cutbirth. "The Impact of Campaign Agendas on Perception of Issues." *Journalism Quarterly* 60 (1983): 226–232.

Wilmoth, John, and Patrick Ball. "The Population Debate in American Popular Magazines, 1946–90." *Population and Development Review* 18 (December 1992): 631–668.

Wilson, Quintus C. "A Study and Evaluation of Military Censorship in the Civil War." Master's thesis, University of Minnesota, 1945.

_____. "Voluntary Press Censorship During the Civil War." *Journalism Quarterly* 19 (1942): 251–261.

Winter, Kari. *Subjects of Slavery, Agents of Change*. Athens: University of Georgia, 1992.

Wroth, Lawrence C. *The Colonial Printer*. Portland, ME: Southworth-Athoensen Press, 1938.

Yaukey, David. *Demography: The Study of Human Population*. Prospect Heights, IL: Waveland Press, 1985.

"You Can't Run Away." *Newsweek*, 31 July 1967, 17–20.

Zaroulis, Nancy, and Gerald Sullivan. *Who Spoke Up?: American Protest Against the War in Vietnam 1963–1975*. Garden City, NY: Doubleday, 1984.

Zhu, Jian-Hua. "Issue Competition and Attention Distraction: A Zero-Sum Theory of Agenda Setting." *Journalism Quarterly* 69 (1992): 825–836.

Zimmerman, James F. *Impressment of American Seamen*. New York: Columbia University Press, 1925; reprint ed., Port Washington, NY: Kennikat Press, 1966.

NEWSPAPERS

Aberdeen *Daily World*
Albany *Centinel*
Albany *Democrat Herald*
Albany *Gazette*
American Industrial Liberator

American Minerva
American Socialist
Anti-Slavery Bugle
Argus of Western Kentucky
Arkansas *Gazette*
Ashland *Daily Tidings*
Atlanta *Constitution*
Aurora
Austin *American-Statesman*
Bakersfield *Californian*
Baltimore *Afro-American*
Baltimore *Sun*
Boston *Daily Chronicle*
Boston *Evening Transcript*
Boston *Gazette*
Boston *Globe*
Boston *Herald*
Boston *Independent Chronicle*
Boston *Newsletter*
Bull
Catholic Register
Charleston *Mercury*
Chicago *Daily News*
Chicago *Times*
Chicago *Times-Herald*
Chicago *Tribune*
Christian Science Monitor
Cincinnati *Enquirer*
Cleveland *Plain Dealer*
Columbian Centinel
Corvallis *Gazette Times*
Country Porcupine
Denver *Post*
Denver *Times*
Detroit *Free Press*
Everett *Daily Herald*
Frederick Douglass' Newspaper
Freedom's Journal
Freeman's Journal
Gaelic American
Gazette of the United States
Genius of Universal Emancipation
Greensboro *Patriot*
Hartford Connecticut *Courant*
Hartford *Times*
Herald of Freedom
Independent Chronicle
Indianapolis *Journal*

Indianapolis *News*
Irish World
Lexington *Reporter*
Liberator
Liberty Hall & Cincinnati *Gazette*
Longview *Daily News*
Los Angeles *Times*
Lyon *Record*
Manchester *Union Leader*
Masses
Miami *News*
Milwaukee *Journal*
Milwaukee *Leader*
Montgomery *Advertiser*
Nashville *Gazette*
National Anti-Slavery Standard
National Era
National Gazette
National Journal
New England *Palladium*
New Haven Connecticut *Journal*
New London *Bee*
New Orleans *Daily Picayune*
New Orleans *Times-Democrat*
New Orleans *Times-Picayune*
New Yorker
New York *Argus*
New York *Call*
New York *Columbian*
New York *Daily News*
New York *Evening Post*
New York *Herald*
New York *Herald Tribune*
New York *Journal*
New York *Journal of Commerce*
New York *Sun*
New York *Times*
New York *Tribune*
New York *World*
North Star
Northumberland *Gazette*
Ottawa *Citizen*
Pennsylvania *Freeman*
Philadelphia *Aurora*
Philadelphia *Censor*
Philadelphia *Daily Advertiser*
Philadelphia *Evening Post*
Philadelphia *Gazette*

Philadelphia *General Advertiser*
Philadelphia *Inquirer*
Philadelphia *National Enquirer*
Philadelphia *Public Ledger*
Philanthropist
Porcupine's Gazette
Portland *Eastern Argus*
Portland *Oregonian*
Rafu Shimpo
Raleigh *Register*
Richmond *Enquirer*
Richmond *Examiner*
Richmond *Globe*
Richmond *Recorder*
Richmond *Times-Union*
Rocky Mountain *News*
Sacramento *Bee*
Salt Lake *Tribune*
San Diego *Union*
San Francisco *Chronicle*
San Francisco *Leader*
San Luis Obispo *Telegram-Tribune*
Seattle *Post-Intelligencer*
Seattle *Times*
Solidarity
St. Louis *Globe-Democrat*
St. Louis *Observer*
St. Louis *Post-Dispatch*
St. Paul *Star Tribune*
St. Petersburg *Times*
The Nation
The New Republic
The Olympian
The Times of India
The Times of London
The Virginia *Gazettes*
Toledo *Blade*
United States *Telegraph*
Vancouver *Sun*
Wall Street Journal
Washington *Evening Star*
Washington *Globe*
Washington *National Intelligencer*
Washington *Post*
Washington *Times*
Wasp
Westliche *Post*
Worcester *National Aegis*

INDEX

ABOUT THE EDITOR
AND CONTRIBUTORS

LLOYD CHIASSON JR. is a journalism historian specializing in the role of the press in periods of crisis. He received a B.A. degree from Louisiana State University, an M.A. degree from the University of Arizona, and a Ph.D. from Southern Illinois University. All of his degrees are in journalism.

Dr. Chiasson's book, *Reporter's Notebook*, published in 1993, was one of, if not the first, journalism interactive computer textbooks to be marketed nationwide. He has also published numerous book chapters and journal articles on topics including Frederick Douglass, George Ripley, Noah Webster, the encampment of the Japanese-Americans during World War II, the John Brown raid at Harper's Ferry, and the literature of the Antebellum Period.

Dr. Chiasson, who is of French-Acadian and German heritage, is a professor of mass communication at Nicholls State University in Thibodaux, Louisiana, the pride of Cajun country.

DONALD AVERY has written broadly on the colonial and early republic periods, as well as the party press period. A former president and secretary and treasurer of the American Journalism Historians Association, he has served as managing editor of *American Journalism* and on the editorial boards of *American Journalism* and *Journalism Monographs*. He is a professor of communication and chair of the Communication Department at Eastern Connecticut State University. He received his Ph.D. in journalism from Southern Illinois University.

CAROL SUE HUMPHREY is an American historian specializing in the media of the 18th century, particularly the newspapers of the American Revolutionary era. She received a B.A. degree from the University of North Carolina at Wilmington, an M.A. degree from Wake Forest University, and a Ph.D. degree from the University of North Carolina at Chapel Hill. All of her degrees are in history.

Dr. Humphrey's book, *'This Popular Engine': New England Newspapers During the American Revolution, 1775–1789* appeared in 1992. She has also published numerous articles and book reviews concerning the press of the Revolutionary era in *American Journalism, Journalism Quarterly, Journalism History, Georgia Historical Quarterly,* and *Media History Digest.* She is currently writing a study of American journalism from 1783 to 1833, part of a six-volume edition being published by Greenwood Press.

Dr. Humphrey is currently an associate professor of history at Oklahoma Baptist University in Shawnee, Oklahoma.

ARTHUR KAUL is associate professor and chair of the Department of Journalism, School of Communication, at the University of Southern Mississippi. He earned a B.A. in psychology and English from Central Methodist College, an M.A. in humanities from Western Kentucky University, and an M.S. and Ph.D. in journalism from Southern Illinois University. His scholarly interests include media history and ethics and literary journalism. He has published in *American Journalism, Critical Studies in Mass Communication, Dictionary of Literary Biography,* and *Journal of Mass Media Ethics,* among others.

MIKE MAHER is an assistant professor of communication at the University of Southwestern Louisiana, where he teaches writing, editing, and desktop publishing. As this book goes to press, he is a doctoral candidate in journalism at the University of Texas at Austin. His dissertation will address media coverage of population-driven environmental problems. He has done public relations and magazine editing work, as well as freelance writing.

JOSEPH MCKERNS is associate professor of journalism at the Ohio State University. He is the author of the *Biographical Dictionary of American Journalism,* published by Greenwood Press, and *News Media and Public Policy: An Annotated Bibliography,* and articles on the history of the American news media published in scholarly journals. McKerns is a past president of the American Journalism Historians Association, and past editor of *Journalism Monographs.*

McKerns has taught journalism at St. Bonaventure University, the University of Maryland, the University of Tennessee, Southern Illinois University, and Virginia Commonwealth University. He received a Ph.D. in mass communication at the University of Minnesota, an M.A. in journalism at Ohio State University, and an A.B. in communication arts and American studies at the University of Notre Dame. He is the proud descendant of Catholic Irish and Polish immigrants who were coal miners and railroad workers.

DONALD REYNOLDS is a professor in the Department of History at East Texas State. He is the author of two books, *Editors Make War, A History of Newspapers in the Secession Crisis,* and *Professor Mayo's College: A History of East Texas State University.* Dr. Reynolds has also published numerous articles on various historical periods and figures. He received his doctorate in history from Tulane University in 1966.

BERNELL TRIPP is an assistant professor in the School of Journalism at the University of Florida. She has published several book chapters on the 19th century black press and is the author of the text, *Origins of the Black Press, 1827–1847*.

Dr. Tripp received her doctorate in mass communication in 1993 from the University of Alabama.

GENE WIGGINS is a professor of journalism and director of the School of Communication at the University of Southern Mississippi. He earned his Ph.D. in journalism at Southern Illinois University in 1973. He has authored numerous articles on press law and history. His most recent publication is a media law book for the state of Mississippi.

KEITH WOODS is an associate at the Poynter Institute for Media Studies in St. Petersburg, Florida, where he teaches ethics, writing and reporting on race. Prior to that he was a columnist and an editorial writer for the New Orleans *Times-Picayune*. Woods was city editor for the *Picayune* when David Duke ran for the governorship of Louisiana.

ISBN 0-313-29364-3

9 780313 293641

90000>

EAN

HARDCOVER BAR CODE